Diary of an

Angry

Targeted Individual

Renee Pittman

DEDICATION

This is book is dedicated to the Targeted Individual Community worldwide of whom fairness continues to elude.

NOTE: These books must continue to rely on, the research and substantiation, not only of the author, but also others, related to scientific programs. This is done for credibility purposes. It is vital due to the nature of these greatly, deceptive, and highly secret operations.

TABLE OF CONTENTS

"People sleep peaceably in their beds at night only because rough men stand ready to do violence on their behalf."

George Orwell - 1984

The justice system has proven many times over, as not being a resource for targets of government ongoing non-consensual human experimentation.

As a result, victims are forced to singlehandedly seek ethical and moral relief from extreme covert victimization using exposure for now. Why? This is a 'legalized' covert, psychological and physical torture program, of which many are aware, however, that no one wants to admit it exists or much less touch.

This fact continues to be magnified by Targeted Individuals, in fruitless, lawsuit after lawsuit. The question is how did such a vagrant disregard for human lives, men women and children unfold?

Most targeted today agree, there seems to be nowhere to turn.

The Crumbling of the United States Constitution

"Congressman Confirms: United States Is a Corporation!"

Junior Tea Party Congressman <u>Allen West</u> makes a huge confession: "...the President is the Chief Executive Officer (CEO) of this corporation called the United States of America"...

Today as United States citizens watch once held sacred rights Constitutional, Civil, and Human Rights dissolve right before our very eyes, many are searching for the how and why. One promulgated theory is that the factual changes we are witnessing today started in 1871.

On February 21, 1871, Congress passed an Act to provide a separate government for the District of Columbia, Washington, D.C., known as the Act of 1871.

With no constitutional authority to do so, Congress essentially created a separate form of government for the District of Columbia, a ten-mile square parcel of land confirmed by "Acts of the Forty-first Congress," Section 34, Session III, chapters 61 and 62. The Act -- passed successfully when the country was weakened and financially depleted in the aftermath of the Civil War.

As a result of this Act, Congress formed a corporation known as THE UNITED STATES centered in the District of Columbia.

This corporation, now owned by foreign interests, immediately changed the Republic version of the Constitution by changing the word 'for' to 'of' in the title, Constitution *for* The United States of America to Constitution *of* The United States of America. This is also said to be the foundation for the assertion that all capital letters are used in the names of citizens instead of upper- and lower-case letters for example, on Social Security and IRS documents.

Further cementing the United States as a Corporation, owned and operated by foreign interest, was the 1933 bankruptcy of the United States. During this time the U.S was officially dissolved, turned over to international bankers, and converted into a commercial Corporation operating under International Maritime Commerce Law and Bankruptcy Law.

Subsequently, the rights of United States citizens were then turned into Civil Rights under Commerce Law. Arguably, the United States has not been a "government by the people" since 1933.

The Federal Reserve Act of 1913 is said to be the biggest Ponzi scheme in world history. The Federal Reserve Act is an Act of Congress that created and set up the Federal Reserve System, the central banking system, and granted it the legal authority to issue Federal Reserve Notes, now commonly known as the U.S. dollar, and Federal Reserve Bank notes as legal tender. The Act was signed into law by President Woodrow Wilson.

Many Americans believe that the collusion of international bankers became a powerful influence when the Federal Reserve System (FRS) came into being. The end result was that the President and Congress became servants of the FRS main shareholders. The privately-owned Federal Reserve Corporation, belonging to a group of bankers became the only real power in America which then started to vie for world dominance.

Today, many argue that United States citizens are merely corporate of slaves, and sheeple, owned, and ruled by the International Banking Cartel?

The United States as a corporation would explain much about why our President and Congress can "do unconstitutional' acts with impunity. They are lawful employees of the International Banking Cartel operating under commerce.

In this scenario, America's judiciary system is said to be smaller corporate branches called Courts. The judges are actually business administrators and all of America's laws are civil corporate regulations called Statutes. People are treated as corporations in these Courts and these so-called bastions of justice are all about commerce and corporate interest. Courts are pseudo corporate businesses operating in conflict of interest being the receivers of Bankruptcies. All judges, attorneys are members of "inn of court" which ties them directly to the Queens Court in London.

As a result, with clear vision, the realization is that, Federal agencies, state, county and local police, and prosecutors are not in place for the American public but more so than ever before to global interest. They are a structured corporation, designed to enforce the corporate statutes against the corporate enemy now believe to be "The American citizen." For example, many are perplexed why several countries have passed laws against, Genetically Modified Organism, except the United States.

It is documented that many employed by the corporation or government in Washington D.C. have, or have had, political ties and interest to Monsanto resulting in personal interest and profit.

The alphabet agencies, were first called "New Deal" agencies and created by the corporation, the District of Columbia. The original agencies were created factually as part of President Roosevelt's "New Deal". The earliest agencies were established during Roosevelt's first 100 days in office in 1933 and many were created throughout the 1930s.

Today the alphabet agencies are known as the DOD, DOJ, FCC, CIA, FBI, NSA, IRS, ATF, DEA, NASA, INTERPOL, DHS, etc. Their employees receive their paychecks from the Office of Personnel Management (OPM) which belongs to the International Management Fund or IMF, which is the property of the United Nations, which belongs to Israel, and the Royal and Elite Class of Europe.

The IMF describes its effort saying: The International Monetary Fund (IMF) is an international organization that was initiated in 1944 at the Bretton Woods Conference.

The Bretton Woods Conference, was formally known as the United Nations Monetary and Financial Conference, and was formally created in 1945 by 29-member countries. The IMF's stated goal was to assist in the reconstruction of the world's international payment system post–World War II.

The structure was that Countries contribute money to a pool through a quota system from which countries with payment imbalances can borrow funds temporarily. Through this set-up, activity and others operations, such as surveillance of its members' economies. The demand for self-correcting policies, the IMF works to improve the economies of its member countries.

It is headquartered in Washington, D.C., United States of America.

Previously all monetary appropriations had been separately passed by Act of Congress, as part of the power of purse; and the National Industrial Recovery Act through Executive Orders and other means. These powers were used to create many of the alphabet agencies. Other laws were passed allowing the new bureaus to pass their own directives within a wide sphere of authority. After the National Industrial Recovery Act was found to be unconstitutional, many of the initial agencies, the Federal Deposit Insurance Corporation, FDIC, 1933, Federal Communications Commission, FCC, for example created under it remained.

At this point, you may be asking, what does this information have to do with thousands of Targeted Individuals in the United States? Does it really matter? What is the connection to high-tech mass, social population program today unleashed Post 9/11 nationwide and globally?

In an excerpt from the Edward Griffin analysis: *Is the United States Government A Corporation? If True, So What?* (Freedom Force International) The below, well stated, article excerpt, makes it quite clear that the United States being a corporation is essentially a moot point saying:

"Let's take the first question: what would be the practical significance of a corporate government versus a constitutional government?"

In one case, the charter is a corporate charter. In the other case it is a constitution. Both are written documents and both outline the purpose, function, and limitations of the entity they create.

The primary difference, as revealed is that a corporation always is the creation of government, which makes government "a higher source with powers assumed to be derived from the people themselves.

In the case of the United States, however, this distinction is blurred, because the federal constitution was created by representatives of the colonial government. That means the United States was created by other governments, just as it would have been with the creation of all corporations. "The structure of government is important but not as important as the power of government. That is also true of corporations.

Governments and corporations are neither good nor evil by themselves.

They can serve man well or be a huge disservice depending entirely on the terms of their charters and the character of those who direct them. Private entrepreneurs, partnerships, and associations have exactly the same capacity for good or evil. Corporations become evil when they acquire political favoritism giving them unfair advantages over competitors and legal immunity from crimes – however, the exact same thing happens with politically connected individuals, partnerships, and all associations."

"A similar contrast between good and evil is found within governments, whether they are corporations or not. There is little difference between corporations and governments except ownership of stock. I don't want to make too much over the structure of government and too little over the principles of government.

Which would we choose: a corporate government with a charter that limits its powers and with functioning mechanisms to choose our leaders – or a constitutional government in which the constitution is subverted and the electoral system is in the hands of ruling elite?"

One thing is certain, whether a government or corporation, within the USA, a powerful machination has risen, from the darkest bowels of Hell, and has harnessed, to do its deeds, one of the greatest power sources known to man. This is where Targeted Individuals, who are essentially nonconsensual human guinea pigs come into play, literally.

Today, whoever holds and controls the reigns of this power, holds a capability for good or evil. More importantly, it holds the power for complete control over humanity by weaponization of the Electromagnetic Spectrum the Earth's natural energy source, used to meet the challenge. This is not only within the United States of America but globally. The corporate system is flawed and in favor of a Global Alliance, globalization known decisively as the New World Order. The goal total population control. In order to meet this global agenda, we must understand that in reality, since the beginning of time, those who define society as 'subjects' have sought to control the masses and determined this its great desire. This hope today has evolved psychophysical technology, patented, that is so advance, most cannot believe it exists. However, thousands in the ongoing human experimentation program, approved by the corporation of Washington D.C., tell a different story. It is a story of pain, suffering, and people being marginalized as scientific objects.

An excerpt from a Global Research, article entitled "Psychotronic and Electromagnetic Weapons: Remote Control of the Human Nervous System, written by Mojmir Babacek reports:

In March 2012 the Russian defense minister Anatoli Serdjukov stated,

"The development of weaponry based on new physics principles; direct-energy weapons, geophysical weapons, wave-energy weapons, genetic weapons, psychotronic weapons, etc., is part of the state arms procurement program for 2011-2020," Voice or Russia

The world media reacted to this hint on the open use of psychotronic weapons by the publication of scientific experiments from the 1960's where electromagnetic waves were used to transmit simple sounds into the human brain.

However, most of them avoided saying that since then extensive scientific research has been carried out in this area throughout the world. Only a Colombian newspaper, El Spectador published an article covering the whole scale of the achievements of this technological explosion.

Britain's Daily Mail, another exception, wrote that research in electromagnetic weapons has been secretly carried out in the USA and Russia since the 1950's and that previous research has shown that low-frequency waves or beams can affect brain cells, alter psychological states and make it possible to transmit suggestions and commands directly into someone's thought processes. High doses of microwaves can damage the functioning of internal organs, control behavior or even drive victims insane or to suicide. Vladimir Putin also confirm, "Whoever controls the best directed energy weapons controls the world without guns or bullets."

Today, the pot of gold for mass social and global control lies with those pushing globalization, through the use of various electromagnetic frequencies through the weaponized Electromagnetic Spectrum and its use without impunity.

My deciding to document the experiences of my targeting, each day took on the qualities of a diary or journal.

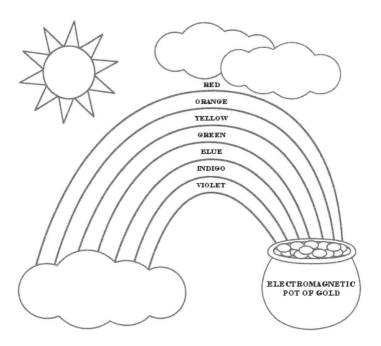

CHAPTER ONE

Awakening to a Monstrous Program

Dear Diary,

I had to ask myself "is this book worth the extreme torturous pain being inflicted on my right femur night after night, slowly draining of blood, in a continued vicious, electromagnetic beamed assault?"

I recognized that those targeting me are still hoping that the painful coercive, attacks, as I try to edit this book, will be unbearable and that I will stop. They are now deliberately, intentionally debilitating the right leg. The only thing left to deplete is bone marrow. I will break for now. I am off to the gym for some pool exercises hoping to restore the blood flow. As I leave through the beamed harassment system I hear the operator saying,

"If we lose our jobs, you will become a total cripple, stop what you are doing!"

Again, I ask myself is it worth to continue?

The answer is, "Yes!"

What choice do I have? I will continue to put my trust and faith in God and not in the powerful spirit of evil that has captivated the hearts and minds of these men. With every life they destroy, they accrue a heavy metaphysical debt in these ungodly widespread efforts.

"If we don't get you will, they will" is faintly, heard in the barrage of threats coming from the vantage point location in my ceiling where the drone, satellite energized radar laser beam is been positioned. As I write, the beam is alternating between my femur then expertly moving up to my left shoulder joint. "Destroy her arm" the operator then says.

It on, I will not and cannot give in. I am no coward and will never cower to this hideous program.

Perhaps, naively, hopefully, after filing another lawsuit the court might recognize my dilemma and morally help in whatever way they can. A court appointed attorney would be a dream. I wish it were this simple; however, courts just don't operate this way.

"Her leg" is said, after I cover the shoulder with Mylar and the pain subsides and the focus redirected again the femur.

This is said over and over again as the beam penetrates to the core typical of microwave weapons that heat from the inside out. When I stand the bone painfully shifts abnormally and there is a cracking noise as the bone slips now from the dried out joint. I almost buckle to the pain.

Should I feel discourage, intimidated, or frightened? Should I just give in, as some targeted individuals have after being beaten down so effectively and having nowhere to turn after their lives have been efficiently and effectively covertly destroyed?

How can I? Not only my life, but also the lives of everyone in our environment, especially family members, are targeted and to subdue the target become a high-tech focus.

The objective being to frighten me, with every breath, and every painful step, I think they will get it, they will see "She's just not scared" and leave. But these efforts are about more than frightening the target. These efforts are about the power of covert technology to control, individuals, groups, and populations and legalized military and law enforcement testing. I cannot stop. I will not negotiate. I don't make deals with the Devil's spawn.

I must face reality. This operation has decided that they will not stop either until I am neutralized one way or another. They will not stop without my life! Exposure has held them at bay albeit for a few years not. I learned quickly that the official program is offended by exposure, and cautious. This is especially true and if you are accurate about who, how and why. The want to harm you secretively.

After filing the Tort Claim, in March of 2013, I received the following excerpted responses by Certified Mail:

"This office has completed the investigation of the above-referenced matter under the Federal Tort Claims Act (FTCA) which you filed March 11, 2013, and is denied."

"The FTCA provides legal remedy enabling an individual to recover damages under which the United States, if it were a private person, would be liable. Our investigation did not find any negligent or wrongful act or omission of an employee acting within the scope of his or her employment that caused harm to you."

The letter goes on to state that should I move forward after Tort Claim denial, that the proper defendant would be the United States..."

My previous efforts have proven ineffective with the same written result to many government officials. The question is how and what can I along with thousands coming forth and revealing their suffering and the same plight? The question before us each day is what will have the greatest impact on the web of deceit surrounding factual government technology testing programs more heinous then many others documented human experimentation efforts historically on US citizens?

What do I have to lose?

The answer then hit me like a ton of bricks, "My life!"

Dear Diary,

When this situation erupted around me, someone told me, "You can't fight the government." I looked her squarely in the eyes and replied, albeit naively, "Yes, I can." I then and now just don't understand why I am not supposed to fight for my life.

Here I set with my sword, my computer.

Dear Diary,

My home has been entered, yet again, in one of numerous covert entries (Google Gaslighting). The covert entry is designed to back up the escalated death threats. In one of my other books, I detail that essentially this specific type of covert entry is designed to show the target how they can easily get to you. Of course, I immediately posted the information on my social network. I find that even this type of exposure to well over 10,000 followers, usually results, as stated before in a brief respite from the effort and backing off after reporting they are going to kill me using the verbal harassment. If so, it will not before I point the finger and tell the world!

The objective of covert entry to a home is to intentionally leave signs, appearing insignificant to others of which only the target would recognize. This time my camera was been taken of the official criminal informants used working alongside corrupt police. It was lying on a chair next to a bag from TGI Fridays, a popular restaurant chain in Los Angeles where I had not eaten but there it sat.

I had noticed the empty carry out bag sitting in the chair for about three days and paid no attention to it believing it was a store bag of which belonged to me and I had taken something out of. Today I picked it up and was amazed to see TGI Fridays written on it. I have not been to TGI Friday, for over two years. As I think back, I remember that the bag appeared on the chair, around the same time that I came in from the gym and found the back door to my family room unlocked.

The game is to get targets to question their reality, aka Gaslighting. I this type of mind game, the target then questions their sanity. You are supposed to think, "Did I put this here," "Did I go to TGI Fridays?"

These are typical psychological warfare tactics PSYWAR / PSYOPS designed to throw a target off balance and more importantly, the effort's hope is to question yourself and become fearful. In "Covert Technological Murder – Pain Ray Beam," I detail several similar incidents of coming in and actually having furniture moved around which is outrageous. Mark Rich's online PDF "The Hidden Evil" details many tactics of official state sponsored terrorism, which includes, covert entry, sabotage of property, and vandalism.

Let me state for the record, I, with a clear mind, 100% did not put the bag there, it was left behind for a desired effect. Silly me, through it all I still find amusement in this operation's tactics and even under the circumstances. Why, because I still am not frightened. I think, these people are having entirely too much fun with what they hope will leave to discrediting with the mental illness tag. The objective is for targets to buy into the and as a result, captured my attention and keep your focus on the covert effort around you. Otherwise you might forget and they can't have that

Dear Diary,

It is odd that the men in the operation center are always asking how I look. It appears that after getting a report on my physical appearance, by one of their foot soldiers following me around, I am then bombarded, and sickened, by their repeated false compliments. Many times, knowing in

7

advance where I am heading before leaving home, by mind reading and real-time viewing watching me prepare, someone connected is there waiting with charades, theatrics officially mobilizing the community.

The modernized Organized Stalking network is nationwide, alive and well as it was in Nazi Germany. Gang stalking was invented by Adolf Hitler during his dictatorship in Germany. During that time, they were called "informers". They wore a costume of brown shirts. Anyone against Adolf Hitler or against his laws were followed and watched and eventually killed!

Victim, after victim, after victim report that the U.S. government is today seeking out those who are considered troublemakers, i.e., political dissidents, activists, whistleblowers, and anyone exposing covert legalized, essentially illegal activities and more importantly the Electromagnetic technology being used, unseen or detectable. It makes the perfect hidden crime until thousands begin spilling the beans. The fact is this type of high-tech targeting is legalized under the guise of the "War on Terror" and the hunt for US citizens bogusly designated and placed on an FBI, DHS "Watchlist." The hope that using this label a person can be silenced and especially someone who uses he truth and telling on the corporation. Their fear is that these troublemakers might mobilized massive protest.

Get the picture?

The Patriot Act, was being used for approval to legally place basically anyone under surveillance and especially those individuals those who refuse to be silenced.

Perhaps they even hope that some of the lower level people they mobilize around all targets, and many paid, will be able to somehow ingratiate themselves with targets and become their Handler. That's funny. Many Mucky Mucks have certainly tried. Everyone, I repeat everyone from nationwide, two to three in each state, FBI/DHS and with me LAPD satellite / drone division, high operation centers are overseeing everything in these situations, and they apparently will sit and watch their handiwork if a target is pushed over the edge and goes postal? This is why many believe aliens and demons are at the helm. I must inform you it is red-blooded human monsters, with empathy muted who are likely programmed themselves. The awareness of human experimentation dating back decades, goes against their programming and means absolutely nothing to them.

It has crossed my mind several times, through research that the Army Electromagnetic Spectrum Management Operation could be spearheading biometric targeting, DNA, iris, gate, facial recognition, to include satellite tracking operations by the USAF are heavily involved. It is something to consider. However, the ideation of "Fusion Centers" FBI and DHS goal are to bring everyone under one roof within a counterterrorism paradigm. The Army Spectrum Management Office (ASMO), and is currently located in Alexandria, Virginia.

Alexandria Virginia. Again, Hmmm…Interesting. This is where many Intel agencies are headquartered. As prior military, Army, these bucket heads sound just like people in the military. However, law enforcement recruits heavily within the military branches of service. The USAF definitely, 100%, is involved, due to an installation being very close to where I live. And victims continue to report Navy involvement as well and essentially all levels of the military at various levels. The fact is these are joint operations, combining not only the military and more importantly military technology now turned on the civilian population.

After I posted on social network continued entries into my home and escalated death threats, and beamed assaults from the Multifunctional Directed Energy Weapon system, sporadically on my heart at times, a horrifically targeted individual in Syracuse, New York, responded, cautioning me, saying:

Dear Renee,

You need to do what you feel is right. However, that kind of talk, about coming into your home & silencing you, doesn't sound like an idle threat. They do kill people they feel are too activist or making things too public. Nancy Schaefer (lady crusader against CPS), Sean Stinn (TI working on solution to our problem), Darrim Daoud (TI activist England), and Markus and Bott (TI activist Germany) and many others.

I know you refuse to live your life in fear, but they are prepared to murder & sometimes do it.

Pamela June Anderson - stuck it out as long as she could. Alva Andersson – All targeted the same way you, I, and many are. All Heroes

Dear Diary,

I am not trying to be a hero. I am just willing to stand and fight for my life against this great evil slowly encroaching globally. I will not cower. It must be the Sun in Leo and Moon in Aries, in me!

Below is a list of which many, targeted activist, and whistleblowers, believe as shown by the excerpts below, are individuals who were factually *Target Individuals*, who died suspiciously. They are believed to have been covertly murdered for exposing mind control corruption by Directed Energy Weapons using extremely low frequency assaults deployed as radio waves.

I cannot collaborate whether true or false personally:

Nancy Schaefer

1. Oddities in the Nancy Schaefer "Suicide" Case

Garland Favorito

Infowars.com

March 30, 2010

On Friday, former Senator Nancy Schaefer and her husband were found dead in their home in Habersham County. Even before a GBI investigation could be initiated, media outlets began pronouncing that their death was a "murder-suicide" and shut off most public comment posting on their web sites. The "murder suicide" theory implies that Sen. Schaefer's husband shot her and then killed himself (or vice versa). Both Habersham County and the Georgia Bureau of Investigation began investigating the case as a "murder suicide" rather than the more obvious "murder made to look like suicide". Like so many people, I have known former Sen. Nancy Schaefer for 15 years and spoken to several people who know her better than I do. They believe that the "murder suicide" theory is highly unlikely for any one of the following reasons...

Alex Jones Infowars link: http://www.infowars.com/oddities-in-the-nancy-schaefer-suicide-case.

2. Sean Stinn Case:

"Biomedical Targeted Individual Dies Suddenly"

"Our friend and TI (targeted individual), Sean Stinn, who was a victim of electronic terrorism has passed," advised Kim Smith in a Facebook notice Saturday.

Stinn, 45, died unexpectedly on Sept. 5, reportedly of a heart attack.

Known as a bioengineer technical genius among the Targeted Individual community, Stinn fought to have evidence regarding electronic terrorism used in court. His father, a career Army man, had also been targeted, according to Stinn.

Stinn's roommate, Steve Wilson, also active in the Targeted Individual advocacy groups, advised on Wednesday about Sean's sudden death. "Sean Stinn, my friend since we went to summer camp at Chase Park in the 197Os and my recent roommate, passed away in his room inside my apartment," Wilson stated.

"He accomplished an incredible feat of acquiring a Bachelor Degree in biomedical engineering and traveled to Europe to make video regarding human rights abuses of mind controlling technology while being remotely tortured. He was brave intelligent and a friend." Stinn was in the process of acquiring Ph.D. in physics and was studying for the GRE exam.

"We were exchanging scientific papers and ideas," Wilson explained. "He had another targeted individual Peter Rosenholm scan [ned] me for RF signals before he moved in. He was tutoring me in math and physics. Sean will be missed..."

3. Darrim Daoud:

Darrim Daoud

"I think it is highly tragic that the young man, who was first to demonstrate against the crime of organized stalking and electronic terrorism, was killed under suspicious circumstances!"

Writes Eleanor White. Eleanor is a well-known Activist and Targeted Individual for over 30 years, from Ontario, Canada

"I believe that the late Darrim Daoud lived, and died, the best hero he had it in him to be, a hero of whom his father and mother can justly be proud, whatever belittling the papers might have to say about their fallen son, the few column-inches they had to spare at the time."

Writes John Allman's Christians Against Mental Slavery, in Great Britain, targeted for over 20 years.

4. Markus Bott

According to the elder Bott, his brother Markus Bott has been assassinated by the German BND on July 11th 2009 because of their activism, revealing the current situation in Germany, involving the modern-day genocide. Bott warned: "If my homepage disappears the BND will have assassinated me as well."

Victims of Organized Stalking, Electronic and/or Psychotronic Harassment, Mind Control 1940s to Present:

5. Pamela June Anderson

"Pam Anderson was respected in the targeted individual (TI) community and had recently been appointed to the board of Freedom from Covert Harassment and Surveillance (FFCHS) now dissolved. However, after 53 years of constant suffering and sabotage, with no end in sight, Pam Anderson had reached the end of her endurance."

"The Suicide of a Secret Government Program Victim Pam Anderson Military Raised Electronic Terrorism Bullied Stalked Organized Government Stalking", September 5, 2012, by Lissa Mires.

<u>6.</u> Alva Andersson

Alva Andersson, another Targeted Individual, victim of Electronic Terrorism dies.

On September 24, 2012 Carmen Lupan of Spain wrote:

Alva Andersson, a beautiful woman, TI and painter, died last week. She was only 38. She couldn't handle the pain and had often suicide thoughts and in the end the pain and suffering were too big to handle and she took her own life - according to a friend of a friend. That's how we receive news about our friends when they die and have been tortured for some years. The world lost yet another beautiful mind and soul that could have enriched culture for many years to come. Every stalker out there, every man with a position to defend, you committed yet another murder. And because of you the world will never be the same, because you walk in the know and have guilty minds and souls.

See also her message (July 30, 2011)

(Authentic Message)

Since December 2009 I have been attacked with electronic terrorism, via directed energy and or satellite, remote neural monitoring using supercomputers with artificial intelligence. This has been developed by and is being used by secret national agencies together with organized stalking. I have not been a political activist. This has made me lose my job several times and destroyed my life completely.

Alva Andersson, School of Hard Knocks, University of Life

7. Aaron Wartz (1986-2013)

Murdered by Erosive No Touch Physical Torture.

March 5, 2013 by Lissakrhumanelife - Published on Jan 14, 2013

Aaron Swartz was murdered by corporate interest…

Targeted Individual June T. Kuwatani's "List of the Dead"

A list of those targeted, stalked and terrorized, who came forward and tried to help?

All Targeted Individuals who have come forward to proper authorities, stayed within the law to obtain a remedy to the insidious violence inflicted upon every aspect of their human lives, tortured, terrorized, stalked, harassed, and had their physical, psychological, and financial lives ruined by their terrorist targeting and who are the victims of summary, arbitrary, and extra-legal executions:

'Summary executions' is the means of summary procedure in which the due process of law and in particular the minimum procedural guarantees as set out in Article 14 of the Covenant are either curtailed, distorted or not followed.

Arbitrary execution' is the arbitrary deprivation of life as a result of the killing of persons carried out by the order of a government with its complicity or tolerance or acquiescence without any judicial or legal process.

'Extra -legal execution' refers to killings committed outside the judicial or legal process, and at the same time, illegal under relevant national and international laws. Accordingly, in certain circumstances 'arbitrary execution' as defined above can be an 'extra-legal execution'.

"Spot a Word to the Wise" Blog"

Thank you for keeping track of those innocent human beings that died as the result of their extrajudicial, due process free - State, Corporate, Educational Institutions recruitment, training, and experimenting who are Sponsoring - Torture, Terrorism, and Human Extermination.

Another Target denied and deprived her rights and liberties, ridiculed by society, and murder by a police system that was designed to protect al in an equal manner are once again, are guilty of Murder in the 1st Degree.

Pamela June Anderson

Died - September 8, 2011 - San Bernardino, California.

Pamela Anderson was a longtime Targeted Individual who came forward to all proper authorities over the years - to no avail. This is due to government sponsored recruitment, training, and secret, ongoing human lab rat experimentation programs.

Robert Sharpe

Died - September 15, 2011 - Glendale, California

Robert was in contact with another Target. He was the victim of Organized Group Stalking and likely Electronic Terrorism

OBITUARY

Robert M. Sharp

Formerly of the Town of Newburgh, NY died September 15, 2011 in Glendale, CA.

MEMORIAL MASS:

11am on Tues, Oct 11, 2011 at Sacred Heart Church, Newburgh, NY. McKenzie Mortuary Services, Long Beach, California, 562-961-9301.

Edmund explained that his brother Robert "Bob" Sharpe had died in Glendale, California at a bus stop from heart failure.

During my conversations with Robert Sharpe he revealed to me that he was a victim of Organized Stalking and that he knew Wanda Dablin. The last email response that I sent to Robert Sharpe was on Monday September 12, 2011 at 5:45pm PST.

Robert responded on Wednesday September 14, 2011 at 4:10pm PST

Dr. Fred Bell,

Died of an apparent Heart Attack, on Sep 26, 2011

Another death, this time someone who was aware of Targets of Electronic Terrorism, with full understanding of the Government Involvement, under the Department of Defense - National Security Agency, CIA and other government agencies, participating in the use of Electronic Biological-Technological Weaponized Technologies:

Dr. Fred Bell died of an apparent Heart Attack, on Sep 26, 2011 in Minneapolis in his hotel room. He died a day or so after he spoke with Jesse Ventura for a Segment on the third season of "Conspiracy Theory with Jesse Ventura"

Alex Jones Interviews Jesse Ventura the Death of Dr. Bell, whom Jesse Ventura interviewed for a segment for his upcoming season, in the now off the air.

Coast to Coast AM – 22 February 2011 - Electronic Harassment & Warfare with Dr. Fred Bell
Dr. Bell Explains all forms of Electronic Harassment

The list continues to grow of covert assassinations.

Here Is A Really Good Movie. It is about how the wealthy, behind the Targeted Individuals program have recruited Civilians to go along with the entire targeting program nationwide. It is classic life imitating art or vice versa. One thing is certain, and you can bet that the architects are gambling with the human lives of Targeted Individuals with focus on the Targeting Audience of recruits.

The general public have no idea that the architect's behind all of it are in direct line with a fictional movie about the rich who gamble upon the human lives of other people. They bet large sums of money - and don't give a (bleep). If those being dragged into it are forced into the demented world of these rich psychopaths and sociopaths and serial (bleep) killers who for nothing other than a wagered bet, the movie depicts would sacrifice the human life of targeted individuals.

In Memory of Kishing Andrew Michael Lai

Andy Lai recently passed away based on his account here:

Rebellious Slave it was sometimes in June.

Remembering Bruno Marchesani

Those who knew Bruno Marchesani were saddened to hear a couple of days ago of his passing on July 19th due to complications from a stroke, as I was informed.

Bruno did a lot for the TI community in the San Francisco Bay area.

He helped organize meetings, rallies, sent email notices to local TI's and helped with our annual table at Conspiracy Con in Santa Clara.

He touched many lives in our community and will be greatly missed. He was also tortured with a variety of ailments, mostly having to do with being targeted. Prayerfully, he is now at peace and in a place where the perps can no longer torment him.

Sandy Cason

Sandy Cason was a sweet heart and will be missed along with Sean Stinn (47), Ted Gunderson (80), Fred Bell, Pam Anderson (53) September 8, 2011, Kelly Shropshire (26) April 9, 2012, Cindy Goldman, Charles Schlund,

Bruno Marchesani (53) July 19, 2012.

Sandy Cason - Recorded a Testimony of Being a Targeted Individual

Man, who died in blast lived in foil-wrapped home, filmed neighbors

Kevin Harris

Neighbors described Kevin Harris, 52, as odd but harmless with a history of mental illness. They made a point to walk at a brisk pace past his house, which was wrapped in foil, neighbors told The Times. Cryptic notes would appear, taped to a tree in the front yard.

A neighbor showed the *Times* one such note taped to the tree Saturday morning. It read: "For your information: My introspection and my adversary's behavior have convinced me that electronic mind reading is now reality."

This would also include something called a life insurance policy called - Dead peasants

From Capitalism a Love Story - Michael Moore

Here is the movie about the rich who gamble via Russian Roulette - as they find their victims who either play or will be killed, and the rich who bet millions upon who will be the last one standing....

Sounds like the global targeted individual - and how they are sold out - to the highest bidders.

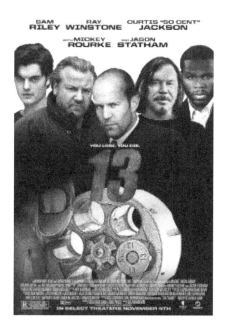

In Acknowledgement

In Remembrance

In Celebration

In Testament

In Support

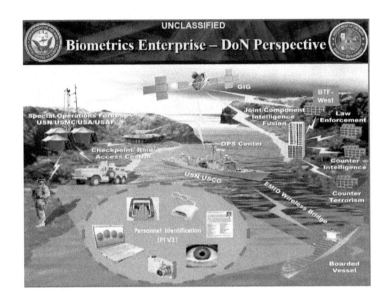

CHAPTER TWO

What exactly is the Electromagnetic Spectrum (EMS)?

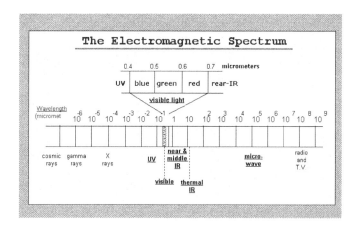

The Communications Act of 1934, as amended, governs radio EMS use in the US and its territories. The act established duality in Spectrum Management (SM) in the US between the President for federal government stations and the Federal

Communications Commission (FCC). The FCC regulates the spectrum use of non-federal operated radio stations, common carriers, and private organizations or individuals.

By Executive Order 12016 of 1978, the President delegated his functions under the act to a new organization created as the National Telecommunications and Information Administration (NTIA) and placed them under the Secretary of Commerce.

The electromagnetic (EM) spectrum is the range of all types of EM radiation. Radiation is energy that travels and spreads out as it goes – the visible light that comes from a lamp in your house and the radio waves that come from a radio station are two types of electromagnetic radiation. The other types of EM radiation that make up the electromagnetic spectrum are microwaves, infrared light, ultraviolet light, X-rays and gamma-rays.

You know more about the electromagnetic spectrum than you may think says NASA Goddard Space Flight

Center website. We encounter portions of the EM spectrum in your day-to-day life.

RADIO: Your radio captures radio waves emitted by radio stations, bringing your favorite tunes. Radio waves are also emitted by stars and gases in space.

Microwave: Microwave radiation will cook your popcorn in just a few minutes, but is also used by astronomers to learn about the structure of nearby galaxies.

INFRARED: Night vision goggles pick up the infrared light emitted by our skin and objects with heat. In space, infrared light helps us map the dust between stars.

VISIBLE: Our eyes detect visible light. Fireflies, light bulbs, and stars all emit visible light.

ULTRAVIOLET: Ultraviolet radiation is emitted by the Sun and is the reason skin tans and burns. "Hot" objects in space emit UV radiation as well.

X-RAYS: A dentist uses X-rays to image your teeth, and airport security uses them to see through your bag. Hot gases in the Universe also emit X-rays.

GAMMA RAY: Doctors use gamma-ray imaging to see inside your body. The biggest gamma-ray generator of all is the Universe.

Are radio waves completely different physical objects than gamma-rays?

They are produced in different processes and are detected in different ways, but they are not fundamentally different. Radio waves, gamma-rays, visible light, and all the other parts of the electromagnetic spectrum are electromagnetic radiation.

The electromagnetic spectrum describes all the wavelengths of light. From dark nebulae to exploding stars, it reveals an otherwise invisible universe.

When you think of light, you probably think of what your eyes can see. But the light to which our eyes are sensitive is just the beginning; it is a sliver of the total amount of light that surrounds us. The electromagnetic spectrum is the term used by scientists to describe the entire range of light that exists.

The EMS is a highly regulated and saturated natural resource. The EMS includes the full range of all possible frequencies of electromagnetic radiation.

The Air Force Spectrum Management Office (AFSMO) mission is to plan, provide, and preserve access to the EMS or the Air Force and selected DOD activities. The Army spectrum Management Office (ASMO) is the Army Service-level office for *ALL* spectrum-related matters. The Navy and Marine Corps Spectrum Center (NMSC) coordinates SM policy and guidance and represents the Navy, and when required, the Marine Corps, in spectrum negotiations with civil, military, and national regulatory organizations. The United States Coast Guard (USCG) Spectrum Management and Telecommunications Policy Division, COMMANDANT (CG-652) Office is the USCG Service-level office for all spectrum-related matters. The National Guard Bureau (NGB) J-6/C4 spectrum management branch is the designated office within NGB responsible for planning and executing SM for assigned forces and providing support to the National Guard (NG) joint force headquarters–state (JFHQ-State) in communications with United States Northern Command (USNORTHCOM).

Army Spectrum Management is under the control of the Army Spectrum Management Office (ASMO). The Army spectrum manager (ASM) directs Army-wide spectrum management activities. This includes the development and implementation of spectrum management policy, coordination of Army spectrum access requirements with the United States (US) government organizations, and the allocation of radio frequency (RF) assignments in support of Army operations. The ASM is the spectrum supportability certification authority for RF dependent systems and provides guidance to material developers with the identification of spectrum for both the continental United States (CONUS) and outside the continental United States (OCONUS) use. The ASM serves as the principle advisor to the Army Chief

Information Officer (CIO)/G-6 in regard to RF spectrum management and regulatory matters and represents Army requirements in both National and International regulatory and policy forums.

The frequency assignment function of EMSO entails the requesting and issuance of authorization to use frequencies for specific equipment. Examples of frequency assignment are providing the frequencies for assignment to a combat net radio (CNR) network, providing frequencies for unmanned aerial systems (UAS), or providing the frequencies for assignment to a line of sight (LOS) network.

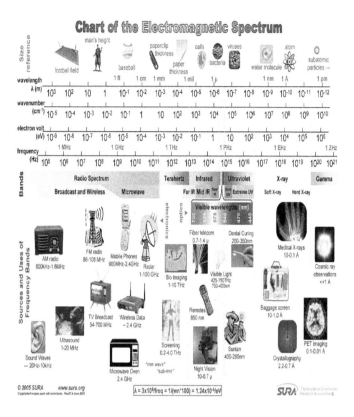

Notice the Electromagnetic Spectrum Ability to:

a. Carry sound waves - An example is that of psychological electronic "Electronic Terrorism" capability from a distance using artificial telepathy or the "Hearing Voices" effect using the spectrum from a distance and originating from a state-of-the-art operation center.

b. Radar / radar laser beam – This is spectrum used in deployment of Microwave and Ultrasound Directed

Energy Weapons, to include mind reading technology connected to EEG technology.

c. Biometric screening is used for real time tracking of a targeted individual through the spectrum bio imaging capability. The system being used is actually a bio-coded system enabling monitoring of a target through downloading of the target's DNA, gait, iris, fingerprint, etc., into a mega computer system.

Dear Diary,

My middle daughter and new granddaughter arrive tomorrow night. Yippee! My youngest daughter, in college in Michigan, arrives the week of Thanksgiving. Both my oldest daughter, who moved back home a few weeks ago, and I are overjoyed!

Dear Diary,

Oh, my goodness. There has been another shooting. This time it was at the Los Angeles International Airport. My oldest daughter recommended we not mention it to her sister scheduled to arrive today. It might scare and upset her. I checked the airport. Terminals 1, 2 and 3 were closed. Terminals 1 and 2 have been reopened. Terminal 3, where the incident took place, will remain closed, I was told by airline staff during my call. Fortunately, my daughter is coming in on a late flight which arrives at 11:00 p.m. tonight.

Dear Diary,

What a great day. We spent the day at a popular Los Angeles French restaurant my daughter use to work so that all of her ex-co-workers could see the baby born after moving back to Denver. The baby's father also worked there. I must admit that my daughter's ex is looking good and I am proud of him. I made the mistake to telling her this, not realizing he was standing behind me in the restaurant. My daughter became extremely agitated. She then had the nerve to tell me to shut up. I was taken aback and thought, "Oh, really!" It was an innocent comment that I made and meant no harm. The oldest girl had already told me to "shut up" earlier that morning in the kitchen.

Yep, they must be mind-controlled if they think they can speak to me this way. I mean, "really!" However, I'm cool. I do not want a repeat of last Christmas where there appeared to be definite manipulation and influence technological effort targeting not only me, but my daughters from the operation center. Many families are test subjects for mind invasive technology and especially this this program is after you. So much chaos, during the planned visit was created, which began with great joy and expectation, that it was completely ruined. I actually ended up spending

Christmas alone a previous time at my home while the three of them, my daughters, at the middle girl's apartment when she lived in Los Angeles. For the operation center, mission accomplished.

Dear Diary

What the heck happened? Can you believe that the Sheriff was called to my house yesterday, a mere four days after the middle girl's arrival called by my oldest daughter? This was after a minor argument. I then was carted off to the psyche ward by the Los Angeles County Sheriff Department on a 51/50? Say it is not so! Unfortunately, it was! As a result, the Thanksgiving family celebration planned for 30 days was cut short in a matter minutes. After just four days, my daughter and new granddaughter returned to Denver and my oldest daughter, having no place to stay, had to leave my home. The youngest girl was scheduled to arrive right before Thanksgiving so she was not affected.

Dear Diary,

They released me from Olive View Psychiatric ER today just shy of 24 hours, after being brought here, involuntarily on a 4 day hold around 11:00 a.m. yesterday. I had to find my way home, 40 miles from where I live, in my pajamas and shoes too big for my feet. The shoes flopped off my feet as I headed towards the Metro Station. I really must have looked mentally ill trying to find the station, but apparently not mentally ill enough for an involuntary hold of 72 hours as determined by hospital staff on the Psych ward. I came home to an empty house, more hurt than angry, at the manipulated machination.

As soon as I arrived, I officially set down and begin to record the experience for this book. I will not be silenced!

Sadly, another holiday gathering with my children has been electromagnetically ruined by these covert monsters. I had so looked forward to having all three daughters together with me this Thanksgiving, to include my grand, and had bought expensive plane tickets. My first grandchild was born on March 21, 2013.

I cannot believe that not one but four Sheriff cars showed up to my house to handcuff me and take me out. This time, the supervisor, with Sergeant Stripes on his shirt came along too. It was as if he already knew in advance that he would have to justify, and approve, my being transported, not to jail, due to a so-called domestic dispute, but to the psych hospital. He then left immediately smiling. Apparently, they do not want me before any judge where I would have an opportunity to explain the dynamics of what is happening around me and a major goal is the have the mental illness tag cleverly applied in the early stages.

This is the third try to have me committed with now two unsuccessful attempts by law enforcement to discredit me. So many targeted individuals have fallen victim to this strategic tactic. After expertly discredited, the result is that no one believes the target, and essentially, sky is literally the limit for the use of extreme psychological and physical torture, and many attempts of mental control of the target.

My daughter told them that I threatened to hit her with the small frying pan which I had just scrambled eggs in. This was after she came downstairs while I was in the kitchen preparing breakfast. There was absolutely no violence at all. She then went back upstairs, and came down with a hammer in her pocket telling me that if I hit her I would be sorry. It was bizarre. I was not angry at all. "You want to fight, come on" baiting me. At that point, after realizing what she was trying to do, and what was happening through likely extremely low frequency manipulation and influencing of her, believe it or not, I said,

"That's it. I am calling the Sheriff's Department and getting you out of my home."

I instead went into my office, hoping to let things simmer down, and began planning for my show Blog Talk Radio show, "The Targeted Individual's VOICE" scheduled to air that very same day at 5:00 p.m. In fact, I was trying to contact my co-hosts to review the show's topics when I heard a loud pounding on my front door and the announcement, "Sheriff's Department!" They must have known where I was in the house because right before the pounding on the door, I literally heard one of them say to the others, "We are getting ready to get her" as they passed the window of my office.

I at that point did not have a clue that my daughter had gone upstairs and actually contacted the Sheriff's department. I jumped up and answered the door with the Mylar enforced knee pads still attached to my knees naively hoping to combat the extremely low frequency microwave attacks coming from across the street and a neighborhood garage set-up. The portable beam hope to stop me every day as I work on various things and combined with attacks overhead also from the operation center. When the Sergeant saw the material tied to my knees, he grinned, and then asked "What is that on your knees?" The material tied to my knees made me a perfect fit for what they already had in store.

Knowing that any subject related to covert use of microwave electromagnetic technology, and Mylar or aluminum foil to deflect the rays, would surely get me committed, quicker, I quickly regrouped and told him that my knees were hurting after a fall.

"The Mylar material", I explained, holds heat to my knees after rubbing pain relief cream on both knees." I said.

I did not tell them anything thing about my books, etc., or the aluminum foil and Mylar covering the headboard of my bed upstairs and wall to combat the beam being sent up close from another neighbor's *bathroom or from many angles and homes around me that I yet again saw first FBI enter then USAF personnel.*

That would be my daughter's department. I watched her pointing to my books on the dining room table, telling the deputies, I was mentally deranged, and had threatened to harm her with the again, very small frying pan. I sat on the couch with my mouth aghast. I first believed that it was an incident which would blow over with possibly them escorting my daughter out of my home or telling us to work it out. She had intentionally taunted me and I foolishly had played right into it. When I told her, she would have to leave she became angry at having to find somewhere else lounge around and decided to have me taken from my home.

I was handcuffed and taken out of my home in broad daylight for the neighbors to see with the street eerily more quiet than usual as people watched from windows. I sat handcuffed in the back of the squad car for about 30 minutes, waiting for a female officer to arrive to search and transport me to the hospital. While waiting, and saddened, I repeatedly asked the arresting deputy to ensure that my adult daughter was not left inside my home since I was being taken away. The middle girl had been in her room during the entire episode and had not seen, or heard, the exchange of words between her oldest sister and I in the kitchen. Yet, I later would learn that she had substantiated everything that my oldest daughter said to the deputies without even leaving her bedroom.

Attempting to help my oldest daughter, nearing 25 years old, yet again, cost me literally and dearly. She was trying to get into the music industry and I had invested a lot of time and money hoping to help her into whatever would make her a productive member of society and support her dream. There would be no family gathering as the effort to separate and isolate targets from family and friends continues and reported by many nationwide. I had already been told through the beamed harassment system by the men in the operation center saying,

"We are going to make your daughter's hate you!" shortly before and after their arrival.

On November 4, 2013, Monday, at 12:01 p.m., I sat in the Psychiatric ER waiting to see a doctor. The female deputy waited with me, until I could be turned me over officially to hospital staff.

About 45 minutes later, a young Asian doctor entered the room with a young female Resident in tow. He introduced himself then asked,

"Why are you here?" "This appears to be a domestic incident?" I looked him squarely in the eyes and replied,

"That's my question." I then begin explaining the argument between my oldest daughter temporarily staying with me because she had nowhere else to go but home to mom.

He then said, "I am just trying to figure out what happened." "Was there any violence? "It says here you threatened her with a frying pan."

I replied, "Absolutely no violence," I told him.

"She came downstairs in what appears to be an attempt to incite an argument then returned with a hammer in her pocket. I should have called the Sheriff's department, as I told her I would, but she apparently beat me to the punch."

"What is this about aluminum on your bedroom walls?" An immediate red flag and alarm sounded with this question, "That your daughter reported" he asked.

"Look I am a writer, and have three books currently available on Amazon in which I detail the covert use of microwave, directed energy weapons today." Aluminum is supposed to be a deflector of the beamed rays,

"Do you hear voices" he then asked.

I immediately replied "No."

"Tell me about the books."

I told him the names of the first three books.

"Remote Brain Targeting, You Are Not My Big Brother and Covert Technological Murder –Pain Ray Beam." He repeated the names back to me.

"Do you think that an imaginary "Big Brother" is following you around?"

"Look" I told him, calmly, "I can write a book about the sky being green and the grass being blue" if I chose to.

"If I am not hurting anyone that is my business" I said.

"The problem is" he then replied,

"Your daughter said that you threatened that you would harm her."

"Look doctor, this is clearly a domestic issue as you stated, and I am sure this is documented in your notes from the police connected to the official effort targeting me who brought me here. There was absolutely no violence in this incident and essentially it came down to my word against hers."

"Furthermore, my daughter, the Sheriff Deputies assured me would have to leave my home immediately, after I was brought here, and in fact, she will be there when I return."

"So, if you are confused as to why I am really here, based on whatever is in your notes, know that I myself, am confused as to why I am REALLY here" emphasizing really.

"We will need further evaluation" he then said.

"Tell me, how can I find your books?"

"You can go to Amazon.com and locate the books written by me."

"There is a total of three in what I call the "Mind Control Technology" book series, and a fourth book, a metaphysical book recently published entitled

"The Heart is Another Name for God."

"I also have a website which you can check out."

I then gave him the link to bigbrotherwatchingus.com and watched as he scribbled it on the top of the notes he had been taking as we talked

"One last thing Doc, I do a weekly internet talk show broadcast, every Monday night 5:00 p.m. In fact, when the Sheriff knocked, I was back in my home office preparing for the show this evening. Is there any way that someone could contact my show's co-host and let him know what has

happened, and also tell him to go on with the show and to use the script I prepared and emailed to him?"

"What is the name of your show," the doctor asked, skepticism never leaving his face,

"The Targeted Individual's VOICE" I replied.

"What do you mean by targeted?" he asked.

I knew of no way to get him to quickly grasp the format for the show except to ask him was he familiar with the recent Navy Yard Shooter, Aaron Alexis.

"Well, my show is about the reality of electromagnetic, extremely low frequency technology, little known to the general public in full use today for subliminal manipulation and influence. I have a fast-growing audience into the thousands" I told him. And, the show has been advertised in advance."

"Hmmm" he said. "I will see what I can do."

During the exchange the Resident had listened quietly. He then turned to her and said,

"You can take over from here. You are officially now a doctor."

He then turned and left the room. She stood in front of me, assessing where to begin her line of text book questions fresh out of school. Before she could get started, and immediately after her asking me to tell her everything again, which she had just witnessed me report to the doctor, I was annoyed. Did she not stand there and hear me tell the entire story?

"Look, I am not a guinea pig here" I told her after her request.

"Why do you feel like a guinea pig" she shot back.

"Really, come on now" I said,

"I am not your practice patient. Can you please contact my co-host about the show which is set to begin in about 3 hours?" It was after 2:00 p.m.

"Do you have a phone number" she asked?

Fortunately, I had written his number down that morning on a Post It sticky note and remembered what I had written as his San Diego residence. I gave her the phone number, and thanked her a few times. She then left the room saying that she would attempt to reach him for me.

Shortly afterwards the ward nurse entered the room to take me to the ward.

The female Sheriff, who also had sat quietly witnessing the exchange, finally removed the handcuffs, and left as me in the care of the hospital staff member.

"Follow me" the ward nurse said as she and I headed towards her office for additional processing. Once seated, she explained that they were experiencing a rather large number of unusual admittances. As a result, there was no room available for me on the actual psych ward. Because of this, I would be held in the holding room next door to her office, which is usually reserved for patients who had to be isolated and strapped to their beds.

"This room is usually for violent and extremely mentally ill patients," she told me.

"If you notice there are straps on the bed. However, you appear to be harmless based on why you are here" she said.

"Thank you, do you have to shut the door?

"No, we can leave it open, nor do you have to be restrained."

Right before shift change, around 3:30 p.m., the young Resident appeared in the office, apparently being shown around the facility by a fellow doctor. When they came into the nurse's office, I asked her could I speak with her for a moment.

"I have additional information I neglected to give to the first doctor" I told her.

"I believe this information is connected also why I am really here I said." My hope was that the information would also add suspicion to the ludicrous reason why I was taken from my home this morning and add to my credibility. The doctor giving her the tour of the facility immediately told me,

"She does not have time right now." The two then abruptly left the room.

However, to my surprise, right before 5:00 p.m. the young Resident returned before going home. I was so grateful to see her face.

"I forgot to tell the doctor during the initial interview that my books focus on legalized technology in full use today specifically by law enforcement and the military in which they do not want publicized."

And also, *"Based on what I heard, before they knocked on my door, my being here has something to do with the decision to take me, not to jail, but to the psych ward in an ongoing effort to discredit me in a relentless effort to have me declared mentally ill."*

"Oh, I see" she said.

"By the way, were you able to speak with my co-host?" I asked.

"Yes, I did get in touch with him. I told him exactly what you said to tell him, "The show must go on.""

"He told me that he had already spoken to your daughter after returning a call you made to him this morning, apparently before the Sheriff knocked. During that time, he learned what had occurred. He said to tell you that he then contacted your guest to inform him of the situation, and the possibility of going on with the show. However, your guest, said, he did not want to do the show unless you were there."

This was a major positive hit for credibility.

After she left I felt a degree of relief and began preparing myself for the mandatory stay, usually, 72 hours. Everything had fallen into place for the show to be rescheduled at a later date. I asked for something to read, a book or magazine to distract my mind and redirect my focus.

On the other side of her office was another room connected, and also used as a holding area. The movie "Independent Day" was playing on the television. Two young African American men were sitting inside talking, laughing, and watching television and another man, I later learned a veteran as well was snoring loudly.

When the shift changed, and the two were discharged, the veteran was transported to the VA.

I sat watching television and reading until I became tired about 11:30 p.m. that night. I tried to stay awake as long as possible to ensure that I would be able to sleep throughout the night. I was totally drained and completely exhausted from the activities of the day and slept soundly.

The next morning, as I sat watching a game show, I was distracted by the sound of a determined walk of a woman in high heels clicking as she walked down the hall which stopped at the open door of the nurse's station. She walked through the door and asked for me by name. I looked up from my couch/bed not far away. One look at her, I knew she was a very, very, sharp woman appearing to be of Hispanic origin.

"Renee Mitchell" she asked as she approached me. It was around 9:30 a.m.

"Good morning, I am Doctor...could you come with me please."

"Good morning" I replied back as she turned and headed out the door with me following. We headed into an office that said, "Resident's Office" on the door."

"Are you a Resident" I asked her.

"No" she replied, "I am a staff doctor here."

"Have a seat" she said as she slid into her seat behind the desk and I on the opposite side.

"So, tell me why you are here?" I then recanted everything as I had identically in less than 24 hours ago. I detailed the situation before I arrived and gave her information on where to locate my books, on Amazon and also the reviews that the books were getting, substantiating my plight through others having similar experiences. I explained to her that typically, many are experiencing, when speaking out about covert government corruption, or specific technology in a covert testing program, efforts evolve immediately to discredit the target. I also gave her the links to my website, and also the link too archived talk show on Blog Talk Radio telling her she could listen to archived shows where there are highly credible interviews from even ex insiders of this program.

She said that she would check out all of the information I have given her out and would get back to me. It was about 10:00 a.m. She then escorted me back to the holding area.

About an hour later, she returned.

"I checked out the information you gave me. I find it fascinating to include your website. However, before I can release you, and to protect the

hospital from liability, is there anyone who can verify that what you are saying is a belief held not only by you but also others?"

"What do you need?" I asked her thinking she had come to the right person.

"Are there other websites, for example, or even someone else I could call to vouch for you, for example, prove that if I release you, that you have a safe place to return also?"

"I have little family and talking to my daughter's right now is out of the question. Didn't you talk to the show's co-host"

"I did" she said.

"The problem is that he mentioned that people are following you all over town as part of what you are experiencing and harassing you" That true to some extent, it is called "Organized Stalking" another tactic of this program

When she told me, this was reported to her by my co-host, familiar, with organized community stalking efforts, by his own personal experiences, which again goes hand in hand with electronic assaults, I quickly had to reevaluate if letting the hospital staff speak with another targeted individuals would help me or hurt me, and result in a delusional diagnosis and longer stay.

"Is there anyone else" she asked.

"You could to reach my landlords" I said.

"But on second thought, I don't want them involved in personal business, especially of this nature, and certainly do not want them to know that I am here."

"I would just ask them about you home life, and if you pay your rent-on time, and things of that nature" she replied.

"Okay" I said.

"I don't have my cellular phone and have been waiting on a new phone, which I purchased and should arrive soon. This is a handicap because this is where I keep phone numbers."

"However, the other day when I needed to find a contact phone number for them to fix the garbage disposal, and smoke detectors in my house, I was able to find them online by typing their names into a search site and miraculously their landline phone number came up on the internet."

"You should be able to get their home number this way also," I told her.

"Okay" she said. "And, would write down at least one other website with content similar to yours?" Mind Justice came to mind instantly, as well as Freedom from Covert Harassment and Surveillance. She writes the site names in her notes. I also gave also to prove how this is a global issue, the Targeted Individuals Canada.com website.

"There are many, many more" I told her and they are accessible by simply typing in targeted individuals, MK Ultra, Electronic Terrorism, Organized or Gang stalking, etc.

About a half an hour later, I again heard the determined clicking sound of the heels as she neared the door. It was exactly 24 hours after my arrival. She entered and said,

"You are free to go. I have begun processing the discharge paperwork, and the ward nurse will finish up and return your belongings and clothes. Take good care of yourself."

I had sat there relieved. Although appearing cool, calm and collected, my stomach had knotted up not knowing what to expect.

"Thank you sooooooo very, very much" I told her elated!

She smiled, told me to follow up with my therapist at the VA hospital, and then left the room.

Criteria for a 72 hour Hold 51/50

A 72 hour hold usually means at least 72 hours. Yet, again, as documented in "You Are Not My Big Brother" another incident unfolded. Although the first time it had taken court intervention, I was now being released after just an overnight stay of approximately 24 hours.

The Regulations Regarding Release from Detention States:

At the end of the 72-hour period, the detained person must be evaluated to determine whether further care and treatment is required. If the person no longer requires evaluation and treatment, the person shall be released. WIC.Div.5, Art.1.5, Sec.5172.

If further care and treatment is required, the person must be informed of the evaluation, and the advice of the need for, but has not been able or willing to accept treatment, or to accept referral to services which must be describe on the certification application. As willingness to accept treatment on a voluntary basis is a pre-condition to involuntary detention, the failure to adequately address the issue of voluntariness may serve as a basis for release or voluntariness ordered by the decision maker.

If the person continues to be a danger to him or herself, or others, or is gravely disabled, the person may be certified for intensive treatment and detained for up to 14 additional days.

Again, I have not, never have been nor ever will be a danger to self or others! You can count on this!!!

Dear Diary,

Now back at home after a family uproar, as I edited this note, the radar laser beam directed again bore down from the ceiling focused on my left shoulder joint. When I stood, the joint now deteriorating began to crack. I did an exercise I found online designed for restoring the blood supply to the shoulder joint, then decided to head to the gym. The only reason, that I have not been reduced to a complete cripple, so far, is because of a pool routine daily and exposure.

Dear Diary,

Was it even wise to have my oldest daughter around me based on the negativity happening in her life right now? Losing the major music deal was a big blow to us all. It was especially hard on her. Those targeting me immediately took full credit for the loss by validating their tampering with her and saying,

"We told you to stop those books and if you do not, we will completely destroy her too!" As a result, an extremely talented songstress and more importantly, songwriter, was left with nothing. The deal had been negotiated and neared finalization.

The objective in these targeting continues to be a search for, and focused on, anything the operation believes will affect the target emotionally or psychologically. They look for anything they believe the target cares for, loves or holds dear, that can be used as a pawn and means of control. And, sadly, in many cases, it works. Whether true or false, after she lost the deal, I knew that their covert tampering was not an improbability. I had seen it before regarding her a few times and again, many targeted across America are reporting tampering with loved ones as well.

This technology can manipulate and track anyone, and everyone, on the face of the earth effortlessly and as easy as a full body scan, and then downloaded into the mega computer system the target's biometric signature. The mind has no firewall.

Based on the characteristic of this technology, it also is not a great improbability that she was also nudged into calling the Sheriff's Department. The episode made no sense. I was not angry at her. Why else would she risk being put out with no place to go herself there trying to recuperate? It makes no sense except to those in the operation center overseeing these situations. They could care less about you, your family or anyone. This is how they earn their living. Why should they care? They go home to their families each day, and night, after 8 hour rotating shifts, and focused covert destruction of other lives, in a fraudulent existent. They pretend to be someone they really are not, working in "Top Secret" programs behind tightly closed doors, well hidden.

Thank goodness, the ongoing strategic effort to discredit me continues to fail again, again, and again. These books are partly the reason and have leveled the playing field to some degree to include the electronic microwave beamed assaults.

Some TIs have not been so lucky, have lost hope, and given up. Or, their bodies have failed them from repeated, long term, covert physical attacks by powerful, debilitating, Directed Energy Weapons.

Make no mistake about it; a life can be taken in an instant and without leaving a trace.

Dear Diary,

I am all alone today on this Thanksgiving morning 2013. The house, which should have been filled with the sounds of laughter, and family love, is so quiet, that you can hear a pin drop. Guess I will get take out!
Someone on Facebook posted "Stand" by Rascal Flatt on my page and I listened to it about 10 times already. It really made me feel so much better

and gave me hope that my efforts are meaningful in the grand scheme, even if it means separation from my family. The fact is they will never destroy the love my daughters have for me and I for them. No matter how they try, incident after incident, they keep coming home to Mom.

"Stand"

You feel like a candle in a hurricane
Just like a picture with a broken frame
Alone and helpless
Like you've lost your fight
But you'll be alright, you'll be alright

[Chorus:]

Cause when push comes to shove
You taste what you're made of
You might bend, till you break
Cause it's all you can take
On your knees you look up
Decide you've had enough
You get mad you get strong
Wipe your hands shake it off
Then you Stand, Then you stand

Life's like a novel

With the end ripped out
The edge of a canyon
With only one way down
Take what you're given before its gone
Start holding on, keep holding on

Cause when push comes to shove
taste what you're made of
You might bend till you break
Cause it's all you can take
On your knees you look up
Decide you've had enough
You get mad, you get strong
Wipe your hands, shake it off
Then you stand, then you stand

Every time you get up
And get back in the race
One more small piece of you
Starts to fall into place...

Cause when push comes to shove
You taste what you're made of
You might bend til you break
Cause it's all you can take

Yeah, then you stand

Yeah, baby

Woo hoo, woo hoo

Woo hoo, woo hoo

Then you stand, yeah yeah

Songwriters

Blair Daly and Danny Orton

Thank you. I will!

CHAPTER THREE

The Mind Controlled Programmed Assassin: An Ancient Science

In front of an envoy from Malek-Shah, a fedavi plunges a dagger into his own heart and another leaps off the tower upon orders from his programmer, Hassan Sabbah, "The Old Man of the Mountain". Sabbath had organized this secret society of Assassins, the Haschishin, in the 11th century at the time of the Crusades. The members of this sect, while intoxicated with haschish, would commit the most violent crimes or acts of daring; all upon a given cue by their leader.

DEMOLAY

When the Templars under Jacque DeMolay were disbanded by the Council of Vienne in France in 1311, among the charges leveled against them was that they had adopted the heretical teachings and practices of this Islamic sect, the Haschishin.

The Templars which fled to Scotland would become the Scottish Rite we know today. Haschish was also the same drug which Wilhelm Wulf, a Nazi psychological warfare specialist hired by the CIA after the war; experimented with in Nazi Germany and in the MK-ULTRA mind control program before the CIA settled on LSD.

In recent years, Aaron Alexis, named the "Navy Yard Shooter," contacted a major and well-known support organization for targeted individuals. This documented as happening right before his murderous rampage asking for help, and seeking direction on what to do. He specifically stating that he, as a government contractor working with the Navy, recognized what was happening to him as Electronic Terrorism. He stated that he was being targeted by electromagnetic, extremely low frequency technology. After the incident, it was documented that this organization also received call regarding Alexis's contact from the FBI.

AARON ALEXIS

Aaron Alexis 15 days before the Navy Vet killed twelve people at the DC Navy yard, Alexis emailed the following letter to freedom from covert harassment and surveillance (FFCHS):

Subject: need assistance on dealing with the direct energy attacks!!

September 1, 2013

Hello,

My name is Aaron. I am ex-Navy, and have been working as a contractor for the DOD. I have recently come under attack after blowing up at Norfolk Airport in Virginia.

The first attack started coming when I was on assignment in Rhode Island. I was hearing what I though was people next door telling lies about me. In truth I didn't know that I was under attack and thought I could escape what I was experiencing, by leaving the hotel I was in. It wasn't until it almost cost me my job that I realized that one, I wasn't crazy, and that two that I had to figure out what was going on.

I am glad I found this site; however, I need assistance because, I have not allowed them to scare me off my job, but I fear the constant bombardment from the elf weapon is starting to take its toll on my body. I am currently in dc now near the pentagon. I think I know the specific group in the military that is responsible for developing and assisting the military with.

Any assistance you can give me and at the same time whatever info can give you on what I know please contact me ASAP. This was written by Aaron Alexis.

A look back over fifty years ago…

Charles Manson

Interestingly a rumor which surfaced sometime afterward the Alexis fatality was later determined to be completely false. This rumor centered on a non-existent letter by none other than Charles Manson written from his jail cell.

The letter stated that he now believed himself part of a government mind control program which included various brainwashing and mind control techniques. It is documented that Manson and his followers were using drugs such as LSD, for mind control.

Was Manson a delta programmed killer? Were the techniques Manson used taught during his own programming/brainwashing? Eerily his technique used to captivate his followers would be, in many ways, identical to techniques used for delta programmed killers or those mind controlled, also known as monarch programmed or Manchurian candidates. What would be the motive?

Along with the theory of why he was programmed and used is linked to the effort of "big brother" attempts to regain control or a revolutionary United States, and a specific agenda to destroy the "Hippie" movement of free love, universal, global love, peace love and brotherhood. Nationwide activism, uprising and protest against war could be heard through lyrics of protest in the music industry, such as "war, what is it good for, absolutely nothing..."

Could the Charles Manson incident have been a useful, strategically and carefully crafted distraction?

This became an interesting topic for me when I heard this rumor. Coincidentally, a few days prior, I was watching a documentary on the discovery channel, on the hippie movement. In the documentary, it was stated that of all the incidents surrounding this era, the Manson murders proved to be more consciousness changing than anything else. This incident greatly impacted the perception of not only free love, as wrong, but that also, brother love and drugs led only to murder of innocent people. Remember, also, the Manson incident had a key element focused on racism. Many would recognize this as divide and conquer. The 60s saw the rise of not only activist against the Vietnam war, but also revolutionary groups such as the black panther party, Angela Davis, Martin Luther king, Jr. And, the assassinations of a united states president John f. Kennedy also his brother Robert.

What is factual about the Charles Manson murders is the fact that Charles Manson programmed an entire "family" of assassins in a California desert with hypnosis and LSD and used the same formula pioneered by the CIA in their MU Ultra mind control experiments.

The question is, "was Charles Manson a MK Ultra victim?" And, were the Son of Sam, the zodiac killer, etc., efforts to take attention away from mass Vietnam war protest? How low would this type of program go to regain population control and support?

It is well known that followers of Charles Manson committed the Tate-La Bianca murders during the late 1960's. If one examines the case closely, says *unexplained mysteries.com* it becomes obvious that Manson used mind-control techniques such as hypnotism, LSD, and other types of mental programming to turn middle-class suburbanites into selfless killers, but one has to wonder just exactly how Manson was able to accomplish this?

Consider that Manson was part of the "Hippie Movement" at the time of the CIA's project, MK Ultra, which implemented the use of drugs in order to conduct mind control experiments.

It appears that part of Manson's own supply of LSD may have come directly from the CIA. A new type of LSD known as "orange sunshine" was being used by the Manson family immediately prior to the Tate-La Bianca murders according to family member Charles "Tex" Watson, who wrote in his prison memoir that it was the use of orange sunshine LSD that finally convinced him that Manson's violent, apocalyptic vision was real.

In addition, Tex Watson recounted in his testimony that Manson used other drugs such as "mescaline, psilocybin, and the THC, and STP" and described a "mental acid" that "drew stuff out of your mind; and the other (body acid)...would be drawing your body."

Later, when asked about the use of drugs in the Manson family "Tex" said, "people seem to think that Manson had all of us drugged out, while he remained sober so he could easily manipulate our minds. This may be true, but a sorcerer such as

Manson uses mind-altering drugs himself in order to contact spiritual beings, and gain supernatural powers."

"He did use drugs to manipulate and control us, and the more drugs we took, the easier it was for him to manipulate us with his philosophy. We all began to reflect his views, a mirror image of destruction, growing worse every day. We mirrored his lifestyle and attitude toward society."

Orange sunshine LSD was manufactured and distributed exclusively by a group known as "the Brotherhood of Eternal Love" who operated out of a beach resort near Los Angeles. The brotherhood had among its drug manufacturers and dealers, one Ronald Stark, who is believed to have manufactured 50 million doses of LSD, and had known connections to the CIA.

It was this very same batch of acid that was available in abundance four months later during the fateful free concert held at Altamont speedway. Four people died at that concert, one of them after being brutally stabbed to death by a group of hell's angels who had been given access to multiple tabs of orange sunshine. Many people who attended that concert noted that the LSD seemed to be "contaminated" and that the general vibe one got from using it was that of extreme negativity, violence, and death. Additionally, orange sunshine was in use among American ground forces during the Vietnam war, having been smuggled into that country from the California coast.

Manson's personal obsession was with "Helter Skelter" and his belief was that this event would ignite a black-white race war in America; the Tate-La Bianca murders and the murder of musician Gary Hinman were definitely staged with false clues that the killers (or perhaps someone else) hoped would be blamed on elements of the "black militant" movement.

Manson has said in interviews that he based some of his philosophy on the science fiction novel "Stranger in a Strange Land" by Robert Hienlien. In a scenario perhaps reminiscent of mark David Chapman's and John Hinckley's infatuation with "Catcher in the Rye" could "Stranger in a Strange Land" somehow have been Manson's programmed-trigger mechanism? Was the concept of Helter Skelter part of Manson's program? It is interesting to note how the "science fiction" character of Valentine Michael Smith, in Heinlein's "Stranger in a Strange Land" very closely parallels Manson's own life: valentine Michael Smith was a human being who returned to earth after being raised on mars where he underwent training in the occult arts; Manson was isolated in prison where he also studied the occult extensively and has quipped that he viewed himself as a man with an alien mind after his release from prison in 1967; both Manson and the fictional "smith" gathered about them a group of followers into a communal lifestyle and practiced a sort of "group mind" telepathy; both attempted to transform the world as we know if via their respective philosophies.

So, it came to pass that Charles Manson was stuck in solitary confinement at Folsom prison when a new inmate was placed in the adjoining cell. It was Tim Leary, who was eventually captured with Joanna Harcourt Smith, who later admitted working for the DEA. "they took you off the streets", Manson informed Leary, "So that I could continue with your work." Charlie couldn't understand how Leary had given so many people acid without trying to "control" them.

With all this in mind, consider that if an ex-convict-turned-hippie like Charles Manson could program people to kill, then why not

The *unexplained mysteries.com* article goes on to say:

In the book, "Helter Skelter," Manson prosecutor Vincent Bugliosi discussed Manson's programming techniques in depth, likening much of Manson's programming abilities to those used by the U.S. military.

Manson was in prison during the time that the CIA was known to be using inmates at Vacaville prison in MK Ultra experiments, a fact that leaves one to speculate that perhaps Manson was some sort of mind-controlled guru created by the CIA and set loose against the "subversive" left-wing elements in order to discredit them.

Since his incarceration for the Tate-La Bianca murders, Manson has again served part of his time at Vacaville.

In a lot of Manson interviews he will say things like "I'm only what I've been trained to be, I'm only what you thought" in one interview he said jimmy carter made me what I am"

Some historians have asserted that creating a "Manchurian Candidate" subject through "mind control" techniques was a goal of MK Ultra and related CIA projects.

Mk ultra used numerous methodologies to manipulate people's mental states and alter brain functions, including the surreptitious administration of drugs (especially LSD) and other chemicals, hypnosis, sensory deprivation, isolation, verbal and sexual abuse, as well as various forms of torture.

Project MK ULTRA can be described as an effort by "America's intelligence agencies who grew obsessed with brainwashing and mind control.

In the summer of 1975, congressional Church Committee reports and the Presidential Rockefeller Commission report revealed to the public for the first time that the CIA and the Department of Defense had conducted experiments on both unwitting and cognizant human subjects as part of an extensive program to influence and control human behavior through the use of psychoactive drugs such as LSD and mescaline and other chemical, biological, and psychological means. They also revealed that at least one subject had died after administration of LSD. Much of what the Church Committee, chaired by Frank Church, and the Rockefeller Commission learned about MK Ultra was contained in a report, prepared by the Inspector General's office in 1963, that had survived the destruction of records ordered in 1973.

To this end, they launched Project Bluebird. During the course of experiments, thousands of Americans, often from the most powerless segments of our population, like mental patients and prisoners, were subject to disgustingly perverse and grossly unethical procedures performed by the best and brightest psychiatrists and medical doctors at the most prestigious institutions in all the land. Bluebird researchers worked tirelessly to create Manchurian Candidates as well as controlled amnesia and hypnotic couriers.

Next came Project Artichoke, which intensified research into interrogation, hypnosis and forced opiate addiction. Armed forces intelligence personnel and the FBI worked alongside the

CIA toward the following end, summed up in a declassified 1952 memo:

Can we get control of an individual to the point where he will do our bidding against his will and even against fundamental laws of nature, such as self-preservation?

On April 19, 1953, Projects Bluebird and Artichoke gave way to Project MK Ultra, which ranks among the saddest– yet most little-known– chapters in our nation's history. Wild stories of the Soviets mastering mind control techniques and creating human robots that would do their evil bidding were readily believed by many of our national security planners, who adopted a "whatever-it-takes" mentality as they embarked upon a 20-year project of unspeakable horrors. These projects began in the early 50s 'officially" and continued until the early 70's.

Project MK ULTRA is documented as having approximately 149 subprojects, Subprojects 123, 124 are described as African Studies in which it appears possibly connected work initiated by Robert Heath before embarking on official behavioral modification testing officially. Subproject 124 appears to also be relevant, to African studies; however, it is unclear exactly how.

The excerpt from "Remote Brain Targeting - A Compilation of Historical Information Derived from Various Sources" reads:

In the 1950's, the now Tulane psychiatrist and coworkers engaged in studies of the human brain that were sponsored by U.S. government agencies and included black prisoners among its experimental subjects. Psychiatric "treatment" of African Americans has included some of the most barbaric experiments ever carried out in the name of "scientific" research and not very long ago. In the 1950s in New Orleans, black prisoners were used for psychosurgery experiments which involved electrodes being implanted into the brain. The experiments were conducted by psychiatrist Dr. Heath and an Australian psychiatrist, Dr. Harry Bailey, who boasted in a lecture to nurses 20 years later that the two psychiatrists had used blacks because it was "cheaper to use Niggers than cats because they were everywhere and cheap experimental animals." Neurosurgeons at Tulane, Yale and Harvard did extensive investigations into brain electrode implants with intelligence funding, and combined brain implants with large numbers of drugs including hallucinogens."

Below is the inventory list of donated materials in the National Security Archive's collection, from John Marks' FOIA request results which he used to do research for his book *The Search for the Manchurian Candidate: The CIA and Mind Control, The Secret*

History of the Behavioral Sciences. (1979) W. W. Norton, published as Norton paperback in 1991, ISBN 0-393-30794-8).

INVENTORY: CIA Behavior Experiments Collection (John Marks Donation)

Date Range: 1940s-1970s

Box #1 - Artichoke Documents--MKULTRA DOCS 1-57

Burch, Dr. Neil/LSD and the Air Force: Smithsonian: Index and Institutional Notifications

Subproject 1: MKULTRA: Plants Isolation and Characterization of Rivea Corymbosa

Subproject 2: MKULTRA: Drugs

Subproject 3: MKULTRA: Testing

Subproject 4: MKULTRA: Mulholland's Manual

Subproject 5a: MKULTRA

Subproject 5b: MKULTRA: Denver University Hypnosis

Subproject 6: MKULTRA: Testing of Plants by HEF

Subproject 7: MKULTRA: Funding; ONR Probably Abramson

Subproject 8: MKULTRA: Boston Psychopathic Hospital

Subproject 9: MKULTRA: Depressants, Schizophrenics, and Alcoholics

Subproject 10: MKULTRA: Personality Assessment

Subproject 11: MKULTRA: Botanicals Popkin (Documents and articles on Luis Angel Castillo)

Subproject 12: MKULTRA: Financial Records

Subproject 13: MKULTRA: CIA Support to Fort Detrick

Subproject 14: MKULTRA: Paying Bureau of Narcotics for White

Subproject 15: MKULTRA: Magic Support; Mulholland Supplement

Subproject 16: MKULTRA: Testing Apartment Rental

Subproject 17: MKULTRA: LSD Studies of [excised] University

Subproject 19: MKULTRA: Magic Manual

Subproject 20: MKULTRA: Synthesis Derivative of Yohimbine Hydrochloride

Subproject 21: MKULTRA: Defector Study: originally Drug Study

Subproject 22: MKULTRA: William Cook and Co. Research: Amanita Muscaria, Rivea Corymbosa

Subproject 26: MKULTRA: Pfeiffer, Finances

Subproject 27: MKULTRA: ONR Funding, LSD Research

Subproject 28: MKULTRA: Pfeiffer

Subproject 30: MKULTRA: Fort Detrick (1)

Subproject 30: MKULTRA: Fort Detrick (2)

Subproject 30: MKULTRA: Fort Detrick (3)

Subproject 31: MKULTRA: Manufacture of Drugs by Pellow Wease Chemical Co.

Subproject 32: MKULTRA: Collection of Plants

Subproject 33: MKULTRA: Collection of 400 for SUBPR #27

Subproject 34: MKULTRA: More Support to Magic

Subproject 35: MKULTRA: Georgetown Hospital: Geschichter

Subproject 36: MKULTRA: Cuba Chapter Conference, Consultant, Subproject involving getting a man on a diverted freighter

Subproject 37: MKULTRA: Collection of Botanicals

Subproject 38: MKULTRA

Subproject 39: MKULTRA: Iowa State Hospital (and Ionia)

Subproject 40: MKULTRA: Funding, Probably Abrams LSD Research

Box #2

Subproject 42: MKULTRA: Safehouse Chapter 7: MKULTRA Interview Notes White, George Hunter Dope Traffickers' Nemesis

Subproject 43: MKULTRA: Combination drug, Hypnosis, Sensory Deprivation

Subproject 44: MKULTRA: Testing of Aromatic Amines at University of Illinois

Subproject 45: MKULTRA: Knockout, Stress, and Cancer

Subproject 46: MKULTRA: Rochester LSD Drugs

Subproject 47: MKULTRA: Pfeiffer Atlanta

Subproject 47: MKULTRA: (1) Pfeiffer Atlanta/Bordertown

Subproject 48: MKULTRA: HEF Cornell Relationship: Artichoke Team Proposals and Reports

Subproject 49: MKULTRA: Hypnosis at [excised] University

Subproject 50: MKULTRA: CIA Imprest Fund for $500

Subproject 51: MKULTRA: (1) Moore Collecting Botanicals

Subproject 52: MKULTRA: (2) Moore Collecting Botanicals

Subproject 53: MKULTRA: (3) Moore Collecting Botanicals

Subproject 53: MKULTRA: Review Pharmacological lit.

Subproject 54: MKULTRA: Brain Concussion

Subproject 55: MKULTRA: Unwitting Drug Tests at [excised] University

Subproject 56: MKULTRA: Studies on Alcohol, Stanford Medical School

Subproject 57: MKULTRA: Sleep and Insomnia at GW: MKULTRA: Lloyd Gould

Subproject 57: MKULTRA: Sleep

Box # 3

C-30 Project MUDHEN Jack Anderson

MKULTRA --To File: Massachusetts (Bibliographic Citations, articles on mind control experiments in Massachusetts): John Jacobs' Kentucky

Subproject 58: MKULTRA: J. P. Morgan and Co. (see Wasson file) Agency Policy and Conferences

Subproject 59: MKULTRA: Unwitting Drug Tests at University of Maryland

Subproject 60: MKULTRA: Human Ecology

Subproject 61: MKULTRA

Subproject 62: MKULTRA: Consulting Work in Isolation/Electric Shock/CNS Drugs

Subproject 63: MKULTRA: (1) Drugs and Alcohol (Butler)

Subproject 64: MKULTRA: Drugs

Subproject 65: MKULTRA: Hungarian Refugees

Subproject 66: MKULTRA: Alcohol and Drug Study

Subproject 67: MKULTRA: CIA Use of Institutes Facilities -- University of Indiana

Subproject 69: MKULTRA: Rutgers

Subproject 70: MKULTRA: "Knockout"

Subproject 71: MKULTRA: Dr. Wallace Chan at Stanford University Testing Drugs

Subproject 72: MKULTRA: Testing Drugs for Effects on Central Nervous System

Subproject 73: MKULTRA: University of Kentucky: Narcotics Farms, Narco-Hypnosis

Subproject 74: MKULTRA: Small HEF Subproject (1)

Subproject 74: MKULTRA: Small HEF Subproject (2)

Subproject 75: MKULTRA: Mass. Mental Health (by Project number of master list)

Subproject 77: MKULTRA: Biological Lab (1)

Subproject 78: MKULTRA: Biological Lab (2)

Subproject 78: MKULTRA: Biological Lab (3)

Subproject 78: MKULTRA: Biological Lab (4)

Subproject 78: MKULTRA: Biological Lab (5)

Subproject 78: MKULTRA: Biological Lab (6)

Box # 4

Document Indexes, Abstracts, and Documents

Subproject 79: MKULTRA: Cutout for Funding Research of a "sensible nature"

Subproject 80: MKULTRA

Subproject 81: MKULTRA: Cornell--Extension of Hinkle—Wolf

Subproject 82: MKULTRA: Hungarian Refugees

Subproject 83: MKULTRA: Graphology Journal and Cover

Subproject 84: MKULTRA: Hypnosis Work

Subproject 85: MKULTRA: Stanford Medical School

Subproject 86: MKULTRA: Stanford Medical School: Tele-control

Subproject 87: MKULTRA: Hyper -Allergic Substances

Subproject 88: MKULTRA: Cultural Appraisal

Subproject 89: MKULTRA: Hungarian Repatriation

Subproject 90: MKULTRA: MIT--A. J. Wiener

Subproject 91: MKULTRA: Drug Testing and Screening of Animals

Subproject 92: MKULTRA: Teaching Machine for Foreign Languages

Subproject 93: MKULTRA: Toxin Study--Cuba Chapter

Subproject 94: MKULTRA

Subproject 95: MKULTRA: Osgood

Subproject 96: MKULTRA: George Kelly

Subproject 97: MKULTRA: Schizophrenics Psychotherapy

Subproject 98: MKULTRA: Mass Conversion Study: Queens College

Subproject 99: MKULTRA: Optics mixed with Biological Warfare--Cuba Chapter

Subproject 100: MKULTRA: CBW Penn State

Subproject 101: MKULTRA: Biophysics of Central Nervous System

Subproject 102: MKULTRA: Adolescent Gangs

Subproject 103: MKULTRA: Children's Summer Camps

Subproject 104: MKULTRA: Sabotage of Petroleum

Subproject 105: MKULTRA: CBW, Disease

Subproject 106: MKULTRA: Electrodes, Russian Study

Subproject 109: MKULTRA: Drugs-CBW Testing

Subproject 110: MKULTRA: CBW MKNAOMI

Subproject 112: MKULTRA: Vocational Studies in Children

Subproject 113: MKULTRA: Gas Sprays and Aerosols

Subproject 114: MKULTRA: Alcohol Study

Subproject 115: MKULTRA: Mentally Disturbed and Environment

Subproject 116: MKULTRA: Lab

Subproject 117: MKULTRA: Cultural Influences on Children

Subproject 118: MKULTRA: Microbiology--Penn State

Subproject 119: MKULTRA: Telecontrol--Texas Christian

Subproject 120: MKULTRA Drug Research

Subproject 121: MKULTRA: Witch Doctor study-Dr. Raymond Prince-- McGill University

Subproject 122: MKULTRA: Study of Neurokinin

Subproject 123: MKULTRA: African Attitude Study

Subproject 124: MKULTRA: African Attitude Study

Subproject 125: MKULTRA: CO2 and Acid Base Research

Subproject 126: MKULTRA: Work on Placebos and Drugs

Subproject 127: MKULTRA: Disaster/Stress Study

Subproject 128: MKULTRA: Rapid Hypnotic Induction

Subproject 130: MKULTRA: Personality Theory, David Saunders/William Thetford; Columbia Univ.

Box # 5

Subproject 131: MKULTRA

Subproject 132: MKULTRA: Safe House -- Not San Francisco

Subproject 133: MKULTRA: Safe House -- Not San Francisco

Subproject 134: MKULTRA: Correlation of Physique and Personality done by Haronian in New Jersey -- Human Ecology

Subproject 135: MKULTRA: Testing on Volunteers

Subproject 136: MKULTRA: ESP Research

Subproject 137: MKULTRA: Handwriting Analysis, Dr. Klare G Toman-HEF

Subproject 139: MKULTRA: Bird Disease Studies at Penn State

Subproject 140: MKULTRA: human Voluntary Drug Testing

Subproject 141: MKULTRA: Unknown

Subproject 142: MKULTRA: Unknown

Subproject 143: MKULTRA CBW/Bacteria University of Houston

Subproject 144: MKULTRA

Subproject 145: MKULTRA

Subproject 146: MKULTRA

Subproject 147: MKULTRA: Psychometric Drugs THC

Subproject 148: MKULTRA: (1) *Marijuana Research*

Subproject 148: MKULTRA: (2) Marijuana Research

Subproject 149: MKULTRA: George White and Federal Bureau of Narcotics

MKULTRA APE A and B--Funding Mechanisms for MKULTRA

ARTICHOKE Docs 38-461 (2)

ARTICHOKE Docs 156-199

ARTICHOKE Docs 200-310 (1)

ARTICHOKE Docs 200-310 (2)

ARTICHOKE Docs 200-310 (1)

ARTICHOKE Docs 200-310 (2)

ARTICHOKE Docs 311-340

ARTICHOKE Docs 362-388

ARTICHOKE Docs 388-461

MKSEARCH 7

MKSEARCH 6 (continuation of MKULTRA 62)

MKSEARCH 2 (continues BW Lab, MKULTRA 78)

MKSEARCH Docs S-2 (BW Lab)

MKSEARCH Docs S-8 (Phase out of work done on schizophrenics probably by Pfeiffer)

MKSEARCH Docs S-7

MKSEARCH Basic Documents

Unlabeled Accordion File--primarily MKULTRA: Subproject 42

Unlabeled Accordion File--Financial records, checks

Box # 6

MKSEARCH 6 Discontinuation of Geschichter Fund for Medical Research

MKSEARCH 2

MKSEARCH 5

MKSEARCH S-14

MKSEARCH 6 – MKACTION

MKSEARCH 4 - Bureau of Narcotics Safehouse

MKSEARCH 3 - Testing at Vacaville, Hamilton

MKSEARCH S-3 Vacaville (1)

MKSEARCH S-3 Vacaville (2)

Lexington: Air Force: Alcohol: Amnesia: Animals: David Anthony: ARPA

SUBPROJECT 107: MKULTRA: American Psychological Association: Army Testing: Assassination: Raymond A. Bauer: Berlin Poison Case: Biometric Lab: Biophysical Measurements: Beecher (Henry K.): Brainwashing

ARTICHOKE Docs 59-155: Bordentown New Jersey Reformatory: Boston Psychopathic (Hyde-Massachusetts Mental Hospital): Brain Studies: Brainwashing

(1): Brainwashing

(2): Project Calling Card: John Marks Chapter 6 Conclusions: Chadwell, W.H.: CBW Work File: Dr. Wallace Chan: Cold War Late 1953-1955 (1): Cold War Late 1953-1955 (2): Communist Control Techniques VII: Cold War Docs

(1) (Project Artichoke, Bluebird): Cold War Docs

(2): Control of Behavior --General: Cybernetics: Defectors: University of Denver: Destruction of Files:

Diseases: Drug Research and Operations Diseases: Drug Research and Operations: Drugs:

Documents ARTICHOKE: Drugs: ARTICHOKE: Drugs: ARTICHOKE (2): Drugs: Subprojects

Box # 7

Ethics: Federal Penitentiary -- Atlanta: Fisher Scientific Company: Flickering Lights: FOIA Important Documents (FOIA correspondence and Court Documents for suit against the CIA): Freedom of Info Act requests

(1): Freedom of Info Act requests

(2): Foreign Countries: Heath: Foreign Liaison: Friends of McGill University, Inc.: Ft. Detrick: Joan Gavin: Genetics: George Washington University: Geschichter Fund: Unlabeled File --MKULTRA Subprojects: Government Agencies: Graduate students: Grifford: Handwriting Hardenberg: Hearings: Hinkle: History: Hospitals: Hungarian Projects: (Defectors, Refugees): Edward Hunter: Hypnosis 50-53: Hypnosis, Cold War period: Hypnosis - Literature: Hypnosis - C I: Hypnosis Documents

(1): Subproject ARTICHOKE: Hypnosis Documents

(2): Subproject ARTICHOKE: Hypospray: Inspector General: University of Illinois: Internal Revenue Service: Iowa State Hospital, Ionia State Hospital, Michigan: Ittleson Foundation: IVY Research Lab: Johns Hopkins University: Juicy Quotes: Lyman Kirkpatrick: John Lilly: Lovell Chemical Company:

Lovell: Lowinger: LSD - Counterculture: LSD - (Old Sandoz File): LSD (1): LSD (2)

Box # 8

Magic: Mulholland: George Merck: University of Minnesota: Miscellaneous: MKDELTA: ARTICHOKE Docs/Clips: MKDELTA Subprojects: James A. Moore: MKNOOM: Mulholland: Mushrooms -- Chapter 8: Naval Research, Military Side -- Chapter 14: Oatis Case: Often/Chickwit: Ohio State University: *Operation Paperclip: Organizational Structure: ORD: World War II*: Martin Orne: Parapsychology (Limited discussion on EMR research also): *The Application of Tesla's Technology in Today's World*

Box # 9

(Original Box 13-- not copied as of 7/2/93) Press Conferences (Excerpts from documents): Pfeiffer Subproject 47: Penn State (clippings): Placebos: Pfeiffer, Carl C.: Pharmaceutical Houses: Polygraph: POW: Prince-- Witch Doctor Study: Prisoners -- Documents Prisoners-Mental Patients (clippings): Private Company: Programming: Prouty: Psychological Assessment: Research and Development Study by Edgewood Arsenal: Personality Assessment -- OSS (Clippings, Book Chapters, Interview Notes): Psychical Research Foundation: Psycho-Pharmacology: Psychosurgery: Psychosurgery (2) (clippings): Max Rinkel: Public Health Service: Puerto Rican Study: Recent

Agency Policy on Experimentation: Recent Events in Defense Department (Includes document from Siemmer): Project Revere: RHIC-Edom Files (Clippings): Chapter 7 -- Safehouse (draft manuscript?): Safehouse Working File (personal notes): Safehouses (Documents): Schein (clipping): Schultes (clippings, notes): Sensory Deprivation (primary clippings): Schultes (clippings, notes): Chapter 7 -- Safehouses-- clippings

Box # 10

CIA Behavior Modification Reports: Side Tone Delay Device II: *Incapacitation -- Non-Lethal*: 4 Assessment: Sleep Knockout Drug (clippings): Alexander H. Smith (clippings): *Soil Microbiology*: Sonics: Stanford: Team Exp. 1: Technical Assistance: ARTICHOKE: Technologies: Toxic Psychic States: Ultra Sonics/Sonics: Tradecraft: Universities (clippings): Wasson, Robert Gordon (notes, clippings): Wendt: White TD Docs: Harold Wolff (clippings): Documents to file (miscellaneous topics)

Box # 11

Sleep Learning: Interrogation: Electric Fish and Animal Radar 1/3: Electric Fish and Animal Radar 2/3: Electric Fish and Animal Radar 3/3: Plants, Sleep Machine, ESB and Sleep, Biocommunications and *Bioelectronics*: History of Program: Animal ESB: Toxicity in mice 1/4: Toxicity in mice 2/4: Toxicity in mice 3/4: Toxicity in mice 4/4

Box # 12

Index Cards.

CHAPTER FOUR

Decades of Testing, Manipulation and Influence

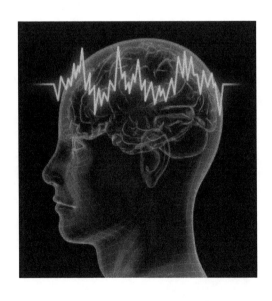

I am not alone in my assertion that these are generational programs where family members are targeted, especially immediate family members, such as fathers or mothers, early childhood of children and many close relatives. It is also my belief that after the rioting and revolutionary efforts of the 60s, a decisive effort was made to deploy this mass control technology on individuals, groups, and specific communities. As a result, the targeting, in decade long testing programs, has been simply passed on to children or those close.

History clearly documents, and I, also in "Remote Brain Targeting" that these programs have been ongoing and dating actually as far back as the Operation Paperclip recruitment, officially on the record, after Nazi Concentration Camp dissolution, of which had a major focus and ideation in the USA, corporate mind control desire. Logically, believe it or not, it took a lot of testing and test subjects, to get the electromagnetic technology to its current state of mind control perfection.

When I began to connect the dots of what was happening in my life, after recognition that this program is a reality, I was able to look back and see situations in my life, where subtle manipulation and influencing, could have played a major role. These were periods, in nearly all cases, where there was some type of conflict which could have destroyed me which was surreal. As a result of this painful reality, I was not surprised at a chat posted online by targeted individuals and a brief statement by another targeted individual after someone posted the first question:

Question from a Targeted Female:

How many TI's have had their minds read, from beginning to end, and then have the Perps harass you for all the wrong things you've done? Am I the only one?

Response from Another Female Target:

You are not alone. Unless you are violating someone else's civil liberties, you have done nothing wrong. THEY are the criminals.

Response from a Male TI:

They have reading my mind from birth. My dad was a target too...

Female TI:

No, you are far from the only one who gets this ill treatment. I'm a victim of synthetic telepathy since 1990. Back then there was no Internet to search for information, no

Facebook where you could vent your anger and get in touch with other victims of this crime for consolation. I have since come to learn that this thing is global and affects people all over the world, regardless of their culture, race, skin color, age, gender etc. As with you, they like to remind me of all the 'bad' things I have done in the past. Mostly sexual things, because these perverts love to rant about such private things. However, since I live a dull and uneventful life there aren't many bad things for the perps to talk about. So, they tend to focus on things they think I 'should' do, like working harder and become more successful in life, get married etc. They keep saying I'm a loser, and that is what made me look more deeply into this thing. It doesn't make any sense why anyone would want to waste time and resources on someone like me. We are merely guinea pigs to these bastards.

Dear Diary,

This morning I was getting ready for a doctor's appointments and those around me announced, after mind reading, where I was heading then showed up looking like lost dogs in heat. They really sicken me to the core. I cannot explain the disgust I feel for them and this hideous program. What is happening today is beyond belief. They are egotistically delusional.

At times it seems to be these men are all about how, specifically, the women look that they are targeting. This devilish technology has produced sexual deviants, who actually think themselves clever and fascinating in their fractured minds. This further confirms that the people involved in this program are factually gravely mentally ill, whether by as stated early their programmed as children, then through employment. Some are sadly, ignorant beyond belief.

It is the technology which is brilliant and not them.

In person, the ones sent around me look like misfits. They look like them smell. Or, maybe it is the lingering fragrance from the filthy tactics which they use, dwell and thrive in on a day to day basis. I have yet to see one who looks intelligent. They can compliment me by leaving me alone. I don't need to be validated by this group of men possessed by evil in their hearts and minds. I don't need them to like me and I not deceived that they do. How could they do these things?

What woman on Earth, with any common sense would want to involved herself with those, now angered at ineffectiveness, and having a capability to hide behind beamed weapons systems attempt murder? These men, at times appear to be among the most emasculated men on earth. At times due to being around a woman for great periods of abnormal time, they become more like jealous twisted lovers.

I despise them and even if this was not happening to me, I never have been attracted to this type.

It is a good thing my self-esteem is high and my thoughts as well, most of the time. However, I am human. I admit I am not perfect and yes, there is rightful indignation. Those who suffer the most are those who have low self-esteem and think negative thoughts about themselves, others, and the world overall. This type of thinking that becomes a playground for this program who goal is to program negativity. Guard your thoughts! They can become a vehicle for control in these operations if you radiate to a lower frequency.

Dear Diary,

After so many Targeted Individuals making the connection of generational targeting by technology within their families, it speaks volumes of ongoing human guinea pigs.

I often wonder, after becoming familiar with this program, if my father was implanted and now in hindsight, can see it as a great possibility. Those around me are a dead give in their efforts as they now attempt to tamper with my one-year old granddaughter hoping it will impact me. With manipulation of children, and electronic weapon torture used on children, I pray the reality will likely proven it may help change the tide for us all. Not many would stand by and watch children being victimized this way and know it is factual . Or will they? We shall see.

To show how ludicrous the operation around me really is, they continue to linger providing accurate info for these books plus as a direct result of their antics. Go figure…

Dear Diary,

I realized, after the fact, that if they could have, they would have nudged my daughter into harming me, then would have locked her up after operation center subliminal programming and have her jailed and her life destroyed. They then would leave the operation center proud of a job well done!

Prior to hospital debacle, I noticed that they were likely implanting fear into my oldest daughter that I somehow would harm her, or go postal on her, and possibly murder her.

Stories of this nature consume the news today and are not farfetched. It is just not going to happen for them with me. There is no influencing in the world that would make me harm another human being, much less someone I love…Sadly, however, the fact is, I cannot now have my oldest daughter around me any longer while this war rages. The good thing is that she is in her late twenties and not a child anymore and should be on her own anyway. I have babysat her long enough. I had to recognize and see it with my own eyes that she is even more vulnerable to manipulation and subliminal nudging when her life is out of sync with no direction and therefore also dangerous to my life and purpose if used for a pawn. In this scenario, she could have become a weapon turned against me and used to destroy me. This part of the reason people around targets are used.

While she was staying here she had been sleeping with the light on every night like a child scared of the dark. When I opened the door to turn it off one night, after midnight, she started screaming bloody murder as if I was coming into her room to murder her. Understanding this program, I though her reaction was possibly by the graveyard shift, telling her I was going to harm her, which they will influence while target's sleep and she even mentioned this to me. She said she had been feeling this way lately. Believe it or not, this is the nature of the heinous manipulation prevalent in these groups using this technology, founded on pure evil.

The message is clear "We can and will get to you" after isolating me from family this Thanksgiving. "We can take you out easily and we plan to." And, essentially, your efforts have become a threat to us and we do not want the technology and how it is being used publicized. "Our jobs will not be jeopardized because of you." "This is our livelihood." And lastly, and ever present, "We are somebody you need to fear and you better know we are important, powerful and have technology to murder you without leaving a trace." Then, as usual, "You're dead," "You're gone" etc., etc., etc.

My response, "Go to back to "Hell!"

The fact is, the veil is lifting and all Hell has broken loose. Better make sure you are standing in the Light of God through thick and thin or else you could become them.

Dear Diary,

The goal is to unlock my doors, while I work downstairs in my office. I live alone. Then when I notice a door unlocked use the satellite to mimic the sound of someone creeping around upstairs hiding, waiting, for me to come upstairs to murder me. The is backed up by the mood beam which can beam synthetic fear.

Whatever....

Death holds no fear for me.

Note to Operation Center deviants, reading along, "You on the other hand better stick around as long as possible before you make you exist. You might not like where you end up.

Here's a clue: *It is a place where you will be jumping over flames and no air conditioner!*

Dear Diary,

I was in my early 20s, when my father began telling me a story of an incident that he experienced while in his early 20s in the early 50s.

At the time it annoyed me hearing him tell the story over and over again. It never made any sense to me until now as even a remote possibility of possible Radio Frequency Identification chip implanting.

I recall how annoyed I would become with him constantly bringing it up. This story had no meaning and sounded absurd until now. I now realize that he likely was trying to make sense of a specific incident that left an indelible impression on him for life.

My father was born in 1927 in Detroit Michigan to a family, which during these times, was considered affluent for African Americans in the early 20s and 30s. His dad, my grandfather, was a well-known and respected minister of a large church congregation, in the city of Highland Park, Michigan, just outside of Detroit. He father had also attended Morehouse College.

My grandfather's siblings, attended and graduated Spelman College and went on to become teachers and a great aunt, gaining worldwide fame as a renowned composer, Evelyn LaRue Pittman and an opera which debuted in Paris in 1956 while studying under famed Nadia Boulanger.

Juliette Nadia Boulanger was a French composer, conductor, and teacher who taught many of the leading composers and musicians of the 20th century. She also performed as a pianist and organist.

My father was one of six siblings. There were three boys and three girls. One of my father's siblings was said to have a learning disability or which at that time was termed as being "slow" in learning. By all accounts, my father's family was a close-knit family with strict rules enforced by a Patriarchal minister parent and a loving mother. I was told that they were not allowed to listen to music and that dancing was considered sinful in the household.

In 1942, at the age of 15, a young neighborhood boy, gasping for air from the short sprint to my grandfather's home, pounded on the door of the family home. As fate would have it, my then 15-year-old father answered the door. The boy anxiously told him that the town bully was pushing around his sister, the one considered slow, and ridiculing her. "He is beating her up, laughing and calling her retarded" the boy reported. Without forethought, my father jumped off the porch and took off running in the direction of which he could see a large slow-moving crowd slowly in the distance.

When he reached the crowd, there stood his sister, with tears in her eyes, being shoved around by several people, but right in the center, initiating the malicious bullying and harassment was they young male of whom many in the town feared.

Without thinking, my father sprang into action tackling the guy who was twice his size and a fight began as the crowd cheered and jeered. They tossed and turned, and my father was able to hold up to the pounding he was getting until one blow landed on the side of his head, and he hit the pavement, and blacked out briefly.

When he came to, after a few seconds, there lying next to him was baseball bat. As he stood and positioned himself, the bully's attention and crowd had again refocused back onto his sister who was now shaking in fear and crying profusely, attempting to break through the crowd barrier to run for help.

Although dazed, my father headed for the crown who had continued down the street a short distance still holding his sister trapped within the circle. When a young girl who lived directly next door to him watched him rise, regain his balance, although, again, slightly dazed, she watched as he began to run towards the crowd, break through the circle reaching the location where the bully stood, who clothes were now hanging partially off her. The last thing, my father recalled hearing was the screaming of the young women, next door, as the bat made a loud cracking noise against the head of the bully. He was pronounced dead on arrival.

It was 3:30 a.m., my father told me, he woke from what he thought was nightmare, frightened, and shaken the night before the incident. It all seemed so real to him. Little did he know that the scene in the dream, exactly as he dreamed it the night before, would play out the next day as a very real nightmare and as a life changing event. He sat in the darkness of the room that night, trying to make sense of the dream, listening to his older two brother snore before finally going back to sleep.

At fifteen years old, he would be charged with involuntary manslaughter, tried and convicted, and sentenced to serve his sentence, not in juvenile detention facility, at the tender age of 15, but in an unprecedented case, for that era, tried as an adult, then placed into a hard-core penitentiary where he would stay for the next seven years until released at the age of 22.

After release, he left Michigan for California where I was born ten years later.

Relatives of my father would later tell me, as a young adult, that during this time, there was great disappointment in my grandfather's handling of my father's affairs during this tragic incident. Many believed that it was a clear case of self-defense and that he should have fought harder for my father to have charges dropped. However, in the staunch, unyielding mentality and character of many preachers, my grandfather, felt that, in spite of everything, a life had been taken, that the circumstances did not matter, and that my father would have to pay.

One story that my father would repeatedly tell me, although at the time, I brushed off it off as silly was an experience he had during the 7-year prison term. He said that he had been acting out, fighting everyone, and was uncontrollable. He was fighting for his life as a young boy placed into an environment of institutionalized, hardened criminals and operated purely on survival instincts.

One morning, he was summoned to a room within the jail where a group of doctors sat around a table. After he was seated, they began to questioning him asking him various thing about his reactions and why. He said he was then led to another room, appearing to be some type of operating room, and then laid out on an operating table. The last thing he recalled was his height being measured as he drifted off to sleep given anesthesia.

Again, I now believe that him telling me this story, over and over again, was his attempt to make sense or gain clarity to what actually had happened to him that day many years ago. Perhaps in his heart of hearts, he knew that his life was forever changed by the meeting and what happened in the operating room.

Was an attempt made to control him by implanting him and numerous others during this time frame for testing with microchips?

During this timeframe experimentation was rampant. In fact, Robert Health, of Tulane University doing testing centering around manipulation of the human brain for control, and also many other government agencies, to include, VA hospitals, Department of Health and Human Services, etc., etc., etc. They were heavily involved in studies surrounding behavior modification.

In the 1920s, the development of the electroencephalograph (EEG)—an apparatus for detecting and recording brain waves—offered brain physiologists the key to unlock the mysteries of the body's pivotal organ of thought, intellect and personality. While giving hope for a specific means of mapping mental-health ailments. The newfound electrical pattern to brain function also opened a monstrous Pandora's Box: to possible radio control of the mind.

In 1934 Doctors E. L. Chaffee and R. U. Light published "A Method for Remote Control of Electrical Stimulation of the Nervous System," an introductory monograph on electromagnetic mind-control methodology as documented in "You Are Not My Big Brother." In 1964, electromagnetic-response (EMR) researcher Dr. José Delgado of Cordoba, Spain, climbed into a bullring and, with the push of a button, triggered an electrode implanted in the brain tissue of a charging bull, halting the beast in its tracks.

Also, in 1934, Russian physiologist L. L. Vasiliev published "Critical Evaluation of the Hypnogenic Method," an article detailing the experiments of Dr. I. F. Tomashevsky in remote-radio control of the human brain "at a distance of one or more rooms and under conditions where the participant would not know or suspect that she would be experimented upon." Reported *Vasiliev*, "One such experiment was carried out in a park with the subject at a distance. A post-hypnotic mental suggestion to go to sleep was complied with within a minute."

The CIA created an EMR laboratory at Allan Memorial, a Montreal, Canada, research facility created in 1943. The heart of Allan Memorial's Radio Telemetry Laboratory (a telemeter is an electrical apparatus for measuring a quantity, transmitting the result by radio to a distant station, and there indicating or recording it) was called the Grid Room. In the Grid Room, an involuntary subject would be strapped into a chair, by force if necessary. Violent resistance was quelled with curare, the powerful plant extract used in arrow poisons by South American Indians and in medicine to produce muscular paralysis. From a head bristling with electrodes and transducers, the subdued subject's brain waves would be beamed to a nearby reception room crammed with voice analyzers and radio receivers cobbled together by laboratory assistant Leonard Rubenstein. Rubenstein, a man who lacked professional medical credentials, believed passionately in the political uses of mind control. Experiments at Allan Memorial's telemetry lab, he declared, would one day help governments "keep tabs on people without their knowing."

Again, there are several within the Targeted Individual community who have said that they were targeted from birth. After hearing these specific remarks, I asked myself, could targeting be generational experiences passed on from family member to family member? I also posed this question to the co-host of my Blog Talk Radio show "The Targeted Individual's VOICE

— Victory Over Issues of Covert Electromagnetic" in early November of 2013. He too had witnessed the horrors of the electromagnetic technologies ability to destroy lives on a powerful personal level. His story is documented in book three, "Covert Technological Murder." He told me also that he believed that his father was likely micro-chipped. His parents travelled all over the world, working in the entertainment industry doing game shows and could have been unwittingly used.

Part of the dynamic of electronic terrorism is to break a person down, in some way. To accomplish this, EEG cloning is also used to map and store specific negative emotions, such as sadness, anger, and depression of the target. It is then beamed back to the target at an opportune time for manipulative control. Brain Mapping is a reality today and is publicized in many professional scientific articles.

The EEG Cloning technology is sophisticated. It is an electronic system used to speak directly to the mind of the listener, to alter and entrain brainwaves, to manipulate his brain's electroencephalographically (EEG) patterns and to artificially implant negative emotional states-feelings of fear, anxiety, despair and hopelessness. The subliminal system does not just tell a person to feel an emotion, it makes them feel it. It electromagnetically implants the emotion into the mind.

There appears to be two methods of delivery with the system.

One is direct microwave induction into the brain of the subject, limited to short-range operations.

The other, as described above, utilizes ordinary radio (AM-FM) and television (UHF-VHF)

Dear Diary,

The garage door is up at the house across the street and I can feel the microwave beam attacking my nervous system rattling it. I can feel the intensity of the beam attacks as I sit working at my computer working on this book. It was getting so intense that I just went upstairs and brought down a smaller, 4 x 4-foot piece, of R-Max 3, the aluminum insulated foam I use, to cover the wall and window where the beam is being sent when I am trying to sleep. The burning sensation and pain immediately stopped.

I just looked out the window again, and could see the person likely directing the beam at me, now standing outside of the garage looking my way through a small opening in my blinds. He must be trying to figure what deflected the beam. Well lo and behold it appears to be a woman and a man directing it from the open garage today. She is now sitting in a chair directly under the open garage door, pretending to be sitting and enjoying the day. I decide to go outside and give them both the finger before going back in. Another male figure comes out, stands next to them, looks at me, angrily, then they both go inside and the garage door goes down.

The objective of this game is to push me to creating a scene, which could result in another attempt to have me involuntarily mentally committed. I am just not buying into it.

The entrapment tactics in these groups are clever. The scenario typically keeps repeating itself in regards to community organized stalking efforts and Standard Operating Procedure and portable technology deployment wherever a target moves. After another tenant moved out of this rental property about six months after I moved in, which is a very nice, four to five-bedroom home with a three-car garage, an elderly aged gentleman moved in who appeared harmless.

He at first appeared to live alone in the large well-maintained property. As I drove by, he would be sitting in the yard in a chair, painting the wooden fence, or watering the grass during the summer months with a straw hat on. From experience, I have learned that it usually takes between six months to a year or a bit longer for the operation to be fully set up at the new location close to a target. This has been pretty consistent since the targeting began around me while living in Arizona. New individuals, involved with the organized stalking network were then into apartments around me and shortly afterwards, I would feel the power of the microwave directed energy weapon coming from the direction of the new resident's home or apartment. This is a well thought out and, more importantly, funded program where people are earning a living doing this.

I have had to call the Sheriff's Department twice already related to this new group operating from this home. Someone continues to enter my residence, and leave the doors unlocked as their calling card. On October 9, 2013, I made a police report after the garage side door was left unlocked and someone entered my vehicle, parked inside the garage and took my Rx glasses. I had another identical pair and when I got them, from their verbal harassment vantage viewing point in my ceiling, "See has another pair, so she does not care" was said. They know when you need glasses to see and to drive.

When the two Sheriff Deputies came out then, I explained what has been happening around me. After they assessed me and determined that I did not look like a nutcase, and my home very clean, orderly, and nicely decorated, one of the deputies actually did make a suspicious circumstances report. I prefaced my reason for calling first by asking were they familiar with the Aaron Alexis incident that was recently in the news. One of the deputies then said he was very familiar with what happened with the Navy Yard shooting. In fact, he said, that his brother-in-law works on the exact Navy facility where the incident happened.

I then explained to them that I have written books about similar personal attacks in the lives of many designed to push people over the edge, by the exact same portable version of this energy weapon technology in which Alexis said was torturing him and following him from location/hotel to hotel.

I told the two deputies that I also do a weekly Blog Talk Radio show entitled "The Targeted Individual's VOICE" and briefly explained the show's content. I did not tell them that I am also tracked by satellite then drones from the operation center. Under the circumstances, that might be way too much information. As a result of my whistleblowing efforts, those targeting me have escalated the level of torture around me to a deathly level while also following me all over town as an act of intimidation I told them.

Many law enforcement officers, I have learned, will not take any type of report for these types of claims, however, these two did. They even asked me how the books were selling right before they left.

I asked, "Why would someone do these things to someone while hiding and attempting, what appears to be physical and mental harm?"

The younger of the two replied, shaking his head, confused replied, "crazy" before heading out to his squad car.

Dear Diary,

I was up working late on my laptop about two weeks ago, editing the script for another upcoming show. I could feel the beam attacking my shoulders and knees and the direction from which it was originating was undeniable. It was around 11:45 p.m. and I decided to call it a night. I shut off my computer and went upstairs. Before going to bed, I usually double check the doors so I came back downstairs. When I did, I looked out the window expecting to see the neighborhood quiet, and everyone likely asleep. However, to my amazement, there stood one of the recent occupants from this house packing up what I have come to know is the small Raytheon microwave pain beam. I could not believe my eyes.

I hurried up the stairs, as best I could, and grabbed a jacket to cover my pajamas and headed over to this house. It took all of about 5 minutes. I knocked several times, knowing he had just entered but there was no answer. Just as I was heading back across the street, around the corner came a younger man wearing the older man's straw hat. It was now just after midnight and he was out walking a fluffy white dog. The house was fully lit so the other person who went inside, and beaming me was obviously awake. I had just seen him go inside shortly before knocking.

As I was crossing the street, heading back home straw-hat man made a bee line straight for me. He asked me what I was doing. I told him that I had just witnessed a man who appears to reside in his home directing the beam at me while I worked in my office. I told him that I saw him packing up the beam and know exactly what it looks like. He looked at me then told a blatant lie that just did not make any sense whatsoever. He said that the man, was his nephew, had just gotten home and was dropped off in front of my house. Even this made no sense. It was completely illogically that a person would be dropped off in front of a house two doors down and across the street. They usually are dropped off directly in front of the house they are going to.

We stood talking for a brief period and he then expertly switched the topic and began telling me an outrageous story of some woman, of which I did know and how she could not be trusted. I was searching for a break in the conversation so that I could excuse myself and go inside. I had seen enough. This I would learn would be one of a series of incidents involving the men in this home. The females showed up later. I guess they were needed to give the appearance of a genuine family dwelling. About a week after filing the "suspicious circumstances" report on October 9th, I was heading out to check my mail box and the guy that lives directly next door to me was sitting out his trash cans.

After publishing "Covert Technological Murder – Pain Ray Beam ," detailing technology deployed from neighboring locations, I had been eager for an opportunity to tell another neighbor that I was on to what was happening around me, and from their homes that I put it in writing.

During our conversation with this neighbor he confirmed that the room, where I could feel the beam attacking my head, was not his bedroom but his bathroom. Many nights, I had seen a bright, extremely fluorescent light illuminating from the room, and also periodically from the smaller garage of his also three car garaged home and told him so. As a result, I had stopped speaking to him, waving, or even looking his way when leaving my home. This was after realizing that the beam attacking my head was definitely coming from his direction which beamed cooked the hair off my head. His house was closest to mind and directly next door. When I told him what I believed was happening from his home, he quickly said, "There is no one in my home except for me and my wife" smugly.

It was when I told him that, I knew, from experience that neighbors are aware on this technology by allowing officials to use it in a room near the target, specifically law enforcement and the military to include organized community stalking efforts, his facial expression changed. This was the reaction I had hoped for.

He said, "Oh so you are saying neighbors around you are allowing the use of the technology officially inside neighboring locations"

"Yes," I replied.

"That is exactly what I am saying."

As we stood talking, I told him, that I can also feel the beam coming from there pointing to straw hat's house. I pointed to the house across the street where a large number of official men were seen going and coming.

When I pointed to the upstairs bedroom of this house, which was in the direct path of my bedroom upstairs, and then the smaller garage, in the pathway of my office, I heard a young man say,

"Excuse me" are you talking to me or about my house. Don't point over here. If you have something to say, say it to our faces."

He had been sitting in the car parked in the driveway, another place to deploy the portable weaponry I had learned. I turned around and glared at him, as he opened the door and stood now next to his car. My next-door neighbor stood watching me quickly become angry.

"How dare you say anything to me" I responded angrily.

"I can point anywhere I want to."

As the argument began to escalate, surprisingly my next-door neighbor who had stood by listening said,

"She was not talking to you, young man but to me." He told him.

By then I had gone from zero to 100 and knew it would take a moment for me to calm down.

"See what I mean" I told my neighbor.

"The reason he said something was after I pointed to the location of the beam coming from two locations where he resides, the upstairs bedroom and smaller garage, is because he knows that what I am saying is factual."

I said, "For your information, they are trying to technologically slowly murder me with the beam coming from at times your home, this house, that house, and that one. The beam is also coming from the house directly behind me on the other block and another house next door to it simultaneously," I told him.

The young man stood looking now quiet. I don't think he expected my neighbor to come to my rescue, in fact nor did I by saying "She was not talking to you."

The objective of these types of targeting is to covertly torture the subject, and they do not want anyone to know it. More importantly I don't think neighbors are factually told of the deathly effects of these weapons which they consent to have set up in their homes. When he saw me telling on them, this young male decided he had better speak up. The neighbor next door to me, said, "So you are saying, that several neighbors are using this technology, and that they are sending it from several houses and that you wrote about it in your books?"

"Yep."

The look on his face told me of my accuracy especially in regards to deployment. From what I now learned was really his bathroom. He then abruptly excused himself, and walked quickly into his home saying goodnight.

This incident happened October 30, 2013

On October 31, 2013, my older daughter and I were coming in from the gym, and we pulled up to the mail boxes to check the mail. Both car doors were open. I looked towards the straw-hat man's operation house, and observed a new face standing out front; appearing to be waiting for me to turn the corner. When I did they made eye contact then went inside saying "You know the drill." He 100% had the persona of an FBI agent. When we pulled up and stopped at the boxes, I heard this man say to a bull dog that was sitting next to him, "Get her" as the dog headed in the direction of my open car door and my daughter screamed and said, "Mom, close the door" and rushed back to the passenger's seat. When I did, the dog returned back to the man standing in front of this house.

When I went into my home, I again called the Sheriff's Department to make a police report that this man had attempted to turn his dog loose on me, probably, angry after my confrontation with the younger male the night before at this location. They are offended by exposure. As long as they are controlling the situation and the target is playing by their rules, those manipulating and influencing, a target's life they are very happy. However, if you are defiant, they appear to become murderously angry.

When a lone deputy arrived, I told him what has been happening, recanting everything. I told him how I had followed someone from this house recently and knocked on the door after he entered the house. This was after feeling the beam and seeing him packing it up one night after I went upstairs to go to bed peeking out the window first. I told him of my interaction with the older male appearing to spearhead the operation, and also about the argument with the young man sitting in the driveway inside his vehicle, the night before. He said that he would go over and talk with them.

Getting the previous two deputies to take even the report I knew was huge. I have found that in fused efforts involving the military, and all levels of law enforcement, as part of the injustice of Electronic Terrorism, whenever a target moves into any area, it is known that they are targeted beforehand, within the community and the local police, InfraGard, etc., in advance. When he returned, after speaking with the occupants of this house, he told me that he had been told by the man that answered the door that he did not have a pit bull nor did he know what I was talking about. The officer told me that he believed him and the only dog he saw was a very small fluffy dog. In the two hours it took for the deputy to arrive, the car with the man with the dog was no longer parked in the driveway.

The funny thing is that, after I decided to call the Sheriff, I walked pass this house, deciding to write down license plates. I could hear a larger dog barking in the backyard as I passed. I told the deputy this. However typical to my experiences, previously in Arizona, it is my word against theirs and these incidents can be turned into successful efforts to discredit the target.

"So" he said, "You said they are using microwave to unlock your door?"

"No, that is not what I said," I replied as he now stood on my porch and I stood in the doorway talking with him after he returned from across the street.

"I said that they are directing the microwave portable extremely low frequency energy weapon radiation at me from the garage and upstairs bedroom."

"That impossible" he then told me.

That technology is only used by the military."

"Come in for a minute" I told him.

"Ma'am, I have other calls" he said now very reluctant. "Just for a minute" I just want to show you something.

He followed me into the kitchen, and I opened up

"You Are Not My Big Brother" sitting on the counter.

I flipped to the image section, where there stood a man, in a sheriff's uniform, no less, whose face I had blacked out, standing next to portable microwave directed energy, extremely low frequency weapon also known as the microwave pain beam.

I then picked up "Covert Technological Murder…", saying many are trained to covertly enter homes without leaving a trace of entry. I then went to the Chapter entitled "Gaslighting" turning to the page that proves that law enforcement, military, and others, contractors mobilized to terrorize a target, in these fused efforts.

Also, little known to most people the satellite radar laser can be used with pinpoint accuracy to turn door latches quite effectively and also tamper with other electrical instruments inside a home. (See: The Shocking Menace of Satellite Surveillance by John Fleming) In this scenario a door could be unlatched so that those, part of the community stalking/harassment effort, could play their role and enter a home to frighten the target by moving things around which sounds absurd but has a great impact. I then flipped the page to the section detailing covert lock picking and entry classes for Los Angeles County law enforcement.

"That's LA Clear" the deputy said.

"Bingo" I replied as I directed his attention to the recent past schedule of classes for Summer/Fall 2013.

I then told him that when a person is targeted in this manner, they are being tortured to elicit some type of reaction out of them. Perhaps, what is more unethical and immortal of all is the inability of a target, targeted for many, many different reasons, to at times prove what is happening and discrediting playing a primary role, strategically as a result.

"I am thankful that you at least went going over there" I told him.

The deputy then turned and headed to the door, shaking his head. I closed the door behind him.

My oldest daughter was sitting in the family room. When she was asked to verify that the dog did come from where the man was standing, and out of the yard of the military/law enforcement house, she immediately said, she did not want to get involved as she looked away..

CHAPTER FIVE

The Dynamic of Perception Management

Dear Diary,

Electronic terrorism entails three specific uses of the technology in these centers mainly, (1) EEG thought reading, (2) Artificial Telepathy directly into the human brain to harass the targeted individual and (3) Directed Energy Weapons to coerce the target into doing something to sabotage themselves.

However, in the games of relentless psychological operations, PSY OPS, "Perception Management" is pivotal.

Below are Examples of Perception Management:

Sitting, watching and monitoring me all day and night, the objective is to search for, or create, any type of useful fear electromagnetically. Fear is the number one objective because it is well known that a person can be controlled through it.

Each night, as I have always done for years and years, I check all doors, in this case downstairs, to make sure they are locked, and lights are off to include in my garage before going to bed. Those sitting watching me perceive this, or interpret this as possibly useful, or as a sign of something they could use to materialize fear.

Three things happened last night. First of all, the house behind me is 100% using portable "see through the wall radar" and the portable microwave beam. Last night as I looked out at the house from my upstairs bathroom and they knowing I was watching then turned on the lights which have never been on since I moved here and opened the blinds so I could get a clear view of the dimly lit kitchen.

Each night, I position the French door curtain on my family room door, a certain way, using a tie. I double check the door as being locked, whether opened or not that day. If the tie has been moved or disturbed it could then be used to determine if someone has entered or has given the appearance of entering my home. Because the operation around me has entered several times, as I have mentioned, I finally had to put a lock on the side gate leading to my backyard from the front. The only way now to enter would be to hop the wooden fence connecting my backyard. Why make it easy for them?

This morning, after obviously monitoring my thoughts before I went to sleep last night, I woke with this door unlocked and the curtain tie disrupted from how I placed it as hopeful proof of entry. The problem is that, as I stated, the technology can do all of this to include, again, turn the latch on a door. I was then hit with a dose of cloned EEG fear. If I did not know it possible, it could have been paralyzing. In reality, no one had hopped the fence at all and my door was likely unlocked by the operation center, this time.

Dear Diary,

This is just pathetic. I just can't see this box of rock controlling me. They believe they can and will…

Dear Diary,

Many targeted Individuals continue to experience the same types of reported technological sexual stimulation humiliation from the electromagnetic technology from these operation centers and around them. This morning I woke with another targeted individual posting on my social network the specific, disgusting, sexual terrorism effort in his life electromagnetically.

Men and women are being targeted in heinous ways many just will not believe. The number of targeted individuals within the United States has slowly encroached on a half a million by some estimates. Many continue to report that a large part of the terrorism is focused violations of a sexual nature designed to humiliate the target. Both men and women work in these centers. .

Facebook Post from a Male TI:

The sexual harassment from the perps, especially the female perp who is the sickest one of all, continues. She just keeps aiming at my penis and testicles morning, noon and night. She or it is like the terminator, programmed to torture me continuously. I know of no sicker 'person' than this lunatic being. She tells me that I am crazy and that I am going to be put away. Can you believe her twisted...?

Dear Diary,

Last night was the first time, I felt the intensity of the beamed focused on the top of my head now switched to a higher level of intensity. I had not felt this extreme sensation since during my writing of "You Are Not My Big Brother." It is now regular as write this fourth book. After about two weeks of microwave cooking of my scalp, my hair literally began to fall out in the specific area of focus. My beautician was able to successfully work her magic and cover the area... However, the ridicule of me being bald is another source of joy for those doing this to me.

The beam is coming from the ceiling downward, directly above me at this very moment.

Dear Diary,

Believe it or not some of the lowest men on this planet are working in these state-of-the-art operation centers using and creating sexual voyeurism for their personal satellite perversion and real time entertainment. Image the creative ways they think up to make their 8 hour shifts interesting. Case and point:

While engrossed in work, for the past three days, I could feel my body becoming exceptionally heated. Without thinking, and not wanting to stop the flow of what I was working on, I would simply take my shirt off and work in my bra. Today I noticed that when this happened, after a blast of heat hit me, the men watching me in the operation center, also reading along with what I was writing said, "Look, there she goes." They then started to comment on my breast like dogs prompting me to get up and put a T-shirt. The heat appeared to be radiating from the wall directly next to me, again, and the bathroom of the neighbor who pretended he was on my side and came to my defense.

When I decided to post this happening, right now, I heard the scratching noise in the wall where they were entering stop and my body heat returned to normal. I wonder how many women; they are heating up using this technology, heating them down to their underwear or less just for the entertainment of these predators.

Intelligent men do not hide and enjoy these activities, sexual deviants do. Those that are intelligent, and about something in life, have more important things to do, in life, than to focus on mindless sexual perversions. Individuals who focus on sex repeatedly usually have little else going on inside their heads.

Not only has our government created covert technological monsters, these weak-minded men, clean shaven, uniformed, and suited are or have become deviants, sitting at the helm of this technology looking for empty headed sexual stimulation of victims. Their weak minds are just not strong enough or capable of separating themselves from their loins. I am not the only one who gets this or sees it this way, copy and paste this link.

Dear Diary,

As each shift comes and goes, they realized, apparently to their utter surprise that yes, "She is writing another book." Admittedly these books were written under extreme duress.

"I am just NOT SCARED!"

I am not required to become personally involved with these devilish cowards, nor do I not need to be validated by anyone. More importantly, at this point, I do not care if no one believes me. The truth will eventually come to light. Historically, rest assured, it always has.

Dear Diary,

Here is yet another Targeted Individual posting on Facebook suffering similar organ deterioration after attempting to expose what is happening through the media:

Female TI:

They know I have sent my TI testimony to William Ross who made a video called "MILABS Who Are Those Responsible". He is working on a new video based on some of my testimony. I was severely punished...tortured last night while I slept. They used some kind of radiation force to hold the top half of my body down while they used a directed energy weapon (DEW) to zap my right hip. They go after my joints trying to cause me to suffer from arthritic pain. It was punishment for the information I shared. It does not kill me but it does cause torture and no marks are left behind for me to prove it happened. Whoever has done this to me will suffer consequences! I have ways of finding out who my perpetrators are. Each and every single one of them will be exposed!!!

Renee Pittman:

I have lost two hips and they are now working on both knees in a slow steady process. I have experienced them holding my arms down as you mentioned with the force of some powerful type of beam where you literally cannot move them. This means, in my opinion, that you are likely targeted by a military technology testing operation. In my case, I have donated a body part per book deteriorated by the focused beam, 24/7 on my joints, etc. They believe that they, can, will and are, torture you into submission and not publicizing what they are really doing. The torture will definitely escalate to make you stop. Many others have been silenced this way.

Targeted Individual:

Well, it is having the opposite effect on me. You would think that they would catch on by now. The more they piss me off, the more I am going to fight back and expose them!

Renee Pittman:

With you taking a stand through it all, I have decided we must be related!

Dear Diary,

While at the gym the other day, a female veteran who apparently, she stated, now works at the West Los Angeles Veterans Hospital in Westwood, California, was holding court and giving everyone in the hot tub pointers and advice on how to get service connected benefits from the VA. Essentially, she was telling people to misrepresent themselves. I became angry and an argument ensued. Many people go to the VA and do not seek compensation. I am among the many that did not. I later went back and explained my situation, so that she would fully understand my reaction.

Admittedly, I was a train wreck when I arrived on the VA facility in late 2001. I document my story in "You Are Not My Big Brother." Now years later, I am being severely victimized, and tortured into submission, because those around me thought they could and would use technology to create wrongdoing on my part regarding my compensation. When they failed and I wrote these books, they were blind sighted.

Those using this technology will brainwash a person easily, into what they believe if unaware. However, they cannot change the truth. Brainwashing is the objective of mind control in its purest form. This is also why awareness is key. Without awareness that advanced mind invasive technology exists and is in full use, many covertly targeted are doom to unscrupulous agencies, testing it on the civilian population seeking to destroy through the technological effectiveness. As the threats continued to come into the open,

My question to them is:

Can you return two microwave energy weapons cooked and deteriorated hip joints after relentless focus of the beam in your failed effort to brainwash me into wrongdoing? Can they stop the slow focused damage and deterioration now to my knees and every other bone, and joint in my body? I have witness that this is a slow process designed to mimic natural deterioration. The beamed focus of operations around targets 24/7 for years is to intentionally shortens your lifespan? And they have plenty of time. It took a few years to damaging my hips while this targeting program laughed and ridiculed me through the beam communication system.

The problem is that I can't say that those around a group of homeless female veterans actually had evil intent their hearts while I was on the Long Beach VA facility. The problem is that no matter what this group does or says to me, it will never change my benefits. The decision is final after a thorough investigation into to my records. The problem is that a full investigation was ran in which this program received nothing of value to make a case. This is why those targeting me then decided to place me into the Electronic Terrorism / surveillance, technology testing program. It appears they are hoping to see if mind invasive technology, patented and through extremely low frequency technology slow-cooking, dream manipulation, thought reading, ongoing verbal denigration would get the results they sought and if not push a target over the edge.

I guess they felt I was a perfect candidate for guinea pig testing which many will confirm across the country as they live this reality on a daily basis as I do. I simply am not! They thought I was a fool and someone easily used and influenced which I am not. This program sought to take advantage of my personal pain while vulnerable which was healed by the VA. When they witnessed me, picking myself up, resurrecting my life from the dead, then become proactive, the situation around me then became a whole new ballgame.

I with many began to be victimized and abused in ways that the average person cannot even comprehend which is high-tech humanly possible. They began to attack my children, everyone around me in a decisive effort to control and destroy my life though covert technology hoping watching loved ones targeted would break me.

What is left for a group of lowly souls doing this specific work for a living and given the green light to test this technology to its murderous limits? Nothing! Plausible denial by "Big Brother" has been expertly crafted from every angle, within the cover-up and setting the stage for hidden activities apparently decided long before approval to use this technology was put into place for military and law enforcement person experimentation.

The deceptive confusion of who, what and why designed for ongoing secrecy is systematically designed and at every level of this type of official technological programs. Those pulling real strings, within a global effort, and a high-level chain of command are enforcing a population control program for the New World Order. It appears that the orchestrators are determined this time around that MK Ultra, exposure to the public will never happen again. They are banking on and have determined that what is happening cannot be proven even in the court system as illegal by legalization under National Security Orders. What they did not expect, is that those they look to destroy perceived as inferior test subjects are genuine fighters who will "Stand!"

Because I am monitored around the clock, those in the operation center sat watching and listening to what this lady was saying at the hot tub this day. Her revelation is yet another example of efforts to help veterans on VA facilities. It should have been confirmation. It is documented, in "You Are Not My Big Brother" that I did not misrepresent myself in any way. I have done nothing wrong and will not bend! But, these self-serving workers of iniquity, again, hired for these testing programs, do this for a living.

Or perhaps it is really, in their case, the refusal to be used that egotistically motivates and challenges them. Or, could it be disbelief of the technology's ineffectiveness in the official herd mentality prevalent in these centers fused with delusional and misguided self-serving goals to conquer other human beings? They continue to try and try to break me down and to bend to their will. The fact is, many have suffered covertly throughout their lifetimes and to the end.

These pitiful souls will never control me. It is just not in my DNA. These bottom dwelling cowards can't go after the real people on this planet draining the planets of resources and profiting millions and billions while doing so. Apparently with this type of surveillance, they cannot stop drugs or Human Trafficking. Their prey is those who they believe have no chance to effectively fight back against this cruelty. They sit comfortably at their computer terminals pushing the buttons of destruction of lives believing in delusion, they are God and playing God. It is my experience that they target and torture those they feel they can use and it appears for sport indicated by the laughter and amusement.

My brief period of losing my way has proven to not be a declaration of lower intelligence, but confirmation of the human experience and the emotional challenges in life. How surprised they were when they recognized that I would put on my suit of armor and fight for my life as anyone should. I was even told, "We did not expect you to be as intelligent as you are." Intelligence has nothing to do with it. This statement in and of itself wreaks of human guinea pig testing on those perceived as ignorant by this ego driven program, proving a specific type of people they believe who can be used and viciously abused.

There is no honor in what these groups are doing which is highlighted by cowardly hiding, allowed by the technology and not wanting you to see their faces, and hoping the use of extreme efforts to ensure that the target does not know who specifically is running the show. The effort to stop the judicial process is also indicative of human guinea pig testing as is the quest for labeling of the mental illness tag.

In my case, as I have said again, and again, "I am not lunch!"

Again, those operating in these programs seek to not only disrupt and destroy the target's life, but also families which includes as exampled small children. This is a clear sign that this is 100% a ruthless technology testing program of which:

a.   They can never come into the open without exposing themselves and this heinous program

b.   Will sit and watch innocent lives being taken resulting from their inability to come into the open, or in many cases, after manipulation of the actual event deeming human souls valueless, and loss of life

c.   Believe they are untouchable

And if the individuals in a previous chapter, believed to be murdered by this program are any indication of the reality of a high-tech monstrosity, and true, these operations, will if they can murder without blinking an eye as long as the blame is not directed to this program and who is behind it!

Dear Diary,

I woke and headed downstairs to my laptop. My 14-year-old vehicle needs repair. While working, the operation center is now targeting the front portion of my thighs. It is painful to walk because the muscle is inflamed. I have folded Mylar and aluminum covering my right hip joint to help a little. When I stand I can feel the slight relief from the protection of the covering. By 2017 I need the second hip replacement after the 2012 surgery. Day by day, targeted, as I limped in pain, the ridicule and laughter of their handiwork continued the taunting and degradation.

As I call around to get work done on my car, they continue to repeat, "That car." The car is 14 years old for goodness sake and worth less than $7,000. They remind me of jealous men and women who scratch and destroy a vehicle, which has happened several times with mine and it motivated by the people this program uses.

Vicious, vindictive, childish, behavior can erupt in some people when they do not get their way or, are, looking for something they believe will deeply affect another person. These malicious, petty, groups constantly look for something to target, such as even an object. They believe it will get to the person. This reminds me of adolescent behavior and that of the underdeveloped.

These men have been essentially totally emasculated as real men. This includes even focus on how my hair looks repeatedly. This to me sounds exactly like jealous women instead of real men. They sound like girls worried about how another female looks. As a result, they took great pleasure in a beamed bald spot on my head. They believe this is big time PSYOPS. As I have often said, I have no attachment to objects. In my opinion, material possessions can prevent you from real contributions in life, and doing things that really matter.

I will bet these clowns are driving around pretending that they are more than what you really are as they heinously destroy lives.

I am not my, car, hair, or skin. I am the soul within.

To drive home my point about the childish nature of those in these groups, here is a glimpse why they repeatedly believe that damaging vehicles, also reported by many will infuriate targets and continue to make a big deal about doing so. It is just plain pathetic that these lowly individuals are working in these operations with this mentality and actually destroying people in more ways than one.

The mentality, that would allow another human being to even consider doing this, says a lot about whom and what they really are and the low standards of the people employed in these centers and used around targets in communities.   *It   is   outrageous.*

CHAPTER SIX

"There's no "B" on earth like a mother
frightened for her kids."~ Stephen King

Dear Diary,

Eight years ago, when I first became a target, my oldest daughter was living with me in Anaheim, California. This was in early 2006. In fact, when the targeting increased around me, there were many signs also that she was being used and targeted which I did not recognized immediately.

Initially, I wondered if the targeting may be connected to my oldest daughter, who was 22 years old at that time. This was just prior to my moving from Anaheim, California to Scottsdale, Arizona for what I had *hoped would be a fresh start and new beginning for my life in early March of 2006.*

In "You Are Not My Big Brother" I document subsequent events surrounding my daughter which led to my belief that she was also targeted. This explains how she was used against me. What is also factual is that these men get a thrill by having the ability to watch young attractive women, inside their private residences, which includes watching them showering and, in the nude, while getting dressed as a perk.

I have also learned that they are not above, showing up, knowing where the women are going in advance for the day covertly, to attempt to become involved in the target's life and even sexually stimulate a woman around one of them for their personal sexual gratification.

The first red flag which painfully pulled at my heart strings was when her younger sister, the daughter, told me of an incident in which the oldest girl ran out of her small apartment after hearing someone talking and it coming from her ceiling. I had been settled in Arizona about three months when this happened in about June of 2006. Actually, it was a neighbor who told her sister, what had actually occurred.

The oldest girl, as I mentioned before was a budding and talented artist/musician/songwriter living in the Arts District in downtown Los Angeles by 2009. One day she fled her small studio apartment running to a neighbor's home, and described hearing strange men commenting from her ceiling. It was reported that she was frightened to death. They and commenting about her body making sexual comments. This was before recognition of the reality of this program sunk in and this type of real-time surveillance became a reality.

There had been several incidents of which she first ignored, until the reality hit her, that she was being watched inside her home and the voices of the men doing so were real and not her imagination. It was the Los Angeles Police Department who had attempted to use her sexually, then set her up for blackmail, or Black male undercover officers. Nor was she, as are many targeted individuals having these experiences mentally ill.

Human voices coming from the ceiling, any targeted individual will confirm, is key during the beginning stages of satellite tracking, and capable, even as a result of portable microwave technology deployed from close by those usually within the target's vicinity. Many targets also report that there appears to be a testing phase for the voice messaging transmission system, in which those in the operation center will initially call out a person's name to see if the target responds which acknowledges that communication has been made established.

In 2009, while staying in Arizona to fight a manipulated entrapment effort in my life, for a second time, again, detailed in "You Are Not My Big Brother" the court approved me to go home for a seven day visit while my case was reviewed in the Superior Court. All three daughters were meeting up at the oldest daughter's residence in the Arts Share. By 2009, I was well aware, without a doubt that I was being targeted, how and why, and had also pulled together a website for credibility, which included laws and official patents, and detailed this program with the patented technology for substantiation.

When I arrived for the visit, I told my daughter's what I was experiencing and played a radio talk show program, on Coast to Coast radio, of an interview with someone who validated Electronic Terrorism, along with callers to the show who also validated the existence of the technology, their experiences of the use and its subliminal capability. It was very important for me, at that time, for my daughters to believe me.

It hurts tremendously when those that you love turn away and label you crazy about events that are factually happening, but are extremely difficult to prove. In reality, my beginning to document what was happening to me daily, and later the first book, was a result of wanting to prove to my children that what was happening to me was very real. My children needed me to be an example for them and not as a falsely declared raving lunatic. Parents should be someone children to look up to. Your successes, or failures in life, impacts them in many ways and believing that a parent is mentally ill can have a devastating effect on young women, who need their mother's guidance, as they step into the world as young adults.

It would be the second incident that confirmed to me that my oldest girl was in fact targeted and likely also being manipulated and influenced. During the visit, I mentioned that the first sign of Synthetic/Artificial

Telepathy, after the target's biometric signature is uploaded into the Brain Computer Interface (BCI) for "Remote Brain Targeting," are the voices of those assigned to you then call you name repeatedly as if in mid-air. Again, this is to make sure that the biometric connect is effective. I and many, many other targets first recall hearing someone calling out our names at various times. In my case, I was resting one day and right before I woke, and my brainwave activity indicated to the computer software in the operation center that I was waking, my name was called. One day it was a woman's voice, saying Renee, and the next day it was a man saying simply, Renee. At that time, I did not know this technology is actually called within the Military Industrial Complex, aka, the Department of Defense, officially, the "Voice of God".

During the visit, ever present attempts to convince my children of my sanity and to trust and believe in me, I mentioned this as usually the beginning stages of what happens to someone. I have never seen a relived look come over my oldest girls face after telling them this. The look read, "Thank God, I am not crazy." She then said, "That has been happening to me Mom. I was walking towards the Metro Link Train Station on my way to work a few mornings ago and someone kept calling out my name. When I looked around no one was there."

The fact is now targeted also, set the beginning stage for those in the operation center to attempt to use my oldest daughter, later against me, and to also manipulate and influence her after strategically set-up.

During this visit, again documented in "You Are Not My Big Brother" the black men in the operation center repeatedly commented on my daughter body, while nude after showering, expressly for me to hear in hope of agitating me also during the visit. And it did. Three of them later followed us, all four of us, the three girls and myself out to a social event and tried to entice the oldest girl into one their vehicles after I left after midnight, tired, and a friend told me they would bring them back to her place safely.

I have received several emails since I began writing on this subject from women reporting that this global technology is being used in many heinous ways and especially used in sexual efforts which I experienced firsthand personally. Not only are women reporting that they are being sexually stimulated electromagnetically, but that they are also being manipulated and influenced into relationships with the mindless deviants at the helm of this technology.

In fact, during an interview on Coast to Coast with George Noory of a well-known targeted individual, Dr. John Hall, in late August of 2013, this specific topic came up and the target detailed the sexual effort by these men by a definitive name calling it satellite war weapon "Tech/Sex" meaning technological sexually stimulated efforts by men picking out women they want to bed down or use for their entertainment.

In other words, women are being sexually technologically raped by these horrible creatures and sadly the sexual technological stimulation also reported by men.

In the correspondence I have received from numerous women, nationwide, many are also reporting that women, and young girls are being manipulated and influenced, and young boys emasculated. Could this motivate Human Trafficking? The reports state that people are actually being used in human trafficking, sex trafficking, prostitution, sexual slavery, and in many other forms of depravity by covert subliminal influencing of the seedier men involved. Many targeted individuals also report that they have been influenced into drug use influence, before realizing they are targets, and after becoming targets making them even more easily manipulated. Drugging a person or motivating subliminal drug use encouragement is nothing new and results in submissive mental states thereby making the target easily controlled.

Here is one of several excerpts which can easily be found online related to the subject of mind control technologies role in sexual manipulation and control. This is what I call the sexual perversion distraction agenda. This agenda, on a higher level, is simply designed to keep humanity operating on the level of lustful animals, and physical gratification and thereby stifling spiritual growth and spiritual advancement.

I cannot say enough about the fact that many experts agree that 70% of those being targeted are female predominantly by men

in these facilities. In my case, I fit a specific type. Many efforts towards healthy relationships with someone are repeatedly sabotaged by this targeting.

The excerpt, below, is one of many from: Roberts.Court.com – Alternative News, Video & Supreme Court blog, Monday, April 06, 2009:

Question? Is the dominate symbolism today of sexual programming, an effort to still man's soul and keep man and woman from ascension to the next dimension of spiritually?

Has this become a reality through use of brainwashing methods, to include technology, employing the use sexual powers, and impressions, to controlled humanity, subconsciously, through the media? For example, television and music industry, is today playing a powerful role by those really pulling the strings for continues mass population mind control? The music industry of the 60s and 70s were of love, peace and unity. It appears that this message was distasteful to those seeking to separate, divide, conquer, destroy and promote globalization. It appears, full control of the powerful medium of the media, for use as another form of brainwashing or mind control evolved. Sex began to play a major role.

Illuminati Brainwashing, Masonic Child
Indoctrination and Subliminal Sex Manipulation

The symbols of the Masonic Lodge are permeated with sexual meaning. The "Tubal Cane" pin worn by some Masons symbolizes that male genitals (tubal=two balls, cane=male phallus). The familiar Masonic square and compass represents the male mounting the female in the sex act. The "G" within stands for the "Holy Fire," the act of sexual regeneration.

Beware the age-old Illuminati sex scam from the Order of the Masons as well as the American mass media. The oldest scam next to prostitution is the suspension of children in sexual ignorance so that they are indoctrinated through emotions which they do not understand. The ceremonial emblems and rituals throughout the Masons as well as in television, movie and video game programming have significant subliminal sexual overtones. 9/10s of the most popular video games played by teenagers are sex and violence oriented. These games are literally programming children for "endless war" based solely on the mass media "official story" of 9/11. These covert sexual messages are most effective on children held in sexual ignorance and who are not empowered by parents with comprehensive sex education or provided the parental duty of sex education at the proper time in their development. Sex education is critical for children to develop what Freud called the "reality principle."

As the parental duty was known for thousands of years for protecting children from the slave-makers, today's slave-makers function through mass media. Like a basic carnival scam, children are easily enticed into the arenas of power and influence through subliminal manipulation and educated parents will choose to empower their children with the truth. Experts in Europe are familiar with Nazi Mind Control methods of sexual repression at childhood which builds a more sadistic and authoritarian population easily manipulated by dictators and top-down government. Only a parent can protect such children through the all-important parental duty of early sex education. Both the government Illuminati and advertisers are targeting children and want them to remain ignorant of this manipulation for as long as possible. Ignorance of human power systems sets children up for manipulation by wrongful authority.

Dear Diary,

I would never have believed that young beautiful women are being used by the depraved animals sitting at the helm of this technology until I witnessed it with my own eyes as an attempt with my oldest daughter after she became a target. It first began with her making outrageous comments about considering becoming a stripper influence. When I questioned her about whether this as a real ideation came from she laughed it off and said, she was just joking with me and did not know where the thought came from. By that time, I was beginning to suspect from where the suggestions came.

However, later, as the obvious targeting progressed around her, I was able to sabotage an effort to get her involved with a call-girl ring, catering to wealthy Jewish men in Beverly Hills, California.

After returning from Arizona, 2007, I ran into the woman who was the outreach coordinator for female veterans for the United States Veterans Initiative. I later moved into the house she ran for transitional living for women in Los Angeles. After I had begun to heal, and settled, she phoned me one day, suggesting that we meet up and go out to a social spot in Beverly Hills. She then said, "We could meet a lot of old rich, Jewish men that way." I was completely taken aback. Never have I given any impression of being interested in something of this nature at all and had no interest to go with her. It was just plain ridiculous and completely out of character for me, for her as well, to view this as exciting and out of the ordinary for her to suggest it.

During this time, I was also going to a recreational program at the Veterans Hospital facility located on Temple Street in downtown Los Angeles twice a week.

During the Christmas holiday of 2010, our group of both men and women were invited to a Christmas dinner sponsored by a Veterans Service Organization in Westwood, California. We departed by bus around 10:00 a.m. a few days before Christmas, with the celebration scheduled for noon which would be dinner and gift exchange.

When we arrived in the large banquet room, I sat at the table with the other veterans, and chatted. I watched as an older white Jewish man made his way over to our table and immediately made his way over to me and parked in the chair right next to mine. He was harmless I felt, as he began to tell jokes and had the whole table laughing at first. However, underneath the table, to my great surprise, he had begun rubbing on my leg immediately. I thought he was simply an eccentric elderly gentleman and guided his hand always from my legs a few times.

When we stood to get in line to be served lunch, he stood also and followed me very closely. He then whispered in my ear, "I am very wealthy and live in Beverly Hills." My feeling was, "Okay, so why are you telling me this, and what does it have to do with me?"

After he realized that I was not buying, did not have a clue, and I intentionally moved my seat to seat between two other veterans, he then moved back to table he had originated from across the room. I did not miss a look of confusion on his face. These two incidents, alone still did not register with me as anything other than odd and I blew it off.

However, as I searched for a place to rent, my oldest daughter was working at a record store in Los Angeles and was with me. We briefly rented a weekly room in a hotel while I searched for suitable housing, at a location not far from where she was working. This was in mid-2008. When we both interviewed for a place, the landlord asked if we would have the first and last month rent and deposit if approved. I said, I would, with my daughter standing nearby, but she might not. When I said this, my daughter became indignant, and angrily said,

"You don't know what I have." We returned back to the hotel and I left to get groceries.

When I arrived back home, my daughter was on the phone speaking in a hushed voice, and taking down what appeared to be a name, location and address. As I unpacked the groceries, she decided that I could hear her conversation and left the room, and walked outside a short distance from earshot and sat in the stairwell. Later that night, just around midnight, with her believing I was sound asleep, she quietly slid out of the queen-sized bed we shared, dressed quietly, and then left.

My first instinct was to attempt to follow her, but my right ankle was still very painful after the car accident in 2007 which had brought me home to Los Angeles from Scottsdale, Arizona with pens and screws now holding it together. I stayed awake with my mind racing wondering where she had gone

I began to think about the two odd occurrences between the Outreach Coordinator and the man attempting to tempt me into what sounded like a sexual proposition. These two incidents with my daughter's behavior, hinted at this program hoping to use her sexually and even the thought of the possibility greatly saddened me. Around 3:30 a.m. I heard the door unlock and lay still in bed, with the light off, as my daughter undressed and got back into bed. I laid there for about 45 minutes pretending to be asleep until I heard her doze off. I needed to find her purse for verification.

I could not turn on the light. This time it was I who eased out of bed. I literally tore the room up looking for her purse to see if she had any money in it. I searched and searched and search, our luggage, her clothes pockets, eased my hand under the mattress, before realizing that the only place it could be was under the pillow. If so, I would not be able to ease it from under her.

The next morning, with a heavy heart, I question her about where she had gone just after midnight. She told me she went to hang out with some friends. Based on what I witnessed, and everything combined, I did not believe her and a fierce argument erupted as she denied what I thought possible again based on the other incidents.

We parted ways. She had a job, but the room was very expensive for just a weekly rate. I later found out that she had moved in with one of her friends briefly before moving into the Arts District in late 2008 and I found a small apartment in Signal Hill, California before going to another women's program on the Long Beach VA facility.

To this day, she has denied what I suspected. And I am accurate, as a result, has been easy prey to be used for manipulation and influencing in an intense effort to discredit me. Police set people up this way all the time for this reason. The use of those closest to a target is vital in involuntary mental health detention and ultimately committing. If anything was really happening with her, I decided that day that my efforts of relentless exposure, if right or even a remote possibility, whether I was right or wrong, could play a major role in stopping any involvement if true or factual around her.

She has and still has so much potential and has always been a brilliant writer since child by even winning the "Young Journalist" award in elementary school in Colorado. In fact, for about a year, she had been pulling together an album after getting the contract with the record company in London. I had hired the best attorney in the entertainment industry to negotiate the deal for her as most parents would, and felt a sense of relief that this child now coming of age and would finally embark on a career and more importantly self-sufficiency. I was not thrilled about the music industry but I could not change her mind.

The producer for her album was an eccentric, although a well-known Grammy award winning producer and well-known. He had worked with many of the greats. However, this man came with a boatload of personal baggage from many wives, loss of his home, vehicle, and back taxes and child support issues. These facts essentially stopped his money-making capability. At first, he was agreeable to the record deal with his ex-wife, an attorney assisting him in negotiations with the London music company. However, after a disagreement with my daughter, they split for good. He decided that the label was not giving him enough money for the advancement and that he wanted more money and if not, he backed out.

My daughter and he had written the lyrics together for many of the 13 songs to be used on the album. She and I had just had a meeting with two very talented graphic artists ready to design the album cover in West Hollywood. However, a few days before the arrival of my daughter and granddaughter, we both received a bombshell in late October of 2013. The label, due to the producer's indecisiveness and arrogance had pulled completely out of the deal. What a blow.

More importantly, those targeting me were taking full credit for destroying the deal through the ongoing harassment using the verbal communication system. If true, the question now became for me, had people been used around my targeted daughter to sabotage the effort, could the producer have been influenced? The fact is anyone can be targeted and anywhere on the face of the Earth.

When my daughter use to talk to the producer about what I told her are my experiences, she would always relay back to me that he, as one of the few people, in the early stages who actually believed every I said as true. Why? I later learned that he had been visited by the Department of Homeland Security himself before which meant he was also on the Watchlist for his religious beliefs. Once on this list, high-tech targeting is legally. Could he have become, it stands to reason, in the search for human guinea pigs, likely a person of interest because of his Islamic name, although of African American dissent. The answer is yes! Whether targeted or not, one thing was certain, his life was totally destroyed. It made no sense for him to pull out of a lucrative deal. The fact is Fusion Centers, across the U.S., where this technology is used and information filtered, motivated by and set up by the Federal Bureau of investigation and Department of Homeland Security with high tech terrorism divisions was watching everyone.

The very fact that Department of Homeland Security personally visited him was huge and would indicate, that he along with many Americans have been downloaded into the mega computer and DARPA effort called Total Information Awareness. Total Information Awareness is/was a documented effort designed to have biometric information on ALL U.S.A citizens maintained in a central data base.

The fact is I have noticed my daughter, on the days preceding her attempt to again have me involuntarily committed to the psych ward through patented Synthetic Telepathy. One day, I heard her say, out of the clear blue, "Thank you." I asked her who she was talking to and she became agitated that I asked. She then said that she did not know what I was talking about. The fact is, by many reports, these men, will compliment you all day long followed by strategic degradation. This is a tactic designed to ingratiate themselves with targets, again a PSY OPS operation and they love doing so while they watch you shower.

It has not ever worked with many, because it is illogical to believe the operators at the helm who compliment then torture mercilessly, and are slowly killing, like the target who are reporting these technological experiences. In fact, at this very moment the men are focusing the beam yet again on my heart muscle as they read along with this note prove they are not friends. These men, believing they are controlling lives, may not have wanted to see her prosper and move to a higher level and out of their grasp. They were comfortable with her operating on their level and these efforts are constant in attempts to change the target and to get the target to see things their way and recreate the target's life. These efforts are about controlling lives plain and simply.

The worldwide music distribution deal was null and void. They are I realized as I learned more, that fame could have opened her up to a different live of influence, and technological manipulation and control prevalent in the entertainment industry. She may not have made it to that level and I encouraged her to pursue the publishing side of the business using her song writing gift which is highly, again highly profitable. In fact, the record deal also included a publishing deal for songs she had written so she lost a lot.

Would they seek to destroy my daughter's life and career to get to me and silence me, or through the producer, who may very well be a targeted individual himself? The only people who easily grasp what is happening today are those that are living it and know of, the brilliance and global power and high-tech influence of this technology. The answer, which can be substantiated by thousands targeted, in growing number nationwide and globally is that those sitting in these centers would do so absolutely! If they will torture individuals to slow death, you can bet they will do anything. No one is exempt in this massive program designed for ultimate global control, and of which is active in every NATO country on the planet today and covertly has been for a long time.

I constantly remind myself, and must not forget that there is a greater force at play, and that it is working side by side and hand in hand with a decisive agenda to uplift humanity and that this omnipresence is working for the overall good. I remain focused and recognized daily, that no matter what, all things are truly, inevitably, working together for good. This has been the key to my survival. Walk through the storm, but keep walking no matter what.

No one can stop what God has ordained for you or anyone. Trust and believe it!

Dear Diary,

The younger men in the operation house across the street appear to be Air Force. I live about 20 minutes from a major Air Force air base. One night, when I first moved in to a rental before purchasing in 2014, as I was leaving for the gym, peaking through the window was someone who looked identical to the non-African American Air Force person I had seen before setting up a larger version of the microwave pain beam in the apartment I moved from in Los Angeles.

Make no mistake about it, when these operation centers were named "Fusion" it 100% is an accurate concept, and depiction of the new paradigm of Police State enforcement, after 911, the unification of military and law enforcement, from massive counterterrorism divisions where Human Rights Advocates, activists, and whistleblowers are targeted.

THE US CONSTITUTION IS MIA

The first ten amendments to the United States Constitution are collectively called the "Bill of Rights," because they deal with individual rights and freedoms that cannot be and should not be abrogated by the government. The Bill of Rights enumerates freedoms not explicitly indicated in the main body of the

Constitution, such as freedom of religion, freedom of speech, a free press, and free assembly; the right to keep and bear arms; freedom from unreasonable search and seizure, security in personal effects, and freedom from warrants issued without probable cause; indictment by a grand jury for any capital or "infamous crime"; guarantee of a speedy, public trial with an impartial jury and prohibition of double jeopardy. In addition, the Bill of Rights reserves for the people any rights not specifically mentioned in the Constitution and reserves all powers not specifically granted to the federal government to the people or the States.

Today, these basic, humane rights, deserving of all human being, on Earth, are a thing of the distant past, in what many that are awake view as efforts towards world dominion.

CHAPTER SEVEN

No Touch Torture and PSY OPS

Dear Diary,

I am hit wherever I go by the Multifunctional Directional Energy Weapon system around the clock on and on and on. These weapons cause every symptom related to radiation toxicity, and injuries known to man and I continue to document excruciating pain. They can also cause blindness, brain damage, skin damage, and over time a complete physical transformation of the human body. I will never walk normally again I thought at first. The surgeries restored my ability to function normally. Not to out done, my legs continue to be a major focus. However, as stated, with my documenting every occurrence, literally step by step the operation pulls back.

They are killing me slowly in a failed coercive effort and the hits to my heart are escalating, however years later if still alive, a target then questions if it is all about fear through Electromagnetic Terrorism? I stumbled on a credible report detailing the technological coercive effort below written by Alfred McCoy below:

Alfred McCoy released his new study of coercive interrogation and "no touch" torture and writes:

"Torture and Impunity: the US Doctrine of Coercive Interrogation," the website, "Desperado Philosophy" reports." "McCoy provides a concise summary of his investigation in an essay on the indispensable Tom Dispatch in which he outlines the nasty pincer of impunity at home and rendition abroad. This led Desperado Philosophy to review the extraordinary 60 minutes interview between Lesley Stahl and José Rodriguez, the former head of the CIA Clandestine Service, and the chief executor for the regime of "enhanced" interrogation imposed during the years following 9/11."

The Desperado Philosophy report further states "the interview received scant attention at the time, and quickly disappeared into the media whirlwind of scandals and crisis, or was dismissed as nada de nuevo. The transcript makes for sobering reading, and reveals what Gitta Sereny would call a "corrupt personality"; corrupt as in broken, together. Even Lesley Stahl, well-seasoned after decades of exposure to venality and corruption in every shape and measure, appears perplexed by the moral vacuity and lack of self-reflective conscience exhibited by Mr. Rodriguez... We have slightly edited and compressed excerpts from the transcript below."

Today, "No Touch Torture" is no longer exclusive to high powered federal agencies as a form of pain, physical and psychological coercion. Today a total standard operating procedure package, has been passed down to hundreds of agencies in electronic harassment programs, use of ELF frequencies, Synthetic Telepathy, and various other "Black Bag" technologies, which can alter consciousness, among other things. Details and a review of the transcript can be found on the Desperado Philosophy website:

Dear Diary,

During the tapings of "The Targeted Individual's VOICE" and numerous times while speaking with my co-host over the phone, I can hear the great pain and struggle in his voice as he is tortured like many mercilessly. There is, by him, an honorable attempt to endure, and continue to function normally, under these great and painful attacks. He too has been crippled refusing to submit after awakening. Make no mistake about it, the pain disseminated by this advanced energy technology is powerful and the user has the ability adjust the setting of intensity at will.

Dear Diary,

I must confess that with the knowledge I have acquired in this battle that I now perceived the drugging of society in a different light with an agenda. The point is, drugs are for profitable and some appear to be continued extensions of MK Ultra drug testing both legal and illegal. Drugs have become a means of accomplishing altered and pliable states of consciousness for population control.

As previously stated, LSD was callously distributed at locations such as night clubs and bars to unsuspecting random people in MK Ultra, who were likely then tracked and monitored from operation centers long before these centers were officially legalized. Satellite usage dates back, on the record, to the Cuban Missile Crisis. And, as revealed, Subprojects, 2, 9, 17, 27, 31, 43, 46, 55 and 59 reveals also testing at even many Universities.

These tests also reveal unwitting drug tests centering on a combination of drugs, along with the effects of several drugs on the central nervous system. The study focused on pharmaceutical company involvement with depressants (which likely led to specific anti-depressant development) and noteworthy, 147 and 148 focusing specifically on a concentrated version of THC from marijuana.

I personally believe that marijuana deserves special attention and suspicion today, as many people profess the great benefits of marijuana for health reasons. However, the marijuana used today is many times more potent than it was when I was a teenager. Why I was not surprised while doing research when I stumbled across a specific grade of marijuana actually cultivated and even called MK Ultra. It is defined below:

MK Ultra Strain of Cannabis

This strain, named after the methods of mental manipulation employed by the CIA's Project MK Ultra, this Indica-dominant strain stands apart due to its powerful cerebral effect. A cross between mostly-sativa hybrid OG Kush and Indica G-13, this strain is bred by TH Seeds and won 1st place Indica at the High Times Cannabis Cup in 2003 and 2nd place in 2004. Indoor growing is facilitated by the plant's short stature, and its above average yield delivers particularly sticky, dense, pungent flowers. MK Ultra is renowned for its 'hypnotic' effects that are fast-acting and best used when strong medication is desired. As evidenced by its collection of awards, this Indica is one of the strongest in the world. It might be best for a day when not getting off the couch would be fine.

Dear Diary,

I, personally, would not trust any drug once documented to be part of any testing connected with the mind control programs and agenda of MK Ultra. I cannot think of a better way to steal a country or the world then a laid back, mellow, becoming a passive population than by drug use that, as stated above, makes you not want to get off the couch. As my dad would say before he passed, "There is no mind better than your normal mind!" It is conscious and aware and evolved by coping with the trials of life. It is Light! Life must be lived on life's terms. There is no escaping this no matter how painful.

It must be clearly understood that MK Ultra was the ultimate mind control study, and that it too, as is the program running rampant today, as extension of it, was an officially sanctioned human guinea pig testing program designed as such before official inception.

With this technology it is not farfetched that a target could be easily nudged into drug usage or even criminal activity. For example, while out shopping recently, the thought was beamed into my head, and have been several times before, that I should steal something out of Walmart of all places. This thought materialized, obviously from the operation center, *although I have money in my bank account and my debit card with me to pay and also a Walmart credit card to pay for an item which cost $10. What happens to people unaware who believe the high-tech suggestion beamed by highly perfected mind invasive technology is their own?*

Imagine a targeted individual unaware of this capability, or unaware that they are even targeted, stealing, while being monitored around the clock by real-time imaging?   The result would be a perfectly executed electromagnetic entrapment set up. This manipulation could then be used as one way of getting rid of the targeted individual, or even used to get the target entangled in the jail system.   Those attempting this with me are a sign of the confidence they have in obvious successful manipulation of others and the success.   They also suggest target's commit suicide.

Please tell me why in God's name I would even think of taking something with money in my purse?   It is just outrageous and absurd. Again, pathetic people will never control me with nonsense.   Dumb asses!

Dear Diary,

I was given, as mentioned previously, six months after denial of my Federal Tort Claim Act filing to file a Civil Complaint against the United States of America. Ultimately this effort failed as it has with everyone trying for judicial intervention.

It is done!

Dear Diary,

This image is an actual depiction of locations I am being hit consistently on my body by the Multifunctional Direct Energy Weapon System especially while I try to sleep at night.

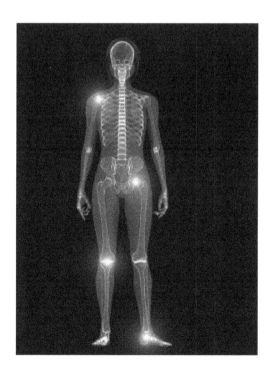

Dear Diary,

I just went outside to set the trash out for trash day in the morning. The neighborhood is quiet; however, when the night shift arrived across the street, I briefly felt the intensity of the beam until I adjusted the protective material against the wall and covered the window with it before coming outside. While outside, I could hear, literally come from thin air, threats from the surveillance location.

I guess now I can say it is cute. I say this because, before I realized the capability of the radio wave technology to throw the voices of those operating it nearby or from the operation center, I at first, probably like many targets, thoughts neighbors were calling me names and threatening me from inside their homes. The technique used is called Voice Morphing.

In 1999 the Washington Post did an article explaining how the technology works, and how it is being used in PSY OPS.

The original article reads:

When Seeing and Hearing Isn't Believing
By William M. Arkin

Special Correspondent to Washingtonpost.com

Monday, Feb. 1, 1999

"Gentlemen! We have called you together to inform you that we are going to overthrow the United States government." So, begins a statement being delivered by Gen. Carl W. Steiner, former Commander-in-chief, U.S. Special Operations Command.

At least the voice sounds amazingly like him.

But it is not Steiner. It is the result of voice "morphing" technology developed at the Los Alamos National Laboratory in New Mexico.

By taking just a 10-minute digital recording of Steiner's voice, scientist George Papcun is able, in near real time, to clone speech patterns and develop an accurate facsimile. Steiner was so impressed, he asked for a copy of the tape.

Steiner was hardly the first or last victim to be spoofed by Papcun's team members. To refine their method, they took various high-quality recordings of generals and experimented with creating fake statements. One of the most memorable is Colin Powell stating "I am being treated well by my captors."

"They chose to have him say something he would never otherwise have said," chuckled one of Papcun's colleagues.

A Box of Chocolates is Like War

****

Most Americans were introduced to the tricks of the digital age in the movie Forrest Gump, when the character played by Tom Hanks appeared to shake hands with President Kennedy.

For Hollywood, it is special effects. For covert operators in the U.S. military and intelligence agencies, it is a weapon of the future.

"Once you can take any kind of information and reduce it into ones and zeroes, you can do some pretty interesting things," says Daniel T. Kuehl, chairman of the Information Operations department of the National Defense University in Washington, the military's school for information warfare. PSYOPS seeks to exploit human vulnerabilities in energy governments, militaries and populations.

Digital morphing — voice, video, and photo — has come of age, available for use in psychological operations. PSYOPS, as the military calls it, seek to exploit human vulnerabilities in enemy governments, militaries and populations to pursue national and battlefield objectives.

To some, PSYOPS is a backwater military discipline of leaflet dropping and radio propaganda. To a growing group of information war technologists, it is the nexus of fantasy and reality. Being able to manufacture convincing audio or video, they say, might be the difference in a successful military operation or coup.

Allah on the Holodeck

****

Pentagon planners started to discuss digital morphing after Iraq's invasion of Kuwait in 1990. Covert operators kicked around the idea of creating a computer-faked videotape of Saddam Hussein crying or showing other such manly weaknesses, or in some sexually compromising situation. The nascent plan was for the tapes to be flooded into Iraq and the Arab world.

The tape war never proceeded, killed, participants say, by bureaucratic fights over jurisdiction, skepticism over the technology, and concerns raised by Arab coalition partners.

But the "strategic" PSYOPS scheming didn't die. What if the U.S. projected a holographic image of Allah floating over Baghdad urging the Iraqi people and Army to raise up against Saddam, a senior Air Force officer asked in 1990?

According to a military physicist given the task of looking into the hologram idea, the feasibility had been established of projecting large, three-dimensional objects that appeared to float in the air.

But doing so over the skies of Iraq? To project such a hologram over Baghdad on the order of several hundred feet, they calculated, would take a mirror more than a mile square in space, as well as huge projectors and power sources.

And besides, investigators came back, what does Allah look like?

The Gulf War hologram story might be dismissed were it not the case that washingtonpost.com has learned that a super- secret program was established in 1994 to pursue the very technology for PSYOPS application. The "Holographic Projector" is described in a classified Air Force document as a system to "project information power from space ... for special operations deception missions."

War is Like a Box of Chocolates

Voice-morphing, fake videos, holographic projections... They sound more like Mission Impossible and Star Trek gimmicks than weapons. Yet for each, there are corresponding and growing research efforts as the technologies improve and offensive information warfare expands.

Whereas early voice morphing required cutting and pasting speech to put letters or words together to make a composite, Papcun's software developed at Los Alamos can far more accurately replicate the way one actually speaks. Eliminated are the robotic intonations.

The irony is that after Papcun finished his speech cloning research, there were no takers in the military. Luckily for him, Hollywood is interested: The promise of creating a virtual Clark Gable is mightier than the sword.

Video and photo manipulation have already raised profound questions of authenticity for the journalistic world. With audio joining the mix, it is not only journalists but also privacy advocates and the conspiracy-minded who will no doubt ponder the worrisome mischief that lurks in the not too distant future.

"We already know that seeing isn't necessarily believing," says Dan Kuehl, "now I guess hearing isn't either."

William M. Arkin, author of "The U.S. Military Online," is a leading expert on national security and the Internet. He lectures and writes on nuclear weapons, military matters and information warfare. An Army intelligence analyst from 1974-1978, Arkin currently consults for The Washington Post, Newsweek Interactive, MSNBC and the Natural Resources Defense Council.

Dear Diary,

Digital Voice Morphing is also used on targeted individuals mimicking the target's voice and also profusely used on those in the target's environment. I simply cannot stress this point enough. When used on the target, those directing it use it to make the target think that they are admitting wrong doing, in their own morphed thoughts which is the key. Again, awareness to the subtle brainwashing and resulting ultimately entrapment is key.

This technique can also be used to create admittance of some type of deviant behavior by the target or that deviant thoughts are actually part of their genuine thoughts or desire for deviance. When used on those in the target's environment, thoughts against the target are beamed into their heads to stir up and promote negativity in the environment. This actually was how the Thanksgiving family hope was destroyed. When the target tries to explain this technological capability to others, the person attempting to convince, adamantly denies this capability is being used on them. I have found that believing it is happening to them, means they are crazy too. As a result, some suffer the harassment in silence until set-off.

Dear Diary,

Ironically, these books exist because of the machination of those targeting me. These books exist, using tactics they felt would impact me emotionally, physically or mentally which I decided to document. Yes, the conflict created in my family was the hardest to deal with at first; however, I am over it. I love my daughters and new granddaughter and know they love me.

184

Right now, I've got work to do!

Thank God for watching over me. Thank God for protecting my loved ones in advance. It is probably best, I realize if they are not around me right now to be continually used as pawns. At times, warriors must walk alone!

Dear Diary

Shift change coming around 10:00 p.m. The one leaving on this current shift spent all night trying to get my attention with comments as I worked focused on this book. He then decided to focus on torture. "Goodbye hideous vicious deviant" I thought!

As I have documented before, the shift that comes in from 10:00 p.m. to approximately 6:00 a.m. in the morning I have found to be the cruelest and vicious of all to include the weekend shifts in these operations. Torturing a person while they sleep, and also experimenting on them using various mind-altering frequencies, seems to be big during this timeframe and great for Delta sleep programing. Again, awareness is key and what my efforts are all about. I hope I can help shed light by personal experiences.

Dear Diary,

In my case, I have noticed that whenever a homeowner approves their house to be set up with technology, always the location closest to the target, front back and both sides, the homeowners appears to go on paid vacations. I noticed, them literally missing in action for long periods of time. I have not seen the lady, directly, across the street from where the direction of the beam is coming right now for quite some time and have seen complete strangers going and coming from her home.

Her sister lives in Las Vegas so she may be there visiting I thought. Oddly, the other day, I did see her nephew cutting her grass. Usually she is out front with him. A dimly lit light stays on in the living room and turns off whenever I turn my office light off to go upstairs to bed each night as if the operation is closing down as I do, but it doesn't.

Sometimes I work in my home office until after midnight. I also saw the same lady that I have seen around me several times, before moving to this rental property actually talking to the nephew one day. One day as I was preparing to leave, I had gotten in my car in the garage, and opened the garage door and she came out to talk with the nephew and I watched her through my rear-view mirror looking back at me then noticing me watching, turned her back.

This woman makes it a point to always keep her back turned from me so that I can never fully see her face. But her height, build, cannot be denied. It is the same woman I have seen, again several times over the years. Essentially the same group assigned to a target continue until successful.

Dear Diary,

They appear to be strategically recruiting, young impressionable men and women for these organized stalking efforts. Many are looking for a sense of purpose and power in life.

I cannot reiterate enough that it is important for a targeted individual to remain as calm as possible. The powerful microwave non-ionizing energy effect creates powerful anxiety and agitation which is useful to those in these operations if you react. You then live the synthetic mental illness tag goal.

Dear Diary,

The party is over for me, as I prepare for bed; however, it has just begun for the graveyard shift working in state-of-the-art operations centers, again nationwide.

I will be on slow kill energy weapon assault, using extremely frequencies while sleeping until early morning.

Dear Diary,

I had a horrible dream last night regarding my middle daughter. My granddaughter was in it also.

She contacted me the other day and told me she wanted to come back and stay with me, and bring my new granddaughter, so that she can go to school full time in California. Of course, I was happy, but I was also cautioned fully aware of the mental tampering technologically. The intensity of the effort around me as I attempt to write this book is horrific and naturally, it will likely spill over to my daughter and even granddaughter. These people don't care who they destroy.

CHAPTER EIGHT

"We have seen today the dark side of those activities, where many Americans who were not even suspected of crime were not only spied upon; but they were harassed, they were discredited, and at times endangered... illegal, secret intimidation and harassment of the ability of Americans to participate freely in the American political life shall never happen again." ~ Frank Church - COINTELPRO

Counter Intelligence "PROGRAM"

COINTELPRO was a series of covert, and at times illegal, projects conducted by the United States Federal Bureau of

Investigation (FBI) which was aimed at specific targeted individuals. The effort combined PSYOPS of infiltrating, discrediting, and disrupting domestic political organizations National Security Agency Operations who citizens were speaking out against corruption. Project MINARET targeted the personal communications of leading Americans, during the Cold War, including Senators and Civil Rights leaders, activists, journalists and athletes who criticized the Vietnam War. Intelligence activities and technology has for quite some time played a pivotal role in target of specific individuals.

The National Security Agency was created in 1952 as part of the Defense Department but with no written charter. The NSA's primary mission was and is today that of electronic intelligence gathering. To perform these requirements, such as gathering intercepts of foreign electronic communications, the NSA had a staff of thousands as far back as the 1970s.

The Senate Select Committee's questioning revolved around the use of this capability to target American citizens, particularly dissidents. Project MINARET was created in 1969 to spy on peace groups and black power organizations was the subject of some focus.

95th Congress 2nd Session I

Committee Print

Unclassified Summary:

Involvement of NSA in the development

of the data encryption standard

Staff report of the Senate Select Committee on

Intelligence United States Senate

APRIL 1978

Printed for the use of the Select Committee on Intelligence

U.S. Government Printing Office 25-983 Washington: 1978

Senate Select Committee on Intelligence

(Established by S. Res. 400, 94th Cong., 2d Sess.)

BIRCH BAYH, Indiana, *Chairman*

BARRY GOLDWATER, Arizona, Vice *Chairman*

ADLAI E. STEVENSON, Illinois CLIFFORD P. CASE, New
Jersey

WILLIAM D. HATHAWAY, Maine

JAKE GARN, Utah

WALTER D. HUDDLESTON, Kentucky CHARLES McCoy.

MATHIAS, JR., Maryland

JOSEPH R. BIDEN, JR., Delaware

JAMES B. PEARSON, Kansas

ROBERT MO RGAN, North Carolina

JOHN H. CHAFEE, Rhode Island

GARY HART, Colorado

RICHARD C. LUGAR, Indiana

DANIEL PATRICK MOYNIHAN, New York

MALCOLM WALLOP, Wyoming

DANIEL K. INOUYE, Hawaii

ROBERT C. BYRD, West Virginia, Ex *Officio Member*

HOWARD H. BAKER, JS., Tennessee, *Ex Officio Member*

WILLIAM G. MILLER, *Staff Director*

EARL D. EISENHOWER, *Minority Staff Director*

AUDREY H. HATRY, *Chief Clerk*

Unclassified Summary:

Involvement of NSA in the Development

of the Data Encryption Standard

Introduction

The Senate Select Committee on Intelligence recently completed a classified study concerning allegations that the National Security Agency (NSA) was improperly involved in the development of a data encryption standard (DES). The DES resulted from efforts of the National Bureau of Standards (NBS) to certify a single DES to be used for all Government. (Non-classified data).

The interest of the committee stems from its oversight responsibility for NSA and as a result of several allegations made about NSA harassment of scientists working in the field of public cryptology.

The classified study, undertaken late in 1977, is based on interviews with both public and private scientists and engineers, including representatives of the following government agencies, private companies, and professional associations:

NSA, NBS, the National Science Foundation (NSF), the Department of Defense, International Business Machines (IBM), and the Institute for Electrical Engineers and Electronics (IEEE).

Over 200 pages of private and public papers and documents were also, analyzed.

Background

Two developments caused the NBS to begin a search for a process which they could propose as a Federal standard to be used for all Government non-classified data stored and transmitted by computer. One was the Brooks Act of 1965 which gave NBS the responsibility to create standards which would govern the purchase and use of computers for the Federal

Government. The second, a general movement which culminated in the Privacy Act of 1974, was an attempt to keep confidential and secure all data on U.S. citizens in the possession of the Government.

In 1968, the head of the NBS Institute for Computer Science and Technology initiated several studies assessing the need for computer security within the Government. As a result of the studies, the NBS decided to foster the development and establishment of a Government-wide standard for encryption devices which would offer adequate security for unclassified Government data. NBS also decided that the best encryption method would be the use of an encryption algorithm.'

Footnote: An algorithm consists of rules of procedure which are used to solve complex mathematical problems most commonly those with frequent repetitive operations. In cryptology an algorithm is used to transform plain text data into encrypted data by using rules of procedure so complicated that decryption is unlikely without knowing the algorithm or rules of procedure through which the plain text was encrypted. This process requires a key which governs encryption and decryption. (1)

Knowing of NSA's experience and expertise in the field of cryptology, NBS officials made contact with NSA and, among other things, asked for NSA's assistance in evaluating the quality of a data encryption standard (DES) algorithm.

NBS issued a federal solicitation through the *Federal Register* of May 1973 encouraging interested developers to submit possible algorithms for consideration as the DES.

That solicitation evoked few responses and a second solicitation was issued in August 1974. IBM, having had some experience with encryption algorithms used in a secure cash transaction system they had marketed a few years earlier, responded with an algorithm to be considered for the DES. NBS, in consultation with NSA, judged the IBM algorithm to be the best of those submitted and NBS decided that the IBM formula would become the Government DES. Before this was announced, however, some private computer scientists and engineers who had been developing their own encryption systems, expressed concerns about the strength of that algorithm and the process through which the IBM algorithm had been chosen.

As a result of those concerns, NBS sponsored two workshops on DES at which many related issues were discussed. At the first workshop (August, 1976) the practicality and economic feasibility of constructing a special purpose computer to attack the DES through a brute force or exhaustion attack was discussed.

Several estimates of the time and cost involved in such an effort were discussed at the workshop. NBS officials said that with their existing machinery, a brute force attack would take 17,000 years. The participants disagreed over the cost, development time, and exhaustion time necessary to construct special purpose computer equipment designed to attack the DES. The majority of those present suggested ranges of 2 to 10 years for construction of equipment which would exhaust the DES-over a 6 month to 10-year period of time at a construction cost of $10 to $12 million dollars. One scientist argued that, given rapidly changing technology, it would be possible by 1990 to construct a special purpose, parallel chip machine for $72 million which could exhaust all possible alternatives within 1 day.

The second workshop (September, 1977) dealt with the mathematical and statistical characteristics of the DES. The conclusion of the workshop was that the DES was a sound algorithm. Concerns were expressed, however, at this workshop that it was not possible to assess all of the characteristics of the DES since IBM had not been willing to share all of the design criteria used in the creation of the DES. IBM replied that in the testing of their algorithms by NSA, certain information was learned which was sensitive and that NSA requested that information not be discussed publicly.

Public attention was called to the DES and related cryptologic developments because of a simmering scientific argument being conducted through some scientific magazines and because of the publicity given a July 1977 letter from a Mr. Joseph A. Meyer to Mr. E. K. Gannet secretary of the IEEE publications board. The Meyer letter pointed to the possibility that some of the discussions and (continued after Footnote)

Footnote: A brute force or exhaustion attack transforms encrypted text into every possible combination in an effort to discover the original plain text.

Publications of members of IEEE's Information Theory Group might be in violation of U.S. export regulations relating to cryptanalytic equipment and information. The letter was circulated to members of the Information Theory Group without comment by Mr. Gannet. Copies of the letter were obtained by the press and stories were written alleging Mr. Meyer was an employee of the NSA and that the letter should be interpreted as NSA pressure on the scientific community to deter cryptologic research activities.

These stories gave rise to additional allegations about NSA activities related to the DES and to cryptologic research in general. The stories also suggested that NSA had exerted pressure on the NSF to persuade them not to fund certain grant proposals for support of cryptologic research.

The following allegations were investigated by the Senate Select Committee on Intelligence: that the NSA exerted pressure on officials in the National Science Foundation (NSF) to withhold grant funds for scholarly research in the field of public cryptology and computer security; that the NSA directed an employee, who was also a member of the Institute of Electrical and Electronic Engineers (IEEE), to write a letter to IEEE warning its members that certain actions related to an upcoming Information Theory Group Conference could be in violation of Government regulations affecting the publication and export of cryptographic information: that U.S. Government harassment brought about a chilling effect in universities doing research in cryptanalysis and even resulted in one university withdrawing already published material from its library shelves; that the NSA, under the guise of testing the mathematical formulae (algorithms) submitted to the National Bureau of Standards (NBS) for consideration as a Data Encryption Standard (DES), "tampered" with the final algorithm in order to weaken it and create a "trapdoor" which only the NSA could tap; that the NSA forced the company (IBM) whose algorithm was chosen, to compromise the DES's security by reducing the key size I used in the encryption and decryption process; and that the DES failed to allow for future technological advancements which will permit successful brute force attacks within the next several years.

Based on its staff study, the Senate Select Committee on Intelligence concludes the following:

- The NSA has not put pressure on the NSF to prevent funding of grants for cryptologic research. However, the very uncertainty and ambiguity surrounding cryptology has prompted some NSA officials to express concern to NSF about certain grants with cryptological ramifications and to suggest that NSA be involved in reviewing these proposals. The NSF has agreed to the latter request, since it views NSA as the only location of competent cryptological expertise in the Government, but has not lessened its interest in, or willingness to fund, good research proposals in this field.

Footnote: The key is the string of binary numbers which directs the encryption process. In a sense, the longer the key, the longer a brute force attack takes. Decryption is possible, otherwise, only if the encrypting key is known; or if the algorithm is weak, thus permitting shortcut attacks.

- The committee has determined that Mr. Meyer's letter to Mr. Gannet of- the IEEE was initiated solely by Mr.

Meyer in his capacity as a member of the IEEE and was not prompted by any NSA official.

- There has been no direct or indirect Government harassment of scientists working the field of computer security. Nor has any university withdrawn library material as a result of NSA pressure. Nevertheless, the very newness of public cryptology and the vagueness and ambiguity of Federal regulations pertaining to cryptology create an uncertainty which in itself is not conducive to creative scholarly work.

- In the development of the DES, NSA convinced IBM that a reduced key size was sufficient; indirectly assisted in the development,\of the S box structures; 5 and certified that the final DES algorithm was, to the best of their knowledge, free of any statistical or mathematical weaknesses. NSA did not tamper with the design of the algorithm in any way. IBM invented and designed the algorithm, made all pertinent decisions regarding it, and concurred that the agreed upon key size was more than adequate for all commercial applications for which the DES was intended.

- While the Intelligence Committee is in no position to settle scientific arguments regarding the exhaustion time necessary to break a DES encrypted message, it can report that the overwhelming majority of scientists consulted felt that the security afforded by the DES was more than adequate for at least a 5-10-year time span for the unclassified data for which it will be used. The committee notes that NSA has recommended that the Federal Reserve Board use the DES in their funds transfer system.

- In order to reduce the potential capriciousness which is possible in ambiguous and uncertain situations, this committee recommends:

- that the appropriate committees of Congress should address the question of public cryptology by clarifying the role which the Federal Government should have in policies affecting public cryptology. That the NSF should decide what authorities and obligations it has to consider the national security implications of grant proposals.

- that NSF and NSA should initiate efforts to reduce the ambiguity and uncertainty which surrounds the granting of research funds; for public cryptology.

- that NSA and NSF should discuss the need for NSA to become part of NSF's peer review process for the review of grant proposals for research in cryptography or cryptanalysis.

- that the NBS should continue to follow developments in computer and related technology in order to be aware of any developments which could lessen the security of the DES. '

Footnote: There are a number of Federal regulations of various types which are interpreted to have some effect on cryptology. Among them are: International Traffic in Arms Regulations (ITAR), 22 CFR 121-128; the Mutual Security Act of 1954, sec. 414-22 USC 1934 42.5m, USC 2274-7.7; 18 USC 798; 18 USC 952; and Executive Order No. 12036. The S box structure is that part of the algorithm which governs the iterative process.

The FBI has used covert operations against domestic political groups since its inception; however, covert operations under the official COINTELPRO label took place between 1956 and 1971. COINTELPRO tactics are still used to this day, and have been alleged to include discrediting targets through psychological warfare, smearing individuals and groups using forged documents and by planting false reports in the media; harassment; wrongful imprisonment; and illegal violence, including assassination. The FBI's stated motivation was "protecting national security, preventing violence, and maintaining the existing social and political order."

"Many of the techniques used would be intolerable in a democratic society even if all of the targets had been involved in violent activity, but COINTELPRO went far beyond that...the Bureau conducted a sophisticated vigilante operation aimed squarely at preventing the exercise of First Amendment rights of speech and association, on the theory that preventing the growth of dangerous groups and the propagation of dangerous ideas would protect the national security and deter violence." - Final Report of the Church Committee.

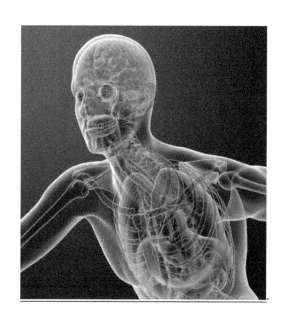

CHAPTER NINE

High Tech Brainwave Mapping

Little known to most Americans, as this decade long program grew to perfection, is the fact that one of the very first lawsuits ever brought before the United States District Court, for Remote Neural Monitoring, was a lawsuit brought against one of the first agencies using electromagnetic, extremely low frequency (ELF) technology the NSA. Today we know that the technology has trickled down as widespread use at all levels of Federal, state and local police departments again unified with military personnel. John St. Clair Akwei brought what are known "Electronic Terrorism" charges against the National Security Agency (NSA). Thank to him for allowing me to use this information, fully, we are all on the same team.

John Akwei

vs.

National Security Agency
Ft George G. Meade, MD, USA
(Civil Action 92-0449)

In this lawsuit, Mr. Akwei alleges the NSA used it resources, including remote physiological devices, to illegally harass and surveil him for over a decade. Mr. Akwei brought his case before the US District Court in Washington DC in 1992. It was dismissed due to the Court being unable to identify any legal cause of action.

This has been a scenario many targeted individuals continue to face. At issue is the fact, as I have stated before, that there is no specific law, with the exception of a few states against the use of electromagnetic technology.

In 1996 Nexus Magazine published Mr. Akwei's evidence dossier which he compiled after the ruling. Based on the intricate working of the NSA many assumed that Mr. Akwei was an actual NSA employee. However, Mr. Akwei is no the record as having never made those claims. In fact, his website today says:

About John Akwei, ECMp ERMp: I am certified in Enterprise Content Management and Electronic Records Management, and I have extensive experience, and proficiency, in Data Management with the goal of Enterprise System efficiency, effectiveness, and productivity. I am available on a consulting basis, for Data Management, Database Optimization, Migration, or Integrity Management projects that your company is involved in.

I search and searched for information on what Mr. Akwei's actual employment status was during this timeframe. My conclusion is that he may very well have been a government contractor, and worked in a similar capacity possibly to that of Edward Snowden. Based on the documents in Chapter 6, many have been allegedly targeting by the NSA at one time or another. Here is John Akwei's well publicized dossier put together after dismissal of his Civil Rights action:

The NSA's Mission and Domestic

Intelligence Operation

Communications Intelligence (COMINT)

Blanket coverage of all electronic communications in the US and the world to ensure national security. The NSA at Ft Meade, Maryland has had the most advanced computers in the world since the early 1960s. NSA technology is developed and implemented in secret from private corporations, academia and the general public.

Signals Intelligence (SICINT)

The Signals Intelligence mission of the NSA has evolved into a program of decoding EMF waves in the environment for wirelessly tapping into computers and track persons with the electrical currents in their bodies. Signals Intelligence is based on fact that everything in the environment with an electric current in it has a magnetic flux around it which gives off EMF waves. The NSA/DOD [Department of Defense] developed proprietary advanced digital equipment which can remotely analyze all objects whether manmade or organic, that has electrical activity.

Domestic Intelligence (DOMINT)

The NSA has records on all US citizens. The NSA gathers information on US citizen who might be of interest to any of the over 50,000 NSA agents (HUMINT). These agents are authorized by executive order to spy on anyone. The NSA has a permanent national security anti-terrorist surveillance network in place. This surveillance network is completely disguised and hidden from the public.

Tracking individuals in the US is easily and cost-effectively implemented with NSA's electronic surveillance network. This network (DOMINT) covers the entire US, involves tens of thousands of NSA personnel, and tracks millions of persons simultaneously. Cost-effective implementation of operations is assured by NSA computer technology designed to minimize operations costs. NSA personnel serve in quasi-public positions in their communities and run cover businesses and legitimate businesses that can inform the intelligence community of persons they would want to track. NSA personnel in the community usually have cover identities such as social workers, lawyers and business owners.

1. Individual Citizens Occasionally Targeted for Surveillance by Independently Operating NSA Personnel

NSA personnel can control the lives of hundreds of thousands of individuals in the US by using the NSA's domestic intelligence network and cover businesses. The operations independently run by them can sometimes go beyond the bounds of law. Long-term control and sabotage of tens of thousands of unwitting citizens by NSA operatives is likely to happen. NSA DOMINT has the ability to assassinate US citizens covertly or run covert psychological control operations to cause subjects to be diagnosed with ill mental health.

2. NSA's Domestic Electronic Surveillance Network

As of the early 1960s, the most advanced computers in the world were at the NSA, Ft Meade. Research breakthroughs with these computers were kept for the NSA. At the present time the NSA has nanotechnology computers that are 15 years ahead of present computer technology. The NSA obtains blanket coverage of information in the US by using advanced computers that use artificial intelligence to screen all communications, regardless of medium, for key words that should be brought to the attention of NSA agents/cryptologists. These computers monitor all communications at the transmitting and receiving ends. This blanket coverage of the US is a result of the NSA's Signals Intelligence (SIGINT) mission. The NSA's electronic surveillance network is based on a cellular arrangement of devices that can monitor the entire EMF spectrum. This equipment was developed, implemented and kept secret in the same manner as other electronic warfare programs.

Signals Intelligence Remote Computer Tampering

The NSA keeps track of all PCs and other computers sold in the US. This is an integral part of the Domestic Intelligence network. The NSA's EMF equipment can tune in RF emissions from personal computer circuit boards (while filtering out emissions from monitors and power supplies). The RF emission from PC circuit boards contains digital information in the PC. Coded RF waves from the NSA's equipment can resonate PC circuits and change data in the PCs. Thus, the NSA can gain wireless modem-style entry into any computer in the country for surveillance or anti-terrorist electronic warfare.

Detecting EMF Fields in Humans for Surveillance

A subject's bioelectric field can be remotely detected, so subjects can be monitored anywhere they are. With special EMF equipment NSA cryptologists can remotely read evoked potentials (from EEGs). These can be decoded into a person's brain-states and thoughts. The subject is then perfectly monitored from a distance. NSA personnel can dial up any individual in the country on the Signals Intelligence EMF scanning network and the NSA's computers will then pinpoint and track that person 24 hours a day. The NSA can pick out and track anyone in the US.

3. NSA Signal Intelligence Use of EMF Brain Stimulation

NSA Signals Intelligence uses EMF Brain Stimulation for Remote Neural Monitoring (RNM) and Electronic Brain Link (EBL). EMF Brain Stimulation has been in development since the MKULTRA program of the early 1950s, which included neurological research into radiation (non-ionizing EMF) and bioelectric research and development. The resulting secret technology is categorized at the National Security Archives as "Radiation Intelligence", defined as "information from unintentionally emanated electromagnetic waves in the environment, not including radioactivity or nuclear detonation". Signals Intelligence implemented and kept this technology secret in the same manner as other electronic warfare programs of the US Government. The NSA monitors available information about this technology and withholds scientific research from the public. There are also international intelligence agreements to keep this technology secret.

The NSA has proprietary electronic equipment that analyzes electrical activity in humans from a distance. NSA computer generated brain mapping can continuously monitor all of the electrical activity in the brain continuously. The NSA records and decodes individual brain maps (of hundreds of thousands of persons) for national security purposes. EMF Brain Stimulation is also secretly used by the military for brain-to-computer link (in military fighter aircraft, for example).

For electronic surveillance purposes, electrical activity in the speech center of the brain can be translated into the subject's verbal thoughts. RNM can send encoded signals to the brain's auditory cortex, thus allowing audio communications direct to the brain (bypassing the ears). NSA operatives can use this covertly to debilitate subjects by simulating auditory hallucinations characteristic of paranoid schizophrenia.

Without any contact with the subject, Remote Neural Monitoring can map out electrical activity from the visual cortex of a subject's brain and show images from the subject's brain on a video monitor. NSA operatives see what the surveillance subject's eyes are seeing. Visual memory can also be seen. RNM can send images direct to the visual cortex, bypassing the eyes and optic nerves. NSA operatives can use this surreptitiously to put images into a surveillance subject's brain while they are in REM sleep for brain-programming purposes.

Capabilities of NSA Operatives Using RNM

There has been a Signals Intelligence network in the US since the 1940s. The NSA, Ft Meade has in place a vast two-way wireless RNM system which is used to track subjects and noninvasively monitor audio-visual information in their brains. This is all done with no physical contact with the subject. RNM is the ultimate method of surveillance and domestic intelligence. Speech, 3D sound and subliminal audio can be sent to the auditory cortex of the subject's brain (bypassing the ears), and images can be sent into the visual cortex. RNM can alter a subject's perceptions, moods and motor control.

Speech cortex/auditory cortex link has become the ultimate communications system for the intelligence community. RNM allows for a complete audio-visual brain-to-brain link or brain-to- computer link.

4. National Security Agency Signals Intelligence Electronic Brain Link Technology

NSA Signal Intelligence (SIGINT) can remotely detect, identify and monitor a person's bioelectric fields.

The NSA's Signals Intelligence has the proprietary ability to monitor remotely and non-invasively information in the human brain by digitally decoding the evoked potentials in the 30-50 Hz, 5 mill watt electromagnetic emissions from the brain.

Neuronal activity in the brain creates a shifting electrical pattern that has a shifting magnetic flux. This magnetic flux puts out a constant 30-50 Hz, 5 mill watts electromagnetic (EMF) wave. Contained in the electromagnetic emission from the brain are spikes and patterns called "evoked potentials". Every thought, reaction, motor command, auditory event and visual image in the brain has a corresponding "evoked potential" or set of "evoked potentials". The EMF emission from the brain can be decoded into the current thoughts, images and sounds in the subject's brain.

NSA SIGINT uses EMF-transmitted Brain Stimulation as a communications system to transmit information (as well as nervous system messages) to intelligence agents and also to transmit to the brains of covert operations subjects (on a non-perceptible level).

EMF Brain Stimulation works by sending a complexly coded and pulsed electromagnetic signal to trigger evoked potentials (events) in the brain, thereby forming sound and visual images in the brain's neural circuits. EMF Brain Stimulation can also change a person's brain-states and affect motor control.

Two-way electronic Brain Link is done by remotely monitoring neural audio-visual information while transmitting sound to the auditory cortex (bypassing the ears) and transmitting faint images to the visual cortex (bypassing the optic nerves and eyes). The images appear as floating 2D screens in the brain.

Two-way electronic Brain Link has become the ultimate communications system for CIA/NSA personnel. Remote neural monitoring (RNM, remotely monitoring bioelectric information in the human brain) has become the ultimate surveillance system. It is used by a limited number of agents in the US Intelligence Community.

5. [No Heading in Original Document]

RNM requires decoding the resonance frequency of each specific brain area. That frequency is then modulated in order to impose information in that specific brain area. The frequency to which the various brain areas respond varies from 3 Hz to 50 Hz. Only NSA Signals Intelligence modulates signals in this frequency band. (See Table 1.) This modulated information can be put into the brain at varying intensities from subliminal to perceptible. Each person's brain has a unique set of bioelectric resonance/entrainment frequencies. Sending audio information to a person's brain at the frequency of another person's auditory cortex would result in that audio information not being perceived.

The Plaintiff learned of RNM by being in two-way RNM contact with the Kinnecome group at the NSA, Ft Meade.

They used RNM 3D sound direct to the brain to harass the Plaintiff from October 1990 to May 1991.

As of 5/91 they have had two-way RNM communications with the Plaintiff and have used RNM to attempt to incapacitate the Plaintiff and hinder the Plaintiff from going to the authorities about their activities against the Plaintiff in the last 12 years. The Kinnecome group has about 100 persons working 24 hours a day at Ft Meade. They have also brain-tapped persons the Plaintiff is in contact with to keep the Plaintiff isolated. This is the first time ever that a private citizen has been harassed with RNM and has been able to bring a lawsuit against NSA personnel misusing this intelligence operations method.

6. NSA Techniques and Resources

Remote monitoring/tracking of individuals in any location, inside any building, continuously, anywhere in the country. A system for inexpensive implementation of these operations allows for thousands of persons in every community to be spied on constantly by the NSA.

Remote RNM Devices

NSA's RNM equipment remotely reads the evoked potentials (EEGs) of the human brain for tracking individuals, and can send messages through the nervous systems to affect their performance. RNM can electronically identify individuals and track them anywhere in the US. This equipment is on a network and is used for domestic intelligence operations, government security and military base security, and in case of bioelectric warfare.

Spotters and Walk-Bys in Metropolitan Areas

Tens of thousands of persons in each area working as spotters and neighborhood/business place spies (sometimes unwittingly) following and checking on subjects who have been identified for covert control by NSA personnel.

Agents working out of offices can be in constant communication with spotters who are keeping track of the NSA's thousands of subjects in public. NSA agents in remote offices can instantly identify (using~ RNM) any individual spotted in public who is in contact with surveillance subject.

Chemicals and Drugs into Residential Buildings with Hidden NSA Installed and Maintained Plastic Plumbing lines.

The NSA has kits for running lines into residential tap water and air ducts of subjects for the delivery of drugs (such as sleeping gas or brainwashing-aiding drugs). This is an outgrowth of CIA pharma psychology (psychopharmacology).

Brief Overview of Proprietary US Intelligence/Anti- Terrorist Equipment Mentioned

Fixed network of special EMF equipment that can read EEGs in human brains and identify/track individuals by using digital computers. ESB (Electrical Stimulation to the Brain) via EMF signal from the NSA Signals Intelligence is used to control subjects.

EMF equipment that gathers information from PC circuit boards by deciphering RF emissions, thereby gaining wireless modem- style entry into any personal computer in the country. All equipment hidden, all technology secret, all scientific research unreported (as in electronic warfare research). Not known to the public at all, yet complete and thorough implementation of this method of domestic intelligence has been in place since the early 1980s.

Editor's Note: I tried ringing Mr. Akwei to find out what was the out- come, if any, of his court case. He firmly but kindly told me that he could not speak about anything to do with the case over the phone and hung up. A subsequent conversation of similar length resulted in the information that he did not wish his address or phone number published with this article. So, if we hear of any developments, we'll let you know.

Table 1: An example of EMF Brain Stimulation

Brain Area	Bioelectric Resonance Frequency	Information Induced Through Modulation
Motor Control Cortex	10 Hz	Motor Impulse co-ordination
Auditory Cortex	15 Hz	Sound which bypasses the ears
Visual Cortex	25 Hz	Images in the brain bypassing the eyes
Somatosensory	9 Hz	Phantom touch sense
Thought Center	20 Hz	Imposed subconscious thoughts

Resources:

These publications have only been discovered since December 1991, after Plaintiff had already notified authorities (Dept. of Justice, etc.) of Public Corruption by named NSA employees. When no action was taken against the NSA employees, I researched the Intelligence Community electronic surveillance technology involved and discovered the following publications.

The Body Electric: Electromagnetism and the Foundation of Life, by Robert Becker, M.D. monitoring neuro-electric information in the brain ESB. (p. 265,313,318)

Cross currents, by Robert Becker. Simulating auditory hallucinations. Remote computer tampering using RF emissions from the logic board. (p. 70,78,105,174,210,216, 220,242,299,303)

Currents of Death, by Paul Brodeur. Driving brain electrical activity with external EM; magneto phosphenes; Delgado. (p. 27,93)

The Zapping of America, by Paul Brodeur. DoD EM ESB research; simulating auditory hallucinations.

Of Mice, Men and Molecules, by John H. Heller 1963 Bioelectricity; probing the brain with EM waves. (p, 110)

The Three-Pound Universe, by Judith Hooper. CIA EEG research; EEGs for surveillance. (p.29,132,137)

In the Palaces of Memory, by George Johnson. EM emissions from the brain; the brain as an open electromagnetic circuit.

The Puzzle Palace, by James Bamford. Signals Intelligence; most advanced computers in the early 'sixties.

The US Intelligence Community. Glossary terms at National Security Archives; Radiation Intelligence (information from unintentionally emanated electromagnetic energy, excluding radioactive sources).

The Search for the "Manchurian Candidate", by John Marks. Electrical or radio stimulation to the brain; CIA R&D in bio-electrics. (p.227)

Secret Agenda, by Jim Hougan. National security cult groups.

Crimes of the Intelligence Community, by Morton Halperin. Surreptitious entries; intelligence agents running operations against government workers.

War in the Age of Intelligent Machines, NSA computer supremacy, complete control of information.

Alternate Computers, by Time-Life Books. Molecule computers.

The Mind, by Richard Restak, M.D. EEG Systems Inc.; decoding brain EM emanations, tracking thoughts on a computer. (p. 258)

MedTech, by Lawrence Galton. Triggering events in the brain, direct to auditory cortex signals.

Cyborg, by D.S. Halacy, Jr, 1965. Brain-to-computer link research contracts given out by the US government.

Psychiatry and the CIA: Victims of Mind Control, by Harvey M. Weinstein M.D. Dr. Cameron; psychic driving; ultra-conceptual communications.

Journey into Madness: The True Story of Secret CIA Mind Control and Medical Abuse, by Gordon Thomas, Intelligence R&D; Delgado; psychic driving with radio telemetry. (p. 127,276,116,168,169)

Mind Manipulators, by Alan Scheflin and Edward M. Opton. (MKULTRA brain research for information-gathering).

The Brain Changers, by Maya Pines. Listening to brain EM emissions. (p.19)

Modern Bioelectricity. Inducing audio in the brain with EM waves; DoD cover-up; EM wave ESB; remote EEGs

Magnetic Stimulation in Clinical Neurophysiology, by Sudhansu Chokroverty. Magneto phosphenes; images direct to the visual cortex.

The Mind of Man, by Nigel Calder. US intelligence brain research.

Neuroelectric Society Conference, 1971. Audio direct to the brain with EM waves; 2-way remote EEGs.

Brain Control, by Elliot S. Valenstein. ESB., control of individuals.

Towards Century 21, by C.S. Wallia. Brain Stimulation for direct-to-brain communications (p21)

Mind Wars, by Ron McRae (associate of Jack Anderson). Research into brain-to-brain electronic communications., remote neural EM detection (PP. 62 106, 136).

Mind Tools, by Rudy Rucker. Brain tapping; communications with varying bio magnetic fields (p82).

US News and World report, January 2nd 1984. EM wave brain stimulation; intelligence community hi-tech (p38).

Ear Magazine. Article on extremely low frequencies radio emissions in the natural environment; radio emissions from the human body.

City Paper, Washington DC January 17, 1992. Article FCC and NSA "complete radio spectrum" listening posts.

Frontiers in Science, by Edward Hutchings Jr 1958 (p48).

Beyond Bio Feedback, by Elmer and Alyce Green, 1977 (p118)

The Body Quantum, by Fred Alan Wolf

Cloning; A Biologist Reports, by Robert Gillmore McKinnell. Ethical review of cloning humans.

Hoovers' FBI, by Former agent William Turner. Routines of electronic surveillance work. (p280).

July 20th 2019, by Arthur C. Clarke LIDA; Neurophonics; Brain-computer link.

Mega Brain, by Michael Hutchison. Brain stimulation with EM waves; CIA research and information control. (pp.107,108,117,120,123).

The Cult of Information, by Theodore Rosnak, 1986. NSA Directive #145; personal files in computers; computer automated telephone tapping.

The Body Shop, 1986 implantation of an electrode array on the visual cortex for video direct to the brain; other 1960's research into electronically triggering Phosphenes in the brain, thus bypassing the eyes.

Evoked Potentials, by David Regan. Decoding neuroelectric information in the brain.

On the website, *The Mother of All Black Operations*, James F. Marino, an Investigative Journalist, Targeted for

Organized Stalking & An Ongoing FBI COINTELPRO sting operation / smear campaigns writes:

This author has been used as an unwitting target of MKULTRA nonconsensual human experimentation for decades via the NSA's SIGNALS INTELLIGENCE EMF Scanning Network - a covert domestic spy program which uses brain scanners deployed via NSA signals intelligence satellites to remotely scan the brainwaves of any American citizen.

The NSA's SIGNIT EMF Scanning Network is an outgrowth of the Pentagon and CIA's MIND and TAMI

(MKULTRA) "mind control" programs, which use EEG Heterodyning technology to synchronize AI computers with the unique brainwave print of each American citizen. This technology enables the NSA to brand us like heads of cattle. Google: AKWEI VS NSA & the Matrix Deciphered to learn more about this Orwellian attack on the American people's Constitutional rights.

Regarding John Akwei, lawsuit, James F. Marino, another well - known TI May 26, 2013 at 8:07 AM wrote:

The judge who dismissed John Akwei's lawsuit against the NSA has a history of influencing cases for the U.S. Intelligence community. The best known of these cases is the one regarding Hamilton Securities. The Judge, Stanley Sporkin, used the Qui Tam false claims statue to keep this case open for over four years, while the Bush 41 Administration and CIA attempted to systematically destroy Hamilton Securities.

Hamilton Securities was owned by Catherine Austin Fitts, who was Assistant director of HUD under Bush 41.

Her revamping of HUD not only decentralized the way housing mortgages were handled, but also prevented many of the abuses of the system that had been taking place in the past.

As a result of this, Fitts and her company became the targets of a smear campaign which resulted in the destruction of her company. Based on the claims made by Catherine Austin Fitts, she was also targeted for organized stalking for a number of years.

Whether John St. Clair Akwei worked for the NSA or not, his lawsuit is a very compelling one, and does describe quite a bit of the NSA's domestic spy apparatus, including a signals intelligence Electromagnetic Frequency (EMF) scanning network that is used to track Americans by way of the unique EMF signatures of their own bodies.

Including the EMF brainwave print of each citizen. Akwei's lawsuit should have been heard in a U.S. courtroom.

Dear Diary,

On a very personal level the John Akwei, battle rings true as personal experiences of many coming forth today and numbering into the thousands and growing rapidly. When I filed a lawsuit in 2009, in Arizona, an attorney said that the judge, who had been assigned my Civil Complaint, has a history of siding with government instead of the little man. In fact, the little man, or in my case, little woman, does not stand a chance in his courtroom was the general consensus. He essentially amplified the hopelessness in getting these cases into the justice system to include admittedly many have no choice to file ProSe. Many aware do not want to get involved and have their lives and careers destroyed as a result for the official demand for secrecy.

This is a tragedy. Because of this those operating in these programs and deploying this technology, continue to target an individual they believe who is not easily broken down until they die and who cannot get any official help and are too poor for attorneys for such a large-scale case, even if you could find an attorney to take the case on. Many powerful agencies, ACLU, Electronic Frontier Foundation have attempting filing cases regarding these issues, for others, and they too have been fruitless.

'The comment following James F. Marino's comment, echoes what many targets have said regarding targeting of their small children also? Again, no one is exempt in the testing programs seeking to control any and EVERYONE!

Dear Diary,

When I read the comments from another target, James F. Marino, I knew that perhaps it was best that my daughters and 7-month-old granddaughter left after only staying for 5 days in early November of 2013. The only thing I can do is to attempt to educate and prepare my middle daughter regarding the tactics, subliminally used to separate and isolate every target from others. However, I have learned that saying nothing is usually best unless something detrimental is being created. People want to perceive life as normal as possible and this program is a heavy burden.

In the constant effort to frighten me into submission, I have already been getting threats related to my daughter and the now ten-month-old even before they even arrived. My granddaughter started walking at nine months and is quite precocious.

The targeting of children is revealed by an online post by a Targeted Woman as sown below

"Autism Mom Targeted by U.S. Government Traitors," posted June 9, 2013, written after Marino's comments on John St. Clair Akwei blog saying:

"Me and my autistic son have been targeted for at least 9 1/2 yrs. or at least that is when I first consciously became aware of the systematic non-coincidences of vibrations, noise campaigns aka sleep deprivation, helicopters hovering over my roof, constant radiation & electrical car problems, COINTELPRO organized stalking/discrediting/blacklisting....and later would come the headaches, metallic radiation tastes in my mouth, hair loss, complete take-over of my ventilation system & water pipes and all sorts of internal GI conditions too heartbreaking to state here

- all would eventually lead me to being hospitalized for 5 1/2 days in 2011 for what I now believe was a complete Acute Radiation GI Syndrome Breakdown of which most people die from. And one would think that hospital deadly illness w/b the worst of my storm BUT IT WAS NOT....

The worst has been what these Satanic, Nazi, Psychopathic Government Terrorists have done to my beloved son who was already Autistic (Asperger's) but very high functioning to a point whereas initially when you meet him, you couldn't immediate detect that he was autistic.

THOSE   DOD/NSA/CIA/NIH/FBI   NAZI EUGENECISTS MF's and their complete invasion of our lives, especially the MANY radiation-emitting military war weapons that we were AND STILL ARE subjected to IN OUR OWN HOMES 24/7, really took a toll on my son's ability and right to an academic pursuit while in high school. Despite these Terrorist Intelligence-Agency NAZIS and their Criminal Contractors constantly bombarding my son and me with noise and stress and sleep deprivation, I am so very grateful to God that my son still was able to graduate H.S on time though having missed out on a lot of academic and social rewards and enjoyment that most other teenagers had b/c he was always so tired and sleepy in the mornings and struggling to even stay alert.

I TRIED EVERYTHING EVERY OTHER TI HAS TRIED AND MUCH MORE b/c tragically they even target TIs' disabled children (imagine what radiation-emitting electromagnetic, scalar wave, microwave & DEW's do to an already-autistic brain.....it has been torture for my son and he's a wonderful young man that most anyone would like)....I tried moving and of course that didn't work as the Remote Neural Monitoring easily tracked our electrical body makeup.....they don't care.....

TI's are merely "OBJECTS" to them and they do it all without fear of punishment too given that ALL complicit corporations and persons that assist these Criminal Intel Agencies, are assured COMPLETE GOVMT IMMUNITY thanks to our corrupt DOJ who has improperly classified these heinous CRIMES AGAINST HUMANITY in order to hide these Government Crimes thereby DOJ having too committed the violation of Executive Order 13526 Section 1.7...well too bad

Executive Orders are NOT judiciously enforceable and too bad today there are NO BASIC LEGAL STATUTES TO PROTECT SO-CALL NATIONAL SECURITY INVOLUNTARY HUMAN SUBJECTS aka TIs. Back to my point... the improper classification of these illegal human-subject research experiments in the name of some ridiculous fake justification of our UNWITTING Torture and Assassinations being secretly committed to protect 'National Security' IS A F'ING NATIONAL DISGRACE!'"

Personally, I am very grateful for Mr. Akwei's lawsuit as it has been very helpful in enabling me to better understand the legal ramifications of this assault on me, my son and THOUSANDS of other fellow Unwitting-American Victims and probably MILLIONS of Global Unwitting Victims too. I found the details of Mr. Akwei's presented case VERY CREDIBLE EDUCATION for a TI who might want to take this on in a court room sometime in the future. Sadly, what is happening today is the most heinous encroachment known to modern man.

Dear Diary,

They truly have a comprehension problem. When taking scholastic tests, there usually is a section of the test in which you are tasked after reading a story to then comprehend what it meant. I have come to realize that this group obviously, barely can read and failed this test of comprehension. I am not scared, let me repeat, I am not scared!

News flash, my continuing to publish books on the subject, using publications as my weapon of choice would indicate to the intelligent, that I am not scared and will stand and fight. These cowards need to move on. However, the grim reality is that they don't have to as longs as they can hide behind technology and also from a distance. Plus, in reality they are simple "Order Followers" for the corporation. For one, I am no coward and engraved in my heart is the reality of how wrong these secret situations are and. America has a right to know!

Make no mistake about it, the black community, as a whole has been historically a major testing site for many, many experiments and for decades as many cases nudged by subliminal focus into crime while watched. I witnessed it with my very own eyes before moving out of this community, However, the fact is the subtle high-tech zombification is prevalent also in many communities, the poor and middle class of all races. Just ask those experiencing this technology nationwide and globally.

Dear Diary,

Lawsuits centering on mind control technology testing date even further back than that brought by John Akwei, against the NSA. In fact, John Ginter told his classic account of electromagnetic (EMR) mind control targeting in 1967 as a San Quentin prisoner. This amazing account was told to Cheryl Welsh, mindjustice.org, on September 30th, 1994 and the actual interview in MP3 format can be accessed on Cheryl Welsh's website.

In 2002, M.I.N.D. (Magnetic Integrated Neuron Duplicator) also known as EEG Cloning, evidence confirmed that the San Quentin ex-prisoner's 1960's account of mind control experiments performed on him were credible. His credibility was substantiated by official documents stating that in 1966, the U.S. embarked on space research using the acronym of M.I.N.D. NASA documented research program in this area confirms John Ginter's accurate 1968 description of M.I.N.D. device.

These studies eerily rang true to me, especially with my father repeatedly telling me what happened to him while incarcerated. The effort to control the masses and research studies began many, many years before John Günter's truthful account and subsequent lawsuit detailing what happened to him.

EEG cloning feeds back the results of Electromagnetic Frequencies (EMF) monitoring in an attempt to induce emotional responses (e.g. fear, anger, even sleep, etc.)

John Ginter

(Authentic Letter)

Pavlovian conditioning with negative psychological stimulus ...

"...Using mind control technology, the experimenters knew what I was thinking and feeling. I filed a court case in 1968 stating, "(A) brain device at San Quentin is being used upon (me) to alter or destroy (my) brain" and "the machine emitted electro-magnetic waves which stimulated petitioner's brain." I think the goal of the behavior experiments performed on us was to develop the computer-brain technology for political purposes and as an intelligence tool. Using Pavlovian conditioning with negative psychological stimulus, manipulators can change your behavior. For example, they verbally attacked my conservative political views all day long for days on end. They would praise all of the persons around me such as the world-famous leader of the Soledad Brothers, George Jackson, who was in a nearby cell. As in brainwashing, they tried to change my values..." –

John Ginter, excerpt courtesy of, targetedindividualscanada.com.

Dear Diary,

The standard PSY OPS is designed for total destruction of the targeted individual through constant degradation, extreme verbal abuse, taunting, mimicking of your deciphered thoughts, EEG cloning of your computerized and downloaded emotions, (specifically fear sent back to you by radar laser) extreme and, relentless physical torture by directed energy weapons (DEW) both up close, in the vicinity of the target and from miles away from the operation center, dream manipulation, hologram beams, and video play of certain images, similar to that depicted in the movie "Inception." Believe it or not!

NOTE: Biological signals arise when reading or speaking to ourselves as our authentic subvocal thought. This happens with or without actual lip or facial movement. Targeting operations using the sub vocal thought patented system are using it as a weapon against targets during various phrases of the testing agenda. People talk to self so quietly it cannot be heard, but the tongue and vocal cords do receive speech signals from the brain. After, the signals are amplified by computer software and read the result is signals which recognize words or sound thus mind reading.

Today, *Silent Computerized Sub Vocal Speech* technology is one of the primary tools being used by law enforcement and other agencies, DOD contractors.

Dear Diary,

In reality, what this operation would love is for me to go outside, bang on the neighbor's doors, create a disturbance, become threatening or violent in some way. This factually is how they push individuals over the edge with massive amount of electromagnetic frequencies attacking the nervous system, verbal harassment, creating extreme anxiety followed with complete and extreme inhumane, degrading comments.

If this were to happen, you can bet the local Sheriff would then show up, five to ten vehicles strong and conveniently shoot a target down in cold blood in the streets. As many are witnessing today, these are not unusual scenarios.

After this happens, the target yet another targeted statistic, in a long and growing list of persons exposing this program diagnosed as mentally ill, delusional, psychotic, a Schizoid, paranoid, and hearing voices written off. Naturally this would be described in the Globalist controlled media to discredit everyone having these legitimate PATENTED TECHNOLOGY experiences, and determined to be nutcases going postal.

The New World Disorder and related to the global population is factually a New World Disorder with technology at the tip of the iceberg.

You must ask yourself, why isn't mainstream America reporting on this technology and it factual use today? How could that be? Could this fact reveal that, in fact, the technology is factually designed for exactly what it is being globally tested for today?

The real 1%, are the thirteen families which makeup the power structure behind what is termed the Secret Government it is believed. This group holding the purse strings, with the world indebted to them, are said to be pulling also the administrative strings through Bilderberg, the Trilateral Commission, and the Council of Foreign Relations, etc. Henchmen for these families include for example, Freemasons, and Illuminati, in place to infiltrate every corporate office, judiciary, and to advance the New World Disorder. They are:

1. The Astor Bloodline
2. The Bundy Bloodline
3. The Collins Bloodline
4. The DuPont Bloodline
5. The Freeman Bloodline
6. The Kennedy Bloodline
7. The Li Bloodline
8. The Onassis Bloodline
9. The Reynolds Bloodline
10. The Rockefeller Bloodline
11. The Rothschild Bloodline

12. The Russell Bloodline
13. The Van Duyn Bloodline

Merovingian (European Royal Families)

The Top 13 Families & the Mormon Leadership (Moriah & the Mormon Leadership)
Interconnected families:

1. Disney - Uno de Los Mayores Engaños de Todos los Tiempos
2. The Disney Bloodline
3. The Krupp Bloodline
4. The McDonald Bloodline

The Rothschilds own Reuters and Associated Press. They also have controlling interest in ABC, CBS & NBC. Rothschild's Swiss banks hold the wealth of the Vatican and the European black nobility, and have for many generations idealized the concept of one world governance.

Dear Diary,

Some would argue that those employed by the Police State such the military, law enforcement, and materialistic contractors are in reality simpleton puppets.

Dear Diary,

In my case, they can hold their breath on me hurting someone else. That is just not going to pan out for them. Actually, me hurting innocent people or being nudged to do so with me is just plain humorous to me. I bet if I went out and purchased a weapon, those monitoring me from the operation center around the clock would sit back, watch, and even allow it.

We must remember that I am monitored around the clock. If this were to happen, it probably would be one of the very few times that I would not hear their constant Electronic Terrorism verbal chatter of threats and degrading name calling.

If, Aaron Alexis reported, he was being followed from hotel to hotel, and obviously monitored how did he get a weapon without those targeting him knowing it? Things that make you go hmmm...

The New World goal is a documented fact by George Herbert Walker Bush and he is on the record saying:

"What is at stake is more than one small country, it is a big idea—a <u>New World Order</u>...to achieve the universal aspirations of mankind... based on shared principles and the rule of law... The illumination of a thousand points of light... The winds of change are with us now..."

Dear Diary,

These people are not joking

In this long-planned agenda, know that the poor and middle class are not considered the "thousand points of light..." One thing is for sure, and documented in George Bush, Sr.'s comments. In this effort, "The winds of change are with us NOW…" And, in the making for a long, long time.

NEW WORLD ORDER

Dear Diary,

While cleaning up my bedroom, I decided to try something different and move the material I sleep on around. Usually, I sleep directly on top of a layer of protection material which is extremely hard because of the directional beam attacks from under my bed up, upstairs. This turned out to be a big mistake and left my legs open to torture from the foot to the top of my thigh. I needed a wheel chair today, to get around, and wished I had one.

Instead of putting the materials directly under me to sleep on top of, I decided that the Multifunctional Directed Energy Weapon System was likely being steered from the floor up when I am upstairs in my bedroom. However, two or three times, I have literally heard the point of the beam, unbelievably, actually tapping directly under me when the radar laser beam tried to penetrate through the thick rubber mat and other material in which I sleep on top of but was unsuccessful. They were testing to see what it was by tapping it.

The tap, tap, tap, had actually woken me twice on two separate occasions, one night in their desperation to get to me. Placing the material between the box spring and mattress proved to be a painful mistake for me this morning as well. I wake with severe pain completely covering my left leg, after sleeping on my left side all night, and realizing that this beam is called the Multi Directional Directed Energy Weapon System" for a reason. It is very capable of manipulation directly under the person sleeping, from the floor up also or directly underneath the mattress. It can be directed anywhere and any direction in which those at the helm choose. Placing the material on top of the box spring and between the mattresses just did not work but I was at least comfortable and able to sleep on my pillow top mattress which felt like sleeping on a cloud for a brief change.

When I woke, the operation ever present, were waiting to see how the successful nightly attack would affect me emotionally. When they realized, I would not let it hurt me or bother me, as they read my mind, and witnessed me instead wake, then go directly to my computer to record the experience, the anger of frustrated, adolescents, pretending to be men, began by typical vicious name calling.

I am not the only woman, reporting to be enduring this type of extreme verbal abuse called specific names. Other targeted women have reported that they are called every nasty name those in the operation can think of.

What a wonderful group of guys! And, they get paid for it.

CHAPTER TEN

Coercion, Community Surveillance, Tools and Gadgets

Federal Communication Commission Radio Frequency Imaging and Surveillance System:

Although technically these devices are not imaging systems, for regulatory purposes, they are treated in the same way as through-wall imaging and will be permitted to operate in the frequency band 1.99-10.6 GHz.

Surveillance systems operate as "security fences" by establishing a stationary RF perimeter field and detecting the intrusion of persons or objects in that field. Operation is limited to law enforcement, fire and rescue organizations, to public utilities and to industrial entities.

What is little known to the average person, unless you are part of a mobilized community organized stalking effort, usually spearheaded by a government agency, is that these radio frequency fields can hear the target talking inside their home, read sub vocal thought, and talk to the target through radio waves thereby creating the "Hearing Voices" effect also known, as Voice to Skull, Neural Decoding, Synthetic or Artificial Telepathy, or the "Frey Effect" named after Alan Frey.

The Below Information is Courtesy of a Targeted Individual, Gleaned from the Website: Gangstalkinghelp.Org (GSH)

Through-The-Wall or (TTW) was developed by the military in the 60's and enjoyed a long service as a military-only technology globally. In 1998 the technology was legalized to be used by law enforcement as well as fire & rescue in the United States. When this happened, corrupt police departments, in my case, the Los Angeles Police Department declared war with the civilian population technologically. Soon other states and countries followed and in 2002, the Federal Communications Commission (FCC) authorized Ultra-Wideband for commercial use. The FCC set forth stricter guidelines for commercial use, such as placing limits on max power output. In 2004, the FCC responded to pressure from developers, creating title 15 exceptions to the restrictions originally set forth.

Current Applications of Through the Wall Ultra-Wideband Technology

Today, the imaging and radar parts of the business are doing well, but they are largely invisible to the public: ground-penetrating radars, radars that measure product levels in tanks and water levels outdoors, automatic braking systems for cars, through-the-wall radars for police, location tags, intruder-detection systems, devices for finding survivors under rubble the list is long.

Ultra-Wideband Radar Capabilities

To understand the potential of the equipment authorized for licensed use by public network service entities let's have a look.

Building Wall Material	LOS error (cm)		NLOS error (cm)		Maximum Number of Walls Penetrated
	Average	Maximum	Average	Maximum	
Sheetrock/ Aluminum Studs	4	10	24	41	12
Plaster/ Wooden Studs	7	16	38	133	7
Cinder Block	4	8	84	157	9
Steel	9	27	350	948	9

Table 1. Performance of UWB Ranging in Four NIST Buildings

In this study, the transmitting device is rated at 1 Watt and the sending signal is omni-directional meaning in all directions rather than directed.

Rated at 1 Watt the system demonstrated the capability to send waves through 12 sheets of sheetrock, 9 cinder blocks or 9 sheets of steel. Another application of this technology is in search and rescue, detecting the faint rising and falling of a victim's chest cavity when buried under several layers of rubble in a disaster scenario.

Ultra-Wideband Radar System Features

UWB evolved and is one of the leading technologies in use today. Many through the wall and security perimeter systems are based on this technology. In the above example, the equipment is a single source system. A single source system can "see" in 2D, record (photos, video, etc., in 2D), and track a target through walls (but if tracking says your belly button if you turn around or sideways it may have difficulty discerning). The systems in use today are multi-node allowing for better spatial resolution (image quality) and viewing in 3D. Because of this several localized regions of the body can be tracked individually and simultaneously (eyes, ears, nose, etc.), this technology is called Multiple in and Multiple Out (MIMO).

Surveillance Systems

Each neighboring residence then could have a node with capabilities to cooperatively add to the collective pool of data on an individual. All of the data collected, analyzed and displayed on a screen at any offsite location. The modern-day term for this is command and control or C2. C2 is a military term, suiting considering the origins of UWB. Various parts of your body external and internal can be tracked simultaneously up to the limits of the system.

Each node is either stationary (residence, business, lamppost, intersection, etc.) or mobile (vehicle, foot patrol, etc.). Each node is capable of switching between modes, the modes are data (forming a data network with other stationary and mobile nodes in range) and radar (sensing surroundings and turning it into useful information for tracking). The data network is at a minimum useful for voice communications, video streaming, and keeping all the nodes synchronized in time and space with other nodes/networks.

Surveillance Systems in Field Operations

I would urge you NOT to approach your neighbors after reading this article. They are all too aware of the scenario and may have agreed to host the equipment in their residence and vehicles. Retaliation, I believe would make matters only worse for you in the long run.

To say your neighbors are the actual operators of this technology would be pure conjecture. Some incite can be had from the FCC regulations.

§ 15.510 Technical requirements for through D-wall imaging systems

"(3) The imaging system shall contain a manually operated switch that causes the transmitter to cease operation within 10 seconds of being released by the operator. In lieu of a switch located on the imaging system, it is permissible to operate an imaging system by remote control provided the imaging system ceases transmission within 10 seconds of the remote switch being released by the operator."

"(e) Through-wall imaging systems operating under the provisions of this section shall bear the following or similar statement in a conspicuous location on the device: Operation of this device is restricted to law enforcement, emergency rescue and firefighter personnel. Operation by any other party is a violation of 47 U.S.C. 301 and could subject the operator to serious legal penalties." [1]

One could possibly conclude that qualified personnel are located at C2 where the system remote controlled rather than neighbors at their residences. The neighbors are cooperating with officials and granting them use of their property for an investigation.

By looking up the definitions it's easy to see and widely accepted that the term law enforcement includes FBI, state police, sheriffs, and city police. Approximately half of the FBI's workforce is government contractors currently, so it's also possible that government contractors have a current work contract with the FBI and are conducting the operation. Also possible is special duty personnel from each component of law enforcement with a chain of command but distinct jurisdictions at the state, county and local levels having a role.

You Ain't No Daisy

Radar provides the firing solution for directed energy. Without radar to find and track an object, directed energy would probably miss. Radar to directed energy is like gun sight to gun. The Wild Wild West term Shoot from the Hip simply doesn't apply.

An Analogy Tumor Ablation

To gain a better understanding and to properly visualize how such a system would function one could look to medicine. It has been shown that tumor ablation (the destruction of tumor cells) when the tumor is deep within the brain is a mature technology being successfully employed by physicians.

Tumor ablation can be done with either electromagnetic or acoustic waves. It works by sending directed energy into the brain to destroy tumor cells. A single node cannot send a high intensity beam through the scalp and brain tissue without destroying healthy tissue. It becomes necessary then to have multiple nodes sending low intensity beams to a convergence point. Thus, radar differentiates between healthy and tumor cells and nodes send synchronous low intensity beams to the tumor site, causing a temperature increase in the localized region of the tumor site with the effect of killing the tumor cells.

Current day See Through Wall technology can image a human's brain in much the same way with sub-millimeter spatial resolution. What that means is the ability to differentiate between regions separated by only a millimeter or less. With this quality of sighting then it becomes possible to send energy from multiple nodes to a convergence point located anywhere in or out of the head region or taking this analogy further a person's body.

Conclusion

Remarkably little attention has been given to the ability of Ultra-Wideband technology to peer into our homes and lives. UWB technology clearly benefits society when responsibly employed by police, fire and search & rescue. Unfortunately, it can be used to invade personal privacy or plan a crime. Additionally, it can be used to create an intense electromagnetic field in a very small localized region of the body. Altering electric potentials in minute structures in the body has been the basis for animal experimentation for decades using electric diodes and wires. To prevent these abuses, changes to current law may be needed to promote democratic accountability even in areas where UWB is used to enhance public safety.

Solutions

The Federal Communications Commission claims authority over rules and regulations concerning UWB operation. A reassessment of the current policy and limits would allow for regulations to catch up with the current state of technology.

Today, whole body absorption limits are the standard for measuring exposure. But current technology has been diverging from this standard and the limits set forth for some time now. A growing number of technologies benefit by sending energy directed rather than in all directions.

The FCC policy and limits for exposure due to signals that may sum in free space exclude mobile and handheld devices

Since exposure diminishes exponentially with increasing distance, additional signal losses occur due to non-line-of-sight conditions from distant sources, and separation from fixed sources is typically large, exposure from fixed RF sources is normally much less than the limit. Moreover, we expect that exposure from devices near a person's body would generally be more significant than exposure from distant fixed RF sources. Secondly, exposure from each portable or mobile device near a person will generally be highly localized, affecting only a specific small area of body tissue and thus may be considered independent of other portable or mobile devices close to the body, which would affect another area or areas of body tissue. Additionally, highly localized exposure would not result in significant contributions to whole-body average SAR."[3]

Mobile and handheld devices increasingly are becoming more efficient, more powerful and more directed in nature. Exposure is primarily a function of how directed the beam is (beam width) rather than the distance travelled from source. A sufficiently narrow beam could travel a large distance with little reduction in intensity.

In addition to policy and limits reassessment, new areas of inquiry would be beneficial to human exposure standards. For example, directed energy can cause tissue heating in highly localized areas of the brain potentially leading to behavioral or cognitive effects. Another example, highly directive point to point technology delivering sufficient energy to trigger action potentials in neurons related to sensation and perception while remaining under whole body SAR exposure limits.

Patented portable technology example of technology readily available for use in community Organized Stalking, InfraGard, and Community Oriented Policing efforts

STEERING OF DIRECTIONAL SOUND BEAMS
United States Patent 7146011

Abstract: Apparatus is disclosed for steering a directional audio beam that is self-demodulated from an ultrasound carrier. The apparatus includes means for modulating a carrier signal with an audio signal and means for adjusting the amplitude and phase of at least one of the audio signal and/or the carrier signal to steer the audio beam to a desired direction. The apparatus also includes means for generating an ultrasound beam in the desired direction driven by the modulated carrier signal. The apparatus may include means for weighting the audio and/or carrier signal by a zero order Bessel functions to synthesize a Bessel distribution source. A corresponding method for steering a directional audio beam is also disclosed. A harmonic generator may be used to generate harmonics of low frequencies in the audio signal. The harmonics may provide (upon demodulation) a psycho-acoustic impression of improved perception of low frequencies. Further, a modulated ultrasonic signal or an unmodulated audio signal may be band-passed into two or more different band-limited signals. The band-limited signals may be amplified and transmitted by ultrasonic transducers having mechanical resonance frequencies substantially equal to a characteristic frequency of the band-limited signals. Ultrasonic processing of the audio signal may include square root methods without generating large numbers of harmonics.

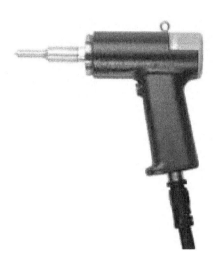

Handheld Ultrasonic Sound Beam

Portable Ultrasonic Generator

Psycho-Acoustic Projector

US Patent #3,568,347

Andrew Flanders, February 23, 1971.

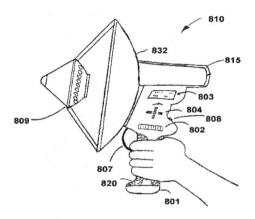

Fig. 10

A system for producing aural psychological disturbances and partial deafness in the enemy during combat situations.

Actual Psycho-Acoustic Projector

Frequency Weapons

Personnel Halting and Stimulation Response (PHaSR)

One of the tools, as documented in "You Are Not My Big Brother" also used by the military in behavior modification and mind-control are the remotely operated electromagnetic frequency weapons. These weapons use microwave, ELF (Extremely Low Frequencies) and acoustics frequencies to covertly manipulate the minds of persons under attack. The use of frequency weapons upon humans toward behavioral control and murder is not new. For well over 50 years, Neuro-Electromagnetic Frequency Weapons have been perfected by their covert use in warfare. These 'classified', 'non-lethal' or 'silent' weapons have also been perfected by experimenting on unsuspecting individuals since their early development. Directing a beam of frequencies to a human brain can cause a series of serious side-effects. ELF waves cause nausea, headaches, accelerated heart rate without cause, to name but a few. In 1974, the first unclassified successful transmission of the human voice directly into the skull of a living person was performed by Dr. Joseph C. Sharp, of the Walter Reed army institute of research by transforming a hypnotist's voice using ELF's. This technique was later developed into the Smirnov scramble method, and used in the Gulf War. It is possible to hypnotize a target without the target being aware and leaving zero trace of evidence.

By emitting frequencies that oscillate in a certain frequency range a victim can be manipulated. There are 6 types of brainwaves: Delta is the frequency range up to 4 Hz and is associated with sleep. Theta is the frequency range from 4 Hz to 8 Hz and is associated with drowsiness, childhood, adolescence and young adulthood. Alpha (Berger's wave) is the frequency range from 8 Hz to 12 Hz. Sensory motor rhythm (SMR) is a middle frequency (about 12-16 Hz) associated with physical stillness and body presence. A target will have trouble moving whenever this frequency is applied. Beta is the frequency range above 12 Hz. Low amplitude betas with multiple and varying frequencies is often associated with active, busy or anxious thinking and active concentration. Gamma is the frequency range approximately 26-80 Hz. Gamma rhythms appear to be involved in higher mental activity, including perception, problem solving, fear, and consciousness. A frequency weapon's shape depends on how frequencies have to be directed to the target. The US Patent and Trademark Office hold vast amounts of patents for machines which can be used in direct or subliminal mind-control systems. Many of which I document in the other books in this series. For example:

a. Hearing System, US Patent #4,877,027, by Wayne Brunkan, October 31, 1989. A method for directly inducing sound into the head of a person, using microwaves in the range of 100 MHz to 10,000 MHz, modulated with a waveform of frequency- modulated bursts.

b. Method and System for Altering Consciousness, US Patent #5,123,899, of James Gall, June 23, 1992. A system for altering the states of human consciousness involving the use of simultaneous application of multiple stimuli preferably sounds, having differing frequencies.

c. Superimposing Method and Apparatus Useful for Subliminal Messages, US Patent #5,134,484, Joseph Wilson, July 28, 1992.

d. Method of Changing a Person's Behavior, Subliminal Message Generator, US Patent #5,270,800.

e. Robert Sweet, December 14, 1993. A combined subliminal and supra-liminal message generator for use with a television receiver; permits complete control of subliminal messages and their presentation.

Also applicable to cable television and computers.

f. Auditory Subliminal Message System and Method, US Patent #4,395,600, Rene Lundy and David Tyler, July 26, 1983. An amplitude-controlled subliminal message may be mixed with background music.

g. Psycho-Acoustic Projector, US Patent #3,568,347, Andrew Flanders, February 23, 1971. A system for producing aural psychological disturbances and partial deafness in the enemy during combat situations. Enough about the frequency weapons. (NOTE: See Patent/Inventor section of bigbrotherwatchingus.com.

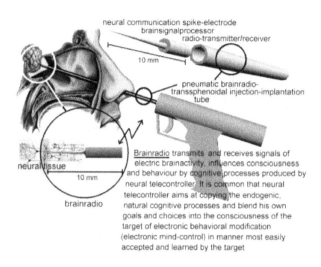

The key to projecting commands in the minds of other people rests in understanding what is being communicated. In the 1950's the UK and USA decided to set up the world's biggest espionage network to ensure all communications between Russians and spies or allies was monitored. This system has continuously been updated since its inception. The system's name is Echelon and consists of a vast network of listening posts, extremely advanced computers, an enormous amount of people, dishes and taps. Echelon captures every communication via Internet, GSM, UMTS, landlines, TV and radio broadcasts, satellite communications (private, military and diplomatic) and listens to every word, well the computers do. The computers work with a list of keywords and when a message contains one or more keywords the message is directed to a specialist who examines its content. If the message is 'suspicious' further action is taken.

This Black Government "Silent Weapons" technology has been developed to monitor the location and manipulate the minds of the general populace. Echelon centers are located around the world including Menwith Hill, North Yorkshire, England. HAARP, Remote Mind Control Computer Center, Alaska. And Pine Gap, near Alice Springs, Northern Territory, Australia.

The NSA is also constructing a network of towers up to 500 feet high, each tower at a distance of 200 miles apart and stretching from the east to the west of the US. The network is called GWEN, Ground Wave Emergency Network, and transmits Very Low Frequencies combined with Ultra High Frequencies and is used in case the communication systems in the US are rendered useless because of a nuclear attack. Coincidentally the frequencies of GWEN coincide with the frequencies being used by frequency weapons. If you start thinking about what can happen to a 500 feet high tower when exposed to a nuclear weapon you kind of start thinking if building high structures is the right strategy for nuclear scenarios. Also, mobile telephone systems like GSM and UMTS also operate in the same frequency areas as some frequency weapons; this means that these systems, like GWEN, can potentially be used as a weapon, by altering the modulation of the frequencies and the direction of the signal.

Of these technologies, the "Pain Beam" is responsible for doing the most physical Damage.

AMERICAN TECHNOLOGY

Acoustic Heterodyne: This device projects sound at an object and you think it's coming from there. This is an old type form of directed acoustics now there is LRAD, MRAD, Phrase Lator and the Magnetic Audio Device.

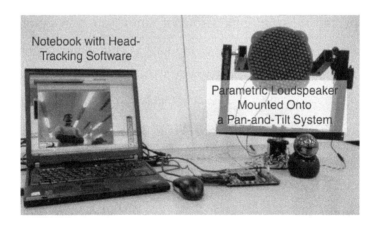

Steering of Directional Sound Beam

US Patent# 20040264707 A1

Apparatus is disclosed for steering a directional audio beam that is self-demodulated from an ultrasound carrier. The apparatus includes means for modulating a carrier signal with an audio signal and means for adjusting the amplitude and phase of at least one of the audio signals and/or the carrier signal to steer the audio beam to a desired direction. The apparatus also includes means for generating an ultrasound beam in the desired direction driven by the modulated carrier signal. The apparatus may include means for weighting the audio and/or carrier signal by a zeroth order Bessel function to synthesize a Bessel distribution source. A corresponding method for steering a directional audio beam is also disclosed. A harmonic generator may be used to generate harmonics of low frequencies in the audio signal. The harmonics may provide (upon demodulation) a psycho-acoustic impression of improved perception of low frequencies. Further, a modulated ultrasonic signal or an unmodulated audio signal may be band-passed into two or more different band-limited signals. The band-limited signals may be amplified and transmitted by ultrasonic transducers having mechanical resonance frequencies substantially equal to a characteristic frequency of the band-limited signals. Ultrasonic processing of the audio signal may include square root methods without generating large numbers of harmonics.

Hyper Sonic Speakers with sound and voice carrying

Ability to isolate Targeted Individual in a crowd in use by law enforcement.

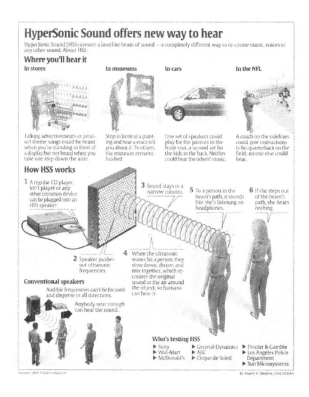

Filigree Electrode Pattern Apparatus for Steering Parametric Mode Acoustic Beam

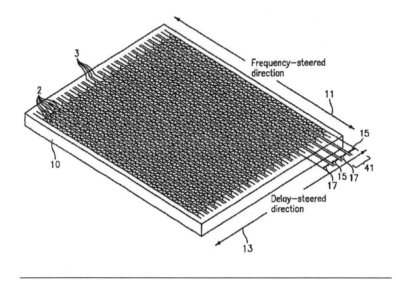

Frequency–steered
direction

Delay–steered
direction

United States Patent 6661739 - A piezoelectric embedded monolithic active surface for transmitting a directed acoustic beam comprising a monolithic active surface, a plurality of piezoelectric elements embedded on the surface forming an array comprising, a plurality of coupled frequency pairs comprising, a first primary frequency row extending in a frequency steered direction the first primary frequency row enabled to accept a first primary frequency signal, and a second primary frequency row extending in the frequency steered direction and located adjacent to the first primary frequency row the second primary frequency row enabled to accept a second primary frequency signal, wherein the plurality of coupled frequency pairs repeat in a delay-steered direction and wherein each of the coupled frequency pairs are enabled to accept a time delayed copy of the first and second primary frequency signals.

AMERICAN TECHNOLOGY

Left, portable Acoustic Beam. Right, law enforcement Magnetic Audio Device

It can project a focused beam of voice or sound over a distance of two (2) miles. This device can go through walls and buildings. This device is based on frequency and tonal pattern which can disorientate a target or group of individuals. This device can be used instead of the CDMA or TM-UWB towers. These devices can be used to talk to individual or targets in the Radio Frequency Perimeter fields.

Long Range Acoustical Device (LRAD):

LRAD mounted on vehicle in background

This device is today used by law enforcement agencies for crowd control, legally, and also in hostage situations supposedly. However, thousands report, that it is being gravely misused as attempts to coercive and control targets through Electronic Terrorism and Stalking campaigns in covert operations where those using it don't want it known nor do they want you to see their faces or locate the agency actually deploying and spearheading the attacks. The LRAD has a range of 1,000 meters.

SOUND SABER: Products are superior to horn devices used as Mass Notification System as the clarity CIS=0.95) and directionality. It achieves its acoustic characteristics with a total harmonic distortion (THD) of less than 1.5 % @ 70 % power (1KHZ. Sine-wave). The physics of its flat transducers lend themselves to the creation of beams to send the announcement where it is needed. The Mass Notification System is the Early Warning Operation System or Emergency Alert System (EAS) is used instead of air raid sirens.

Left, *Sonic Saber*. Right, *Hypersonic Sound* small speaker

PHASOR PAIN FIELD GENERATOR Intended for, military, Law Enforcement Personnel and other agencies and is designed to cause instant, debilitating pain. This pain generator produces a power field of ultrasonic shockwave energy at 140+ db Matrix Output 12VDC. Requires internal Batteries or External, 115VAC, 6" x 6" x 4" in size.

Phasor Pain Generator

PHASOR PAIN FIELD BLASTER: This miniature electronic device is intended for personal protection or field research.Complex sonic shockwaves are internally adjustable for maximizing on target subject.125 db Directional sonic shock waves4"x3" shirt pocket size andoperates on a 9-volt battery.

Phasor Pain Field Blaster

PHASOR BLAST WAVE PISTOL

This device can be used on both animals and people. The unit is fully adjustable for maximizing effect on target subjects. It uses 130 db. of directional sonic shock waves, 3 ½" x 5" Barrel Houses Transducers, and the Electronic Butt Section Houses 8 AA Batteries, external sweep and desired frequency controls.

Phasor Blast Wave Pistol

ACTIVE DENIAL SYSTEMADS is one of the main energy weapons in use today. It is also known as the Directed Energy Weapon (DEW). It is a focused, speed-of-light millimeter wave energy beam that creates intense heat.Active Denial microwave technology uses a transmitter producingelectromagnetic radiationat a frequency of 95 GHZ. And an antenna to direct a focused, invisible beam towards a desired subject which travels at the speed of light. The energy reaches the subject and penetrates the skin to a depth of less than 1/64 of an inch.The waves excite water molecules in the epidermis skin to around 130 degrees Fahrenheit causing an intensely painful burning sensation. Today it is not being used in isolated events. Many targets are attacks repeatedly, which results in intention necrosis of the strategic area and focus of the beam

The model below is an upgraded version in use today by law enforcement especially the Sheriff's department using it in jails.

This device has a 3.2-mile distance and is likely the high-powered version being directed at me from across the street due to its immediate intensity.

PHRASE LATOR

A handheld device that can translate and broadcast voices and talk to you in 50 languages inside the human brain using subliminal messaging. This device is used by the military, law enforcement agencies, and contractors, etc. It is useful when a target is in an environment where others speak a second language than the target to incite negativity towards the target.

SONIC NAUSEA DEVICE

Easily hidden circuit produces a high pitch sound that causes nausea and disorientation in a perimeter field where the device is located and the target has to get away from.operates on a 9-volt battery.

This device was used on me one day at the gym, possibly directed by satellite since no one was in the near empty gym late that night. I instantly become extremely nauseated and nearly passed out in the shower. After about 5 minutes it passed and I returned to normal. While this was happening, I could hear those in the operation center commenting that it actually worked and that I was effectively made physically ill.

EBAY.COM SELLER DESCRIPTION

Sonic Nausea is a small electronic acoustic generating device which can really turn one's stomach. It generates a unique combination of high-pressure sound waves which soon leads most in its vicinity to queasiness. It can also cause headaches, intense irritation, sweating, imbalance, and nausea. Hiding this device in your inconsiderate neighbor's house might put an end to their late-night parties. The abusive bureaucrat's office, the executive lunchroom... the possibilities are endless for that small portion of inventive payback. Its sound wave characteristics make directional source determination difficult. This is the new upgraded 2011 version Sonic Nausea, featuring an enhanced custom-built transducer which provides triple the pressurized output of the previous one. Powered by one 9-volt battery (included). Each unit can cover one average size room. Use with extreme discretion.

NOTE: As you can see the Disorientation Device can be purchased on line and is also called in some locations online, the Sonic Nausea Device.

PATENTS TO DISABLE VEHICLES

As I reported in one of the other books in this series, this technology, both satellites delivered, and portable was used many times to disable my vehicle and recently while shopping to disable the electronic key used to unlock my car door late at night. This could be perfect a set up for a person possibly marked for covert exposure. Anything could happen to targets, activist, and whistleblowers. Another day, the operation center watched me getting dressed, commenting on where I was going. When I went out to start my vehicle, it would not start. I then heard a pick-up truck, black with tinted windows, parked near my garage start up then drive away. It then pulled into the new house designated officially as the new house of covert operation of which I witnessed USAF personnel going and coming. The microwave pain beam and acoustic sound beam, designed to disturb or destroy my neurological system also comes from the upstairs bedroom from this location across the street, during the night, when I am upstairs in my bed. Or at times, comes from the smaller three car garage when I am downstairs in my new office from this location too. A few times, I have observed, the person directing it sitting inside of his vehicle deploying the pain beam also.

1. Engine disabling weapon - Patent5952600A non-lethal weapon for disabling an engine such as that of a fleeing car by means of a high voltage discharge that perturbs or destroys the electrical system.

2. Remote vehicle disabling system – U.S. Patent 5293527 - A compact transportable electromagnetic pulse (EMP) generating system for generating and transmitting EMPs at a target vehicle to disrupt electronics.

Dear Diary,

I felt something that was strange and a new to sensation for me. Lately, the only technology that can effectively reach me due to the protective shield, for a period of time is coming straight down from the top of my ceiling which, again, indicates the operation center today satellite empowered weaponized military drones. For two nights now, they have focused the beam on the top of my skull at for a longer period of time, and intensity. The hair was starting to grow back and now it is being maliciously burned away again. After an intense treatment just a few minutes ago, I just now felt a powerful dizzying feeling inside my brain as well so this was a deep cranial attack. It felt as if pressure had released itself from the top of my skull and the blood could again begin to flow. It was a draining affect.

What a perfect way to give a person an aneurysm covertly. I then decided to search the Targeted Individuals data base and to see if any targeted individual had ever documented this actually happening to them. An obviously angry targeted individual wrote their experience below clearly revealing that it has:

ONLINE TARGET POST:

"This may be a little hard to believe for those of you whom can't even grasp the mind reader concept, but believe me they exist! My father, died from a brain aneurysm in 2004, which was given to him by a directed energy weapon (murder). This is 100% true(as absurd as it may seem) brain aneurysms can be created by directed energy weapons and I had gotten into my first fight in school, the same day, just hours before a healthy 45-year-old died from a brain aneurysm. I will leave it to you to fill in the dots but this is no coincidence... Not only this, but people had been calling me man since middle school. This is absolutely no joke and this is no lie. (I was in 7th grade at the time).

(If you aren't involved with this life 'game' people who are and were involved is instructed to call me that).

(My father was a successful intelligent person whom was nothing but a great parent.)

Re: *Elizabeth Elliot*

Profession: Former Social Worker and Civil Rights Worker

Complaint: Participated in filing Class Action Lawsuit against Judges in Federal Court in Louisville, Kentucky (inclusive of Heyburn, Simpson, et al)

Illness: Diabetic, Kidney Dialysis, Weak Heart Valve - Died May 2012. She was also a victim of Directed Energy Weapons and had UAV's over her home and **stated to me that they were taking her mind. She also spoke with Freedom from Covert Harassment and Surveillance about what was happening to her.**

Another Targeted Individual posted this on Facebook on May 23, 2013 at 8:16 a.m.

Yes, it's happening to many, many witnesses' right here in America and it is violently despicable. I've been subjected to hopeful beam heart attacks, strokes, aneurysms, electrocuted, poisoned, sleep deprivation for weeks (with a few hours' sleep the 3rd day and again) given visual pulse bombs (via computer, this is high tech stuff), sustained some brain injury, sonic weaponry, microwave, DEWs directed energy weapons, the whole enchilada, bio weapons, chemical weapons, I couldn't list it all. I've been irradiated to the marrow and they used the Hi-powered microwave satellite laser weaponry on me like they used in Iraq where they blew people's heads off or shrunk them down to 3 feet tall. Phasers, Masers, all things Scalar, you name it-- every evil weaponry you can imagine. They make it feel like a vice grip is on your head, sometimes you can hear the pressure against the dura matter, they can use lasers to drill into your brain, it's unfathomable. They shattered some of my teeth, ruptured my eardrums more than once. They make some of us bleed from our ears, eyes...

Directed Harmful High Energy Weapons will have effective ranges from the point of contact to several hundred yards. Directed Harmful High Energy Weapons can be used to destroy electronic devices and cause severe interference in computers and alarm systems which can allow forced entry or destruction of vital data. Radar guns are available from surplus stores most anywhere and can be obtained from ex-military sources or even police departments. Radar gun power outputs range from two or three watts to 3 Megawatts! Portable radar guns range in size from small hand-held devices to vehicle mounted long-range high-power models. These devices have very long ranges due to their greater power, higher frequencies and shorter wavelength.

Radar guns emit long or short pulses of high energy capable of causing instant damage or death to living creatures. Semiconductor destruction or malfunction, brain damage & stopping vehicles are other uses for these devices. Other forms of directed harmful high energy include devices such as Tasers, klystron guns (radar guns), ion beam guns, plasma pulse guns, soliton bombs, and many more devices. As I mentioned previously, he is credited with coining the term Electronic Terrorism.

Dear Diary,

The television is on to break the silence in my house, as I wind down for bed. A movie is on that I have never seen before I notice. To my great surprise, I see a creature identical to what was a hologram image beamed into my residence in 2008 by this program again hoping to scare me that demons are targeting me instead of government intelligence agencies and ongoing experimentation, using bizarre technological tactics for confusion and population control.

I am not a big television person, never have been, so I did not recognize the image, I saw as a hologram beam into my Signal Hills apartment in 2008, as a character seen on television or in the movies before today.

I am probably one of the very few today in America who has not watched, "The Matrix," "The Men in Black" trilogies or the "The Lord of the Rings / The Two Towers" series. All I can say is "Wow!" the image below is exactly the hologram image, I saw.

NOTE: A complete list of patents, which can accomplish hologram, portable, and space-based may also be found on bigbrotherwatchingus.com in the U.S. Patents / Inventors section.

HELL IS EMPTY
AND
ALL THE DEVILS
ARE HERE.

WILLIAM SHAKESPEARE

CHAPTER ELEVEN

It's Mind Control, Corruption of Your Thoughts,

Destruction of Your Soul ~ Lyrics by Stephen Marley

Dear Diary,

The problem is that I have never heard a father call his daughter sexy before so when I heard my granddaughter called this it naturally was an alarm. The issue with me, reported by many is that in these programs, is definite attempts to create sexual deviance, to include pedophilia using beamed sexual stimulation reportedly by those awake around children This is a very real technique and part of the most heinous tactic in psychological operations for blackmail and silencing.

It is now late February of 2014 and my middle-born daughter and granddaughter have been home with me for just over a month. While still in Denver, she reported that a male person she spoke with rarely wanted to "Face Time," and see the baby and called her sexy.

Was making the comment a Freudian slip? Or is he like many in specific communities being manipulated and influenced, possibly, into sexual deviance. My granddaughter is multiracial. Do I think he is a pedophile? I cannot say for sure. However, in awareness anyone can be programmed and use as child sexual abuse and child pornography skyrockets all over the globe. The fact is, it can be subliminally influence then sexually stimulated around children.

When I embarked on these publication efforts, one thing I knew for certain, I must be brave enough to broach any subject no matter how distasteful to the public. In reality, I must admit that that the comment was troubling but what is even more troubling, is the possibility that those in these centers, could deem anyone a valueless test subject, and use yet another human guinea pig if they saw fit to harm a child. The goal is to shatter the mind of children, for Trauma Based Mind Control early on.

Make no mistake about it; these programs continue to thrive because new test subjects are added repeatedly and as reported my myself, and many others, creating sexual deviance continues to play a major role to control a person. Mind control is about changing people from who they really are and something they are not. This is the nature of this beast.

Fueling my fire was the fact that after the comment was made, I wondered if my concerns were valid. As a result, I typed into the Google search engine the comment, hoping to prove my concerns to my daughter, as valid, and my intentions not vindictive. The result was numerous responses from women, from a website captioned under, Pedophilia asking what are the characteristics of a person as a child predator." There were many, many responses to this question with one woman stating, that after witnessing the exact same comment from someone close to her family that an extreme sexual incident did followed.

One story struck me to the core. A young mother recalled how when she was changing her daughter's diaper at six months old, the child's father commented "Pretty pussy." She then later again witnessed him commenting about the children on the show "Are You Smarter than a 5th Grader" and him calling the children sexy participating then as well. Later she writes that after leaving the child for a day of shopping, when she returned, the baby would not stop crying. When she changed her daughter's diaper she noticed blood in it.

The person was subsequently arrested and sentenced to a lengthy prison term. Later, the person was on the record as saying that a powerful, irresistible urge captivated him. It stated that it was so strong that he could not resist violating the child and that he did not understand how it happened or why. And, furthermore there were numerous stories of this nature from women having these personal experiences from men, they loved in childhood, to include their fathers and other male figures of trust in their lives.

Many would argue that you cannot create in someone that which is not already there already, or a part of their psyche. However, I beg to differ, this powerful, extremely low frequency technology, if they choose to could very effectively, without leaving any evidence of electromagnetic manipulation create an intense drive for sexual gratification. With this knowledge, his comment, or any comment of this nature regarding a baby, became a red flag for me that I could not ignore.

It is a belief shared by many that some operating at the most "Top Secret" of levels in these programs are sitting, watching, planning, as vultures, lay in wait for anything useful, a small character defect, a dormant negative thought, a past regret, for any weakness to exploit and vulnerability. They are looking for any and every opportunity to test their new toys. Folks whether you believe me or not, people can be programmed to something so sick and depraved. Just turn on the news and witness headlines of children being victimized and abused on a daily basis horrendously.

Regarding the ongoing strategic efforts to isolate me from family, I still communicated on any subject where they or my granddaughter would become prey. In this scenario I did not care whether they liked it or not. Using family members is vital in these situations whether they are receptive or want to hear what you are saying as a warning.

One day, my daughter swore that I had said something to her that I completely did not say. If this happened once, it was okay and I had decided to let it ride. It was trivial. However, when it again happened twice, and a powerful argument ensued in which she would not except that she possibly heard me wrong, I became concerned. Let me state for the record, again, and again, and again, folks, this technology is no joke nor are the intense efforts of those deploying it around family and others.

In my case, I have been blessed to have what is called a memory like an elephant and knew I had not made that statement she was arguing with me that I had.

In reality, something so simple as this type of misunderstanding could be used, as similar incidents had with my oldest daughter, if the situation arose, to portray me as losing my memory, confused, and in need of help. Shortly after arriving, the oldest girl, definitely targeted, banished from my home, but loved from a distance, told her sister, which her sister reported back to me saying, "In a couple of years" we may have to commit mom.

Again, knowing of the pitfalls, I told my daughter when she first wanted to return, with my grand, after the Thanksgiving fiasco, that to be vigilante and that if any negative thoughts entered her mind while around me, whatsoever, related to me, do not let them fester and grow. I told her to be aware of the reality of what is happening around me, because those in the operation center would surely cultivate even a passing thought and use it negatively to destroy our relationship point blank. However, my precocious granddaughter, would become a whole other animal for these technological vicious predators,

Where this group continually read me wrong is that I don't need anyone, around me, nor, will I allow anyone, including family around who could hurt me again, whether successfully manipulated or not.

Because I want my family around, I am always attempting to educate my children on what is happening almost from day one, which I recognize and continue to recognize as completely necessary if they are to survive around me. I like any mother, also want to provide a safe environment for this daughter, along with my granddaughter. She is now in school to become a Civil Engineer.

Because she was not officially targeted as the oldest girl is, she and the younger daughter were more receptive to what I was saying and at the very least listened. Thank goodness for this.

Dear Diary,

If I had not put total and complete trust in God, and what are called "God Shots" aka intuition, I would not have made it this far. I am constantly revitalized by the awareness of the love of God.

In the biblical account of Abraham, he was willing to sacrifice his son for God. Genesis 22 opens with the words "Sometime afterward, God put Abraham to the test" (Genesis 22:1). The story first wants the reader to remember what just happened to Ishmael in Genesis 21. To make this point clear he refers to Isaac as Abraham's "only" son (see verse 2).

Abraham is being "put to the test." He has to ask himself, "Is God the God of love? Is he true to his word? Did he save Ishmael as he promised he would? Will he spare Isaac so that my descendants will come forth from him as he promised?"

Abraham has complete and utter faith in God, and he does as he is told. He takes Isaac to be sacrificed. Why would Abraham willingly offer his son as a sacrifice?

The author of Hebrews helps to shed some light on this. Hebrews recounts a litany of examples of Abraham's faith, but two in particular stand out:

By faith he received power to generate, even though he was past the normal age... So, it was that there came forth from one man, himself as good as dead, descendants as numerous as the stars in the sky and as countless as the sands on the seashore. (Hebrews 11:11-12)

By faith Abraham, when put to the test, Abraham offered up Isaac. He who had received the promises was ready to offer his only son, of whom it was said, 'Through Isaac descendants shall bear your name.' He reasoned that God was able to rise even from the dead, and he would receive Isaac back as a symbol of God's word and promise. (Hebrews 11:17-19).

God had proven himself to Abraham more than once. He knows that God is a God of love who is true to his word. Abraham at his advanced age bore children. Because of this he knows by faith that Ishmael is safe, just as he knows by faith that Isaac will be also.

It appears that even if he can't see how, he "reasoned that God was able to rise even from the dead." just as he had brought forth life from his seed in old age. Abraham is about to commit this deed, when an Angel of

God spares Isaac just as an angel had spared Ishmael.

Dear Diary,

God did not bring me this far to leave me. I have come too far to turn back now. I will not be deceived. God is so much bigger than this! This world is in God's hands.

Dear Diary,

I just ran errands with my daughter and granddaughter. My granddaughter was so happy playing and laughing in her car seat, especially after I purchased her a new toy. When I looked back at her in her car seat pushing buttons on the toy, then bobbing her head to the sounds, I thought, "I love her."

However, shortly afterwards, she threw the toy down and let out a loud scream, urgently for her "Momma, Momma" who was sitting in the front seat alongside me. Usually a drive is uneventful or is instant nap time for her or she occupies herself with various toys attached to her car seat. But the way she started to scream was a fearful scream as she called out for her mother.

Typically, toddlers do cry and many times we don't know why. But, while my granddaughter was crying, the men working this beamed harassment program, that day had been beaming into my head, the child's name, to her, and to me "We are going to kill her!" The radar laser beam beamed around the ear cochlea and this technique is call "Voice to Skull" or V2K, and used for this type of beamed verbal communication. I could hear it and the child could hear it but apparently my daughter could not which was the intent.

Faith and trust in God are imperative. These people are in fact only guaranteeing rent free space in Hell and damnation. There is nothing good waiting for them when it all said and done. You don't live in darkness then see the light at your appointed time to depart this plane. You return to the energy level you resonated to by the law of attraction.

As I finalized this book, in reality, these cowards were greatly concerned, yet were still trying desperately to keep up a front of being, big and bad, and that they ultimately had real power. They don't and I was not and am not going to allow it. This is my God given life.

The fact is that in reality the only power they have is what the target gives them through fear and especially through constant death threats. Death is nothing to fear by the good.

To the skeptics, know that children are not exempt from electronic weapons torture, as detailed in this letter written by Rep Jim Guest in 2007 below:

October 10, 2007
Dear Member of the Legislature and Friends:

This letter is to ask for your help for the many constituents in our country who are being affected unjustly by electronic weapons torture and covert harassment groups. Serious privacy rights violations and physical injuries have been caused by the activities of these groups and their use of so-called non-lethal weapons on men, women, and even children.

I am asking you to play a role in helping these victims and also stopping the massive movement in the use of Verichip and RFID technologies in tracking Americans. Long before Verichip was known, we were testing these devices on Americans, many without their knowledge or consent. With the new revelations of cancer risk beside the privacy and human rights problems with the use of Verichips and RF signals, I am asking for your assistance in stopping these abuses and aiding those already affected. Your attendance is therefore requested at a conference call regarding these issues on Monday, October 29 at 11 am, EST. After a period of brief presentations, we will have a discussion of these issues with the intent of creating a way forward solutions...

Sincerely,
Representative Jim Guest

When this incident happened to my daughter, those in the operation center intentionally allowed me to hear them repeatedly calling my granddaughter's name over and over again. They are after me not her and now using every angle, to include a small child, believing that threats to harm her could be used to stop me.

Dear Diary,

I remain faithful.

These depraved sub-humans, again now paralyzed in cowardly fear of losing their livelihood will destroy any threat by any means necessary.

Two other incidents happened that clued me to the possibility, outside of them telling me they were going to harm her. One night, just before her bath, she was sitting on my bed playing with me a few days later. She again stopped what she was doing, the same expression come on her face which I had observed in the car that day, and she then began to look around to see where the person calling her was coming from. She turned shook her head and said, "No, no" then turned her head and focused for a moment on the house directly behind mine which is 100% one of houses set up with technology without a doubt instinctively.

The second incident happened when she was again playing in my room with a toy that she loves. All of the sudden she threw it down and started screaming for, and calling for, her mother.

As I have said before, these programs have created, covert technological monster and part of their programming is muted empathy and human consciousness or apparently just don't care.

In reality, and target's need not forget, they continue a hope to destroy emotionally anyway they can, but thank God many are stronger. They know I love my grand, and believe, it appears that they can create a situation that would make her mother have to move out in fear. Could they believe it would devastate me, while inadvertently destroying my daughter in transition and temporarily needing my help right now.

In reality, if it came down to me or them, they would likely destroy anyone to include their own mothers.

Dear Diary,

Below is an example, of how sexual deviance can be created and influenced from these operations. Many people receive these types of emails from women, appearing to be seeking to leave impoverished countries, and I am no exception.

However, because I am targeted, and monitored 24/7, the difference is that when I read the emails, I was being sexually stimulated, electromagnetically by the men in this center listening to subvocal thought as I read. Again, I am not lesbian, so this was outrageous to me and key for me to recognize it. Because I am not Gay, technological sexual excitation for me became a whole other animal by these despicable. The fact that I was being inundated with these specific emails, from all women, might be due to my names being Renee and these women possibly believing that I am a man or Rene. I did consider this:

Hi My name is Hannah, I am looking for a good friend. I decided to contact you after viewing your profile please email me at this address and not on Facebook, or acknowledge my email, so that I can tell you more about me. Thanks. Yours new friend, Hannah.

Many, many women have written the exact type of message asking to become friends through Facebook messaging like this.

If you want to be a friend, simply sending a Facebook friend request would suffice. However, this person specifically asks for contact outside of Facebook. Because I began receiving so many, almost on a daily basis, I started reporting the emails to Facebook as spam and Facebook began to catch them.

Whether this Hannah person is real or a shill, one thing is definite, while reading several of these emails initially, attempts were immediately, 100%, made to electromagnetically sexually stimulate me from the operation center I assume hoping to spark an interest in the same sex. It did not work and I literally found the attempts repulsive.

These people are sick puppies.

If this happened once, there would be no question or issue; however, operation center sexual stimulation began to happen consistently with these emails as well, before they were completely and successfully blocked as spam.

This is not my first experience with the unwanted sexual stimulation many targets are reporting as part of the sexual aspect of Electronic Terrorism. We must recognize that if a person can be compromised sexually they can be, as stated previously, blackmailed and controlled very effectively, especially if nudged into deviant acts which they do not want known. These efforts are about control by any means necessary, not to mention, it appears, amusement for the corrupted, evil possessed, weak minded deviants sitting at the helm of this technology.

Image an adversarial business competitor, or partner, political opponent, ex-spouse, male or female, or any target forced into some heinous act, thoroughly manipulation in this manner, unaware of the extremely low frequency capability of patented technology, used for sexual stimulation. In reality, many have not the slightest clue that this capability exists. The technology as many targeted women and men report, being experimented on continues to be reported as capable of bringing the human body to a complete abnormally motivated orgasm.

In "You Are Not My Big Brother" I document how I would be sexually stimulated around my father as those in the operation center tried create sexual deviance with me or to learn if there was any incest activity between he and I. It is sickening and I can tell you that this type of testing is personally traumatizing to the person's psyche having the desired effect.

I guess scanning my brain and memory or listening to my thoughts were not enough for these corrupt pathetic souls which revealed no incident or desire based on mind reading of my thoughts or that this never would happen. It is just sad the many report the same heinous experiences.

Although a distasteful subject, I would not have put that information into that book had I not perceived it as something vitally important for people to know and understand as a definite, again, electromagnetic, patented, capability. I also believe, contrary to what those working in these programs and centers believe, wanting to keep from full disclosure, the use of this technology this way is a must to expose and that people have a right to know the capabilities of this technology and how it is reportedly being used nationwide and specifically to discredit people as insane. These specific efforts I find to be the vilest, and sickest of all in these operations.

In yet another outrageous story, recently one of the many targeted individuals who followed me on social networks reported that she was held up in a hotel, influenced to be there, and that those targeting her were attempting to turn her into a sex slave. To most people reading this would sound like the rant of a crazy person. It would unless you understood that manipulative powerful technology exists and is in widespread use.

I continually used the patents, officially patented at the United States Patent and Trademark Office, to substantiate at the very least that there is the capability. Here, again, is one of the official patents for this technology.

Many who have read my other books know that I have also documented this specific patent before:

US Patent # 6,091,994 (July 18, 2000) Pulsative Manipulation of Nervous Systems

Loos, Hendricus Abstract --- Method and apparatus for manipulating the nervous system by imparting subliminal pulsative cooling to the subject's skin at a frequency that is suitable for the excitation of a sensory resonance. At present, two major sensory resonances are known, with frequencies near 1/2 Hz and 2.4 Hz. The 1/2 Hz sensory resonance causes relaxation, sleepiness, ptosis of the eyelids, a tonic smile, a "knot" in the stomach, or sexual excitement, depending on the precise frequency used. The 2.4 Hz resonance causes the slowing of certain cortical activities, and is characterized by a large increase of the time needed to silently count backward from 100 to 60, with the eyes closed. The invention can be used by the general public for inducing relaxation, sleep, or sexual excitement, and clinically for the control and perhaps a treatment of tremors, seizures, and autonomic system disorders such as panic attacks. Embodiments shown are a pulsed fan to impart subliminal cooling pulses to the subject's skin, and a silent device which induces periodically varying flow past the subject's skin, the flow being induced by pulsative rising warm air plumes that are caused by a thin resistive wire which is periodically heated by electric current pulses.

Then imagine this patented technology used along with the Silent Subliminal Message, patent:

Silent Subliminal Message: U.S. Patent, #5,159,703, October 27, 1992. Inventor - Dr. Oliver M. Lowry

Description

A communication system in which non-aural carriers (in the very low or high audio frequency range or the ultrasonic frequency spectrum) are amplified or frequency modulated with the desired "intelligence," and propagated acoustically or vibration ally for inducement directly into the brain. This can be done "live" or recorded/stored on magnetic, mechanical or optical media for delayed/ repeated transmission to the target. Sound can also be induced by radiating the head with microwaves (in a range of 100 to 10,000 MHz) that are modulated with a waveform consisting of a frequency modulated bursts. This is an excellent method of influencing people without their knowledge.

Purpose:

To instruct or pass messages; in theory. In reality it is used to torment targets. (One unpublicized application was the Gulf war)

Dear Diary,

Resist the Devil and he will flee or in this case the spirit of the devil in human form. But they don't, again many are targeted right up to their death beds. Because of the incredulous nature of the electromagnetic extremely low frequency attacks, many targets are beginning to question, that in terms of good versus evil, that those working in this program must be possessed by the Devil with a Luciferian agenda being heavily promoted all around us and specifically by the music industry today.

Later, about a month after my daughter and I had the initial conversation regarding my granddaughter and the comment, those in the operation center went to work on her attempting to implant that I was in fact the real pedophile. With me, I believe, everyone can be questioned. And if I feel it even a remote possibly, this is what is happening, I will immediately question anyone about anything for sanities sake. I don't allow negativity to rent space in my head without validation of truth. This is how they have not been able to control my thinking. I don't need to be right all the time. I asked people if what is being influenced around me is true.

As I stated, my objective has been to constantly keep my children aware of what is happening. I had already told her to stay alert around me. I am extremely observant and analytical by nature. If something is odd to me, again, I will question it. When I began noticing that my daughter would asked me to watch my granddaughter, run downstairs then, quietly, almost creep back up to see what we were doing I wondered if they were trying to use her and assault me. If this happened once, okay, or even twice, okay, however, by the third time, my intuitive antenna went up.

I finally told her that I felt that, in an effort to now insure that my granddaughter would never be around me again, because the operation center had found someone I love they hoped to use, that it might be possible that those in the operation center were beaming thoughts into her head that I was factually the real pedophile or would harm by daughter, believe it or not. The look on her face was worth a thousand words. She said nothing, nor did she protest my allegation of this possibility.

What was telling is the fact, that, she could not look me in the eyes. This was likely after realizing that what I was saying was in reality being promoted to her by beamed influence and that what I was saying was true. She then factually said, "You better not touch my baby." Although said in a joking manner, I knew that I was right. Bear in mind I raised three girls myself who overall were well adjusted until this program reared its ugly head.

When I realized my accuracy of the likelihood, and her confirmation, I again began to remind her what I had told her when she arrived. Be cautious of any negative thoughts materializing in your head around me and explained to her that the operation center perverts, knowing how much I love you al, combined with the continuous effort to keep family away, are the culprit of negativity as experimentation continues. I told her to remember and know that I love her, and her sisters, and granddaughter, dearly, and would never hurt them. She listened quietly and was not offended at all by what I was telling her. Later the men in the operation center would say, from the ceiling position, "Well, she got her daughter" meaning that my daughter now believed me.

However, I have noticed that in these cases, they undoubtedly will continue to try and try again and again. I learned that they usually wait a few days, after the dust has settled from one incident, before going in for the psychological, technological kill, by redirecting the focus on a new psychological operation.

Dear Diary,

My daughter woke with a severe case of the butt this morning, directed at me. I am willing to bet on my life that she was being programmed all night while sleeping. This too I have also experienced but I know the difference. When I woke and the now full fledge military operation center personnel witnessed me go straight to editing this book, "She doesn't care" was said, which would indicated that if they were working on me all night hoping to implant something beneficial to them, like "Stop that book or else" they likely were working on her too.

I talked with her, and she changed back to herself. They were trying to play on me bugging her yesterday and making a big deal of it, and attempting to help negative feeling linger. Believe it or not!

Dear Diary,

The beam has been focused on the right side of my head with every keystroke today towards finalizing this manuscript.

They don't seem to grasp that I am just not worth losing their souls over. However, in reality, they already have lost theirs.

Dear Diary,

Eleanor White, a Canadian, was a long time, advocate and highly respected activist and whistleblower regarding targeted individuals' issues and experiences. Not only as a target herself, her documentation of this program dated back close to 30 years.

I recently stumbled upon a booklet she put together of suggestions for targeted individuals. The suggestions are helpful and the booklet free. Here is an example of the topics in the Table of Contents:

COPING

WITH THE CRIME OF

ORGANIZED STALKING AND

ELECTRONIC HARRASSMENT

By Eleanor White

LIST OF SECTIONS:

Page numbers are not given here, as this booklet will be updated frequently when new information becomes available.

GENERAL

GENERAL

There are many different ideas and opinions within the organized stalking and electronic terrorism community recommending many ways to cope with these secret, covert crimes. This booklet presents the opinions of the author, who at time of writing has been a target for 33 years. Because this crime includes tactics outside the widely recognized crimes, including classified (secret) technologies, nothing in this booklet is guaranteed to help in any particular case. This collection of coping ideas is provided on a "for what it may be worth" basis.

One aspect of coping is experimenting with countermeasure and detection methods for the electronic terrorism. That is beyond the scope of this booklet.

Others have penned a *hopeful* Bill in desperation for recognition and moral and ethical relief for the plight for thousands of targeted individuals within the United States such as shown below:

Organized Stalking and Directed Energy Weapons Harassment Bill

A bill to provide protections to individuals who are being harassed, stalked, harmed by surveillance, and assaulted; as well as protections to keep individuals from becoming human research subjects, tortured, and killed by electronic frequency devices, directed energy devices, implants, and directed energy weapons.

Section 1. Short Title This bill may be cited as the "Organized Stalking and Directed Energy Devices and Weapons Bill

Section 2. Findings and Purpose

1) The constitution guarantees the right of the people to be secure in their person. The Declaration of Independence asserts as self-evident that all men have certain inalienable rights and that among these are life, liberty, and the pursuit of happiness.

2) As Supreme Court Justice Louis Brandeis wrote in 1928, "the framers of the Constitution sought "to protect Americans in their beliefs, their thoughts, their emotions, and their sensations." It is for this reason that they established, as against the government, the right to be let alone as "the most comprehensive of rights and the right most valued by civilized men."

3) The first principle of the Nuremberg Code states that with respect to human research, the voluntary consent of the human subject is absolutely essential. The Nuremberg Code further asserts that such consent must be competent, informed, and comprehending.

4) There are current regulations implementing the obligations of the United States to adhere to Article 3 of the United Nations Convention Against Torture and other Forms of Cruel, Inhumane or Degrading Treatment including all terms that are Subject to any reservations, understandings, declarations, and provisions contained in the United States Senate resolution of

ratification of the Convention. B) Purpose To establish regulations and penalties for those who use any type of electronic frequency devices, directed energy devices, implants, surveillance technology, and directed energy weapon to purposefully cause any of the following: stalking, harassing, mental or physical harm, injury, harmful surveillance, torture, diseases, and death to any United States citizen.

Section 3. Organized Stalking

If two or more persons willfully, maliciously, and repeatedly follow or willfully and maliciously harass another person and who make a credible threat with the intent to place that person in reasonable fear for his or her safety, or the safety of his or her immediate family, they are guilty of the crime of organized stalking, punishable by imprisonment in a county jail for not more than one year, or by not more than one thousand dollars ($ 1,000), or by both that fine and imprisonment, or by imprisonment in a federal prison.

If two or more persons violate subdivision (a) when there is a temporary restraining order, injunction, or any other court order in effect prohibiting the behavior described in subdivision (a) against the same party, they shall be punished by imprisonment in the state prison for two, three, or four years.

For the purposes of this section, "harass" means engages in a knowing and willful course of conduct directed at a specific person that seriously alarms, annoys, torments, or terrorizes the person, or damages his personal property or possessions and that serves no legitimate purpose.

For the purposes of this section, "course of conduct" means two or more acts occurring over a period of time, however short, evidencing a continuity of purpose. Constitutionally protected activity is not included within the meaning of "course of conduct."

For the purposes of this section, "credible threat" means a verbal or written threat, including that performed through the use of an electronic communication device, or a threat implied by a pattern of conduct or a combination of verbal, written, or electronically communicated statements and conduct, made with the intent to place the person that is the target of the threat in reasonable fear for his or her safety or the safety of his or her family, or personal property or possessions and made with the apparent ability to carry out the threat so as to cause the person who is the target of the threat to reasonably fear for his or her safety or the safety of his or her family or personal property or possessions. It is not necessary to prove that the defendant had the intent to actually carry out the threat. The present incarceration of a person making the threat shall not be a bar to prosecution under this section. Constitutionally protected activity is not included within the meaning of "credible threat."

For purposes of this section, the term "electronic communication device" includes, but is not limited to, telephones, cellular phones, computers, video recorders, fax machines, pagers or synthetic telepathy devices.

The sentencing court also shall consider issuing an order restraining the defendant from any contact with the victim that may be valid for up to 10 years, as determined by the court. It is the intent of the Legislature that the length of any restraining order be based upon the seriousness of the facts before the court, the probability of future violations, and the safety of the victim and his or her immediate family.

For purposes of this section, "immediate family" means any spouse, parent, child, any person related by consanguinity or affinity within the second degree, or any other person who regularly resides in the household, or who, within the prior six months, regularly resided in the household. Section 4. Punishment for threats

Any person or persons who willfully threatens to commit a crime which will result in death or great bodily injury to another person, with the specific intent that the statement, made verbally, in writing, or by means of an electronic communication device, is to be taken as a threat, even if there is no intent of actually carrying it out, which, on its face and under the circumstances in which it is made, is so unequivocal, unconditional, immediate, and specific as to convey to the person threatened, a gravity of purpose and an immediate prospect of execution of the threat, and thereby causes that person reasonably to be in sustained fear for his or her own safety or for his or her immediate family's safety, shall be punished by imprisonment in a federal prison not to exceed one year.. For the purposes of this section, "immediate family" means any spouse, whether by marriage or not, parent, child, any person related by consanguinity or affinity within the second degree, or any other person who regularly resides in the household, or who, within the prior six months, regularly resided in the household. "Electronic communication device" includes, but is not limited to, telephones, cellular telephones, computers, video recorders, fax machines, pagers or synthetic telepathy devices

Obscene, threatening or annoying communication

(a) Every person or persons who, with intent to annoy, telephones or makes constant contact by means of an electronic communication device with another and addresses to or about the other person any obscene language or addresses to the other person any threat to inflict injury to the person or any member of his or her family, or any property or personal possessions is guilty of a misdemeanor. Nothing in this subdivision shall apply to telephone calls or electronic contacts made in good faith.

(b) Every person or persons who makes repeated telephone calls or makes repeated contact by means of an electronic communication device with intent to annoy another person at his or her residence, is, whether or not conversation ensues from making the telephone call or electronic contact, is guilty of a misdemeanor. Nothing in this subdivision shall apply to telephone calls or electronic contacts made in good faith.

(c) Every person or persons who makes repeated telephone calls or makes repeated contact by means of an electronic communication device with the intent to annoy another person at his or her place of work is guilty of a misdemeanor punishable by a fine of not more than one thousand dollars ($ 1,000), or by imprisonment in a federal prison for not more than one year, or by both that fine and imprisonment. Nothing in this subdivision shall apply to telephone calls or electronic contacts made in good faith. This subdivision applies only if one or both of the following circumstances exist:

(1) There is a temporary restraining order, an injunction, or any other court order, or any combination of these court orders, in effect prohibiting the behavior described in this section.

(2) The person or persons makes repeated telephone calls or makes repeated contact by means of an electronic communication device with the intent to annoy another person at his or her place of work, totaling more than 10 times in a 24-hour period, whether or not conversation ensues from making the telephone call or electronic contact, and the repeated telephone calls or electronic contacts are made to the workplace of an adult or fully emancipated minor who is a spouse, former spouse, cohabitant, former cohabitant, or person with whom the person has a child or has had a dating or engagement relationship or is having a dating or engagement relationship.

(d) Any offense committed by use of a telephone may be deemed to have been committed where the telephone call or calls were made or received. Any offense committed by use of an electronic communication device or medium, including the Internet, may be deemed to have been committed when the electronic communication or communications were originally sent or first viewed by the recipient.

(e) Subdivision (a), (b), or (c) is violated when the person acting with intent to annoy makes a telephone call requesting a return call and performs the acts prohibited under subdivision (a), (b), or (c) upon receiving the return call.

(f) If probation is granted, or the execution or imposition of sentence is suspended, for any person or persons convicted under this section, the court may order as a condition of probation that the person participate in counseling.

(g) For purposes of this section, the term "electronic communication device" includes, but is not limited to, telephones, cellular phones, computers, video recorders, fax machines, pagers or synthetic telepathy devices.

Section 5. Assault and battery with an electronic or directed energy weapon

Any person or persons who in the course of organized stalking and harassment, commits an assault upon the person of another with an unauthorized directed energy weapon shall be punished by imprisonment in a federal prison for two, three, or four years or by a fine not exceeding ten thousand dollars ($10,000). For the purposes of this section the term directed energy weapon is defined as any device that directs a source of energy (including molecular or atomic energy, subatomic particle beams, electromagnetic radiation, plasma, or extremely low frequency (ELF) or ultra-low frequency (ULF) energy radiation) against a person or any other unacknowledged or as yet undeveloped means of inflicting death or injury; or damaging or destroying, a person (or the biological life, bodily health, mental health, or physical and economic well-being of a person via land-based, sea-based, or space-based systems using radiation, electromagnetic, psychotronic, sonic, laser, or other energies directed at individual persons or targeted populations for the purpose of information war, mood management, or mind control of such persons or populations; or by expelling chemical or biological agents in the vicinity of a person.

Source: Freedom from Covert Harassment and Surveillance, sample legislation pdf.

Dear Diary,

One thing is certain, if Congressman Dennis Kucinich's Space Preservation Act of 2001, describing the need to curtail and monitor the use of these powerful electromagnetic frequency weapons in many forms, handheld, portable, land, sea and space-based failed, you can bet, this bill will never officially, see the light of day!

There are doctrines also, already in place, which are not being honored today in light of the decisive globalization effort such as below within the United Nations:

Convention Against Torture and Other Cruel, Inhumane or Degrading Treatment or Punishment

The Convention against Torture and Other Cruel, Inhuman or Degrading Treatment or Punishment (United Nations Convention against Torture) is an international human rights instrument, under the review of the United Nations that aims to prevent torture and cruel, inhuman degrading treatment or punishment around the world.

The Convention requires states to take effective measures to prevent torture within their borders, and forbids states to transport people to any country where there is reason to believe they will be tortured.

The text of the Convention was adopted by the United Nations General Assembly on 10 December 1984[1] and, following ratification by the 20th state party,[2] it came into force on 26 June 1987.[1] 26 June is now recognized as the International Day in Support of Victims of Torture, in honor of the Convention. As of September 2013, the Convention has 154 state parties.

ARTICLE 1

For the purpose of this Convention, the term "Torture" means any act by which severe pain or suffering, whether physical or mental, is intentionally inflicted on a person for such purposes as obtaining from him or a third person information or a confession, or punishing him for an act he or a third person has committed or is suspected of having committed, or intimidating or coercing him or a third person, or at the instigation of or with the consent or acquiescence of a public official.

ARTICLE 2

1. No exceptional circumstances whatsoever, whether a state of war or a threat of war, internal political in stability or any other public emergency, may be invoked as a justification of torture.

2. An order from a superior officer or a public authority may not be invoked as a justification of torture, Signs, symptoms, causes, and neurological effects from "electronic stalking and harassment" by electric weapons:

Stress is a psychological and physiological response to events that upset our personal balance in some way. Stress affects the mind, body, and behavior and can cause death.

Chronic Stress is "unrelenting demands and pressures for seemingly interminable periods of time." Many targets have been targeted for years. Chronic stress is stress that wears you down day after day and year after year, with no visible escape as is the agenda once a target is place into one of these technology testing programs. It grinds away at both mental and physical health, leading to a synthetic or manmade breakdown. Instead of leveling off once the crisis has passed your stress hormones, heart rate, and blood pressure remain elevated. Extended or repeated activation of the stress response takes a heavy toll on the body as those deploying this technology are well aware around the clock and relentlessly. The physical wear and tear it causes includes damage to the cardiovascular system and immune system suppression which is also a method of "slow Kill."

Health problems linked to stress resulting from days and days, and day, of around the clock electronic assaults are: heart attack, hypertension, stroke, severe depression, substance abuse, ulcers, Irritable Bowel Syndrome, memory loss, sleep deprivation, thyroid problems and organ damage centering specifically on the joints.

Project Monarch

CHAPTER TWELVE

"The individual is handicapped by coming face-to-face with a conspiracy so monstrous he cannot believe it exist"~
J. Edgar Hoover - COINTELPRO

Dear Diary,

Can the human body withstand such powerful doses of non-ionizing radiation?

The message is clear, and I am reminded over and over again, "You're dead" yet nearing 15 years later I am still alive.

"You can't prove a thing" is faintly heard from the ceiling directly above me where I sit working nearly completing this book, and trying to edit and proofreading determined that if it is my time, when I die, there will be Book IV.

I have found proofreading and editing to be very challenging, due to operation center relentless tampering. In fact, as I powered up my laptop this morning a message immediately come onto the screen saying, the system is locked and to contact the System Administrator. What? I am they official System Administrator, although the operation center does not see it this way.

I also noticed that the Microsoft Security Essential, security and spyware software had been disabled. I was able to get up and running after doing a full system restore. As those in the operation center watched, from their real-time vantage point overhead, I heard, "It looks like she's got another book" said.

Many are crying out for ethical intervention, and revealing credible information backed by clear evidence, of what is really happening today to an astounding half a million human test subjects all over the world. In all cases, no help is forthcoming from anywhere and a target is forced to do whatever they can to protect their own lives. In my case, writing. I hope that others take this proactive path. Hurting self or others plays into the discrediting as mentally official narrative.

The following information was posted on my social network today: My social network page, I hope is a source of verification of the reality, for many trying to prove credibility. I hope that my efforts to supply validation, victim information, and support, for the plight of Targeted Individuals, not only within the United States, but worldwide is helping within growing altruism.

As stated before, the reality is that it takes just three satellites to blanket the Earth with detection ability and by 2020 the US Congress had approved 30,000 drones for US skies. Today there are thousands of satellites orbiting our planet which also fuel military weaponized drones.

Many thanks for this posting:

Electronic Surveillance System Follows Millions of People

by Dr. Charles Kyte –

(Posted here by Wes Penre: Illuminati News March 2, 2004)

****

I received the following letter from Dr. Charles Kyte and found it very interesting. I decided to publish it as-is, so I can let Dr. Kyte take care of the introduction.
Sincerely Yours,

Wes Penre

****

Greetings

I am a research scientist based out of the Mount Sinai School of Medicine. I was informally made aware of illegal neurological-psychological ops and experiments (biotelemetry) [1] conducted at major universities (Mount Sinai School of Medicine, Smith College, Down State Medical Center, University of Southern California, etc.) and cities (New York City, Boston). Are you familiar with this technology? [2] See below.

Charles Kyte

[Son of a Deceased World Order of St. Johns Knights of Malta [3] (Australia): C Wolde Kyte, MD (MA), PhD,

Knight Commander of North & South America]

Reference

World's first brain prosthesis revealed 19:00 12 March 03 Exclusive from New Scientist Print Edition. The world's first brain prosthesis - an artificial hippocampus - is about to be tested in California. Unlike devices like cochlear implants, which merely stimulate brain activity, this silicon chip implant will perform the same processes as the damaged part of the brain it is replacing. [University of Southern California, Los Angeles] Keywords: radio implants, microchips, brain, bioelectrical resonance, DNA microchip,

Electronic Surveillance System Follows Millions of People

Every thought, reaction, hearing and visual observation causes a certain neurological potential, spikes, and patterns in the brain and its electromagnetic fields, which can now be decoded into thoughts, pictures and voices. Electromagnetic stimulation can therefore change a person's brainwaves and affect muscular activity, causing painful muscular cramps experienced as torture.

The NSA's electronic surveillance system can simultaneously follow and handle millions of people. Each of us has a unique bioelectrical resonance frequency in the brain, just like we have unique fingerprints. With electro-magnetic frequency (EMF) brain stimulation fully coded, pulsating electromagnetic signals can be sent to the brain, causing the desired voice and visual effects to be experienced by the target. This is a form of electronic warfare. U.S. astronauts were implanted before they were sent into space so their thoughts could be followed and all their emotions could be registered 24 hours a day.

The NSA's Signals Intelligence can remotely monitor information from human brains by decoding the evoked potentials (3.50HZ, 5 milliwatt) emitted by the brain. Prisoner experimenters in Gothenburg, Sweden and Vienna, Austria have been found to have [missing word] brain lesions. Diminished blood circulation and lack of oxygen in the right temporal frontal lobes result where brain implants are usually operative. A

Finnish experimentee experienced brain atrophy and intermittent attacks of unconsciousness due to lack of oxygen.

Mind control techniques can be used for political purposes. The goal of mind controllers today is to induce the targeted person(s) or groups to act against his or her own convictions and best interests. Zombified individuals can even be programmed to murder and remember nothing of their crime afterward. Alarming examples of this phenomenon can be found in the:

U.S. Microwave Mind Control: Modern Torture and Control Mechanisms Eliminating Human Rights and Privacy

By Dr. Rauni Leena Kilde, MD

September 25, 1999

Helsingin Sanomat, the largest newspaper in Scandinavia, wrote in the September 9, 1999 issue that Scientific American magazine estimates that after the Millennium *[sic]* perhaps ALL people will be implanted with a "DNA microchip".

How many people realize what it actually means? Total loss of privacy and total outside control of the person's physical body functions, mental, emotional and thought processes, including the implanted person's subconscious and dreams! For the rest of his life!

It sounds like science fiction but it is secret military and intelligence agencies' mind control technology, which has been experimented with for almost half a century. Totally without the knowledge of the general public and even the general academic population.

Supercomputers in Maryland, Israel and elsewhere with a speed of over 20 BILLION bits/sec can monitor millions of people simultaneously. In fact, the whole world population can be totally controlled by these secret brain-computer interactions, however unbelievable it sounds for the uninformed.

Human thought has a speed of 5,000 bits/sec and everyone understands that our brain cannot compete with supercomputers acting via satellites, implants, local facilities, scalar or other forms of biotelemetry.

Each brain has a unique set of bioelectric resonance/entrainment characteristics. Remote neural monitoring systems with supercomputers can send messages through an implanted person's nervous system and affect their performance in any way desired. They can of course be tracked and identified anywhere.

Neuro-electromagnetic involuntary human experimentation has been going on with the so-called "vulnerable population" for about 50 years, in the name of "science" or "national security" in the worst Nazi-type testing, contrary to all human rights. Physical and psychological torture of mind control victims today is like the worst horror movies. Only, unlike the horror movies, it is true.

It happens today in the USA, Japan, and Europe. With few exceptions, the mass media suppresses all information about the entire topic.

Mind control technology in the USA is classified under "non-lethal" weaponry. The name is totally misleading because the technology used IS lethal, but death comes slowly in the form of "normal" illnesses, like cancer, leukemia, heart attacks, Alzheimer's disease with loss of short-term memory first. No wonder these illnesses have increased all over the world.

When the use of electromagnetic fields, extra-low (ELF) and ultra-low (ULF) frequencies and microwaves aimed deliberately at certain individuals, groups, and even the general population to cause diseases, disorientation, chaos and physical and emotional pain breaks into the awareness of the general population, a public outcry is inevitable.

[Eleanor White comment: ELF/ULF frequencies on their own cannot be focused and are practically impossible to transmit in the usual manner of radio transmissions. ELF/ULF cannot carry voice.

ELF/ULF can be carried on radio and ultrasound carrier signals, however, and are effective in things like setting up a target to be more receptive to hypnosis, force a target to be unable to sleep, and force a target to fall asleep daytime. This is like the reverse process of reading the brain's natural ELF/ULF electrical activity using biofeedback.]

Recommended reading: Mind Controllers, Dr. Armen Victorian, 1999, UK Mind Control, World Control, Jim Keith, 1997, USA Microwave Mind Control, Tim Rifat, The Truth Campaign, winter 1998, UK
Charles L. Kyte, III

The Mount Sinai School of Medicine
One Gustave Levy Place, Box 1124
New York, NY 10029

Dear Diary,

It is still difficult for some to believe that some are capable of such evil. However, if motivated under false patriotism and again for pay, and allowed secrecy, you would be surprised what some would do outside the public eye.

Dear Diary,

I had a lovely day today. Went with a friend to Spagetini's Brunch and listened to live Jazz, very enjoyable. When I got home and prepared for bed, the beam was hitting me from the house across the street where now several new cars are now parked. I also notice from my window, that the cars parked there also included the same car the man was driving that day with the dog, who left immediately afterwards. Buckle up, Scotty, it is going to be a bumpy ride for me tonight...

Dear Diary,

I see the lady directly across, is back home and her sister is with her. They are setting up a garage sale. What a perfect opportunity to talk with her and subtly let her know that I have been feeling the intensity of the beam coming from her direction to see if there is any validation.

I quickly dressed to run errands, but first get one of the books and head across the street. It was almost as if she knew I was coming. Her house usage is vital because of the location and likely the reason she agreed.

However, many will follow FBI personnel either out of fear or adoration and especially military personnel. This is our programming that they will always do the right thing when it has been proven, time and time again, especially with the COINTELPRO overseers will not.

I cross the street and there she sat. She greets me with a big grin and waves. I looked around first at the things her, and her sister laid out on a blanket, before making my way over to where she actually is sitting inside her garage. I tell her that since I moved here, I have written two more books.

"When I first moved in, I gave you a copy of "You Are Not My Big Brother", did you ever read it?" I ask.

She replies, "No."

I then tell show that, the book I have in my hand, is the latest one, and that she might be interested in it, it is called "Covert Technological Murder." I tell her that in this book, I document that those targeting me have given neighbors technology, set up in their garages, and bedrooms. Or any room parallel to rooms in a target's home, used to the detriment.

She still is looking amused.

This is a good woman, who tried to help me days after moving in as a neighbor.

Because she appears to be amused by my declaration, I reason that the community is not told that the technology can also have a deadly effect. She still has the smug look on her face until I say,

"I wonder if any of the neighbors will lie before a Federal Judge about what is happening from several homes around me, and the fact that, they have allowed technology to be set up in their homes, etc., which is being used for slow, permanent silencing."

At this point her face completely drops and her expression becomes very, very serious. I tell her thank you then slowly continued looking around while easing out of her garage still looking at the things lying out on the blankets.

I feel like I need to purchase something, so I purchase a very pretty Kleenex decorative holder box for 50 cents for my bathroom. Her elderly sister stood within earshot listening to every word I said. I hear her saying goodbye to people who have made small purchases and leave I slowly make way over to her to pay her. After my purchase, she does not say "Thank You" or "Have a Nice Day."

It looks like I hit the nail on the head. If I have, hopefully it will curtail the radiation beam coming from this direction. And, although for a few days, it factually stopped.

Dear Diary,

I came across a very interesting, detailed, older documentaries today explaining electromagnetic technology done by CNN, entitled "CNN Special Report 1985 Electromagnetic Frequency" which is archived on You Tube:

Electromagnetic Frequency Mind Control Weapons

I also found a link entitled "23 U.S. Patented Mind Control Related Devices (1956 -- 2003) \
There was information on the Soviet mind control weapon "The Woodpecker", Stephen Lendman: Electromagnetic Frequency Mind Control Weapons, etc., etc., etc.

Dear Diary

I am doing my laundry and typically, the pervert men watching in real time always watch specifically for my underwear looking for stains. This morning, one of the men, sat waiting. As soon as I picked up a pair of panties to wash, he said "pussy juice there."

Folks, these people are just plain stupid. This comment is clearly a clue to the level in which they operate which is far below most people. No man should have the ability to watch a woman, shower, undress and dress in what should be the privacy of her home or anyone for that matter. This ability includes using very expensive technology to focus on underwear. What a waste of time, energy and resources.

The other day, another targeted individual in boxed me on Facebook and said that she is suffering intense bio-coded radar laser energy weapons attacks. She asked, in my opinion, what could she do and how can she prove it. I told her that these operations, are using radio waves which are undetectable which makes what is happening the perfect crime. I recommend exposure any way she can think of without hurting yourself and destroying her credibility.

Dear Diary,

I had to reinforce the rubber mat and Mylar layered on my bed using two boxes of heavy-duty aluminum foil, 70 ft. long which I broke into 5 feet pieces and layered three times, then thumbtacked to the wall. It has helped a lot. It is amazing to see hundreds of tiny pin holes left in it from the energy weapon's focus.

After posting the comment one of the men made while I was doing my laundry, they kept saying, over and over, "We have got to get her." Why in

God's name would they make such ignorant comments, knowing that I will tell it ALL!

Dear Diary,

I was leaving today; I saw the older male, grandfatherly figure with the straw hat pull into the driveway of the operation house. He then left the engine running then went inside. He came out a short time later with a younger white male in USAF battle dress camouflage attire. It was as if he had been called to the location to escort and shield the face of this man who knew I was watching their every move. His shift must be over and he did not want me to see him leave alone and get into his vehicle.

Dear Diary,

Someone posted how a targeted individual would go about contacting and explaining their targeting to an attorney. Could this advice be helpful in a climate of professional discrediting? I guess it could be if anyone could find an attorney willing to take their case.

A Sample Conversation to Have with Your Attorney

It appears I am considered potentially dangerous to my community and in general the public. It appears I am the subject in problem-orientated policing efforts, State police, public safety, public service, and private business (InfraGard) enlisted to employ "problem-solving techniques" in an "all options" approach to implement the 4D's (Detect, Distract, Deter and Deny).

Since a crime has not been committed and I haven't been charged with anything or arrested what can I do to stop this investigation?

The Washington Post stated in an article that these types of investigations are ruled as inconclusive allowing for the continued gathering of intelligence, surveillance, etc. This appears to be a legalized and effective ploy for lifelong targeting.

Either officially or unofficially, communications equipment, surveillance equipment or escalation of force equipment is being used based on the strategies and tactics set for forth by experts for non-lethal weapons use and applications.

How do I get this to stop?

Post from Another TI:

Why I do not trust police and the courts.

They respond too often to false evidence and false witnessing. Attorneys are trained to cop to evidence even if it is not the TRUTH. I want to learn how to be a lawyer and show them how to do it.

Or shall I save my breath to cool my porridge. (as my mother used to say)

Dear Diary

Many proactive agencies continue to battle against what is happening today and continue to make it public.
Here is an example of what is held in a September 2013 ACLU report. Remember, the effort has been to not only make this technology available at the Federal level, but ALL.

Table of Contents*:*

September 2013

Unleashed and Unaccountable

The FBI's Unchecked Abuse of Authority

Table of Contents

Executive Summary

Introduction

C. Circumventing External Controls

1. Targeting Journalists

2. Thwarting Congressional Oversight

3. Thwarting Public Oversight with Excessive Secrecy

III.   Targeting First Amendment Activity

A. Biased Training

B. Targeting AMEMSA Communities

C. **Targeting Activist**

V. Greater Oversight Needed: The FBI Abroad

A. Proxy Detentions

B. FBI Overseas Interrogation Policy

C. Use of No-fly List to Pressure Americans Abroad to Become Informants

VI. Conclusion and Recommendations

CONCLUSION

What Chemtrails Really Are,

By Carolyn Williams Palit, November 9, 2007, Courtesy of

rense.com.

We are dealing with Star Wars. It involves the combination of chemtrails for creating an atmosphere that will support electromagnetic waves, ground-based, electromagnetic field oscillators called gyrotrons, and ionospheric heaters. Particulates make directed energy weapons work better. It has to do with "steady state" and particle density for plasma beam propagation.

They spray barium powders and let it photo-ionize from the ultraviolet light of the sun. Then, they make an aluminum-plasma generated by "zapping" the metal cations that are in the spray with either electromagnetics from HAARP, the gyrotron system on the ground [Ground Wave Emergency Network], or space-based lasers. The barium makes the aluminum-plasma more particulate dense. This means they can make denser plasma than they normally could from just ionizing the atmosphere or the air.

More density [more particles] means that these particles which are colliding into each other will become more charged because there are more of them present to collide. What are they ultimately trying to do up there -- is create charged-particle, plasma beam weapons.

Chemtrails are the medium - GWEN pulse radars, the various HAARPs, and space-based lasers are the method, or more simply:

Chemtrails are the medium -- directed energy is the method.

Spray and Zap.

This system appears to be in Russia, Canada, the United States, and all of Europe. Exotic weapons can be mobile, stationary, land-based, aerial, or satellite.

It is an offensive and defensive system against EM attacks and missiles. It uses ionospheric particle shells as defense mechanisms [like a bug-zapper shell]* against missiles and EM attacks. That means they spray and then pump up the spray with electromagnetics. When these shells are created using the oscillating, electromagnetic, gyrotron stations, it "excludes" and displaces the background magnetic field. These shells can be layered one above another in a canopy fashion for extra protection from missiles. The chemtrail sprays have various elements in them like carbon which can used to absorb microwaves. Some of these sprays have metal flakes in them that make aerial craft invisible to radar. Spoofer sprays. Sprays like these can be used to create colorful, magnetized plasmas to cloak fighter jets.

There are satellite weapons involved.

Activists are using meters and are getting readings of microwaves, x-rays, and some other kind of emission that they are not sure of, maybe a low-intensity laser.

They are also photographing gas plasma generation due to the heating of chemtrails by electromagnetics. The technical names for vertical and horizontal plasma columns are columnar focal lenses and horizontal drift plasma antennas. Various sizes of gas plasma orbs are associated with this technology. These orbs can be used as transmitters and receivers because they have great, refractory and optical properties. They also are capable of transmitting digital or analog sound. Barium, in fact, is very refractive -- more refractive than glass.

What does that mean? Someone or someone's are very involved in unconstitutional, domestic spying and the entrained plasma orbs carried on electromagnetic beams can be used for mind control programming. The satellites can be programmed to track and monitor various frequencies on different parts of your body. These electromagnetic beams carrying the gas plasma orbs stick due magnetic polarity and frequency mapping and tracking to people's eyes, ears, temples, and private parts. A beam with entrained orbs carries pictures in each orb just like the different frames in a movie. It is a particle beam that is also a frequency weapon.

The satellites download holographic mind control movies, pictures, sounds, and sensations to people through this technology. The Air Force has stated in "Air Force 2025" that their goal is to develop virtual and augmented reality mind control. Depending on the how the computer is programmed or depending on the mood or intent of the person interfacing with the technology, you can be probed, bothered, gaslighted, frightened, manipulated, electronically raped, or tortured. It scans your brain frequencies and deciphers your thoughts. The satellites track you by mapping your bioenergetic signature [body biometrics] and constantly scanning an area to find you.

We are the lab rats for this technology and something is very wrong in the military or intelligence branches somewhere. Because developmental projects in government and military are often so compartmentalized, I suppose someone could be using and developing this technology secretly and without authorization. Then again, behavioral and mind control programs were an authorized policy under MKULTRA. Our country has a history of experimenting on its citizens. We are talking about satellite charged-particle frequency weapons attacking a person 24 hours a day. Psychotronic weapons are considered weapons of mass destruction by the U.N.

"HAARPs" can create earthquakes and can also x-ray the earth to find underground military bases, gold, or oil reserves. These ionospheric heaters can also operate as an over-the-horizon or under-the-ocean communications system. This system can control the weather or create disasters. Taken together with the aurora keyhole through-your-roof satellite surveillance system,

Echelon electronic computer/phone sweeps, plasma-cloaked DOD Drug War helicopters and stealth's, implants, and cameras on the street, it constitutes one, big global and space control grid.

These weapons involve beams. Two beams overlapped will couple into a particle-ion beam that will bounce off of a remote target and send a holographic image back to the satellite for remote spying operations. When you cross two strong beams, you can supposedly* create scalar energies. These energies can be used as untraceable weapons for nuclear size explosions or for defense. These crossed-energies can be used to cause a person's physical electrical system to fail or with a lower frequency, administer a kind of remote electro-shock. Visualize touching a positive and negative electric cable to each other on top of your head. Scalar energies can be utilized in hand-held military guns and on tanks. They can dud-out electronics or cause large, electrical blackouts. Scalar energies are practically impossible to shield against. You need lead ceramics, and a deep underground facility to not be affected by these weapons. Or, you need to be up and above the field of battle.

People who are working on these issues hear tones and hums. If you hear persistent tones and static; have body vibrations, burning sensations, "bangs" to the head, neurological damage, or immune system damage; are hearing electronic voices or hearing the sound of a plasma; suffering from pains deep in your organs or constant headaches; or experiencing other anomalous activity then you may be being targeted by directed energy, mind control weapons. These weapons could be on helicopters, jets, stealth fighters, or on satellites. Directed energy beams and electromagnetic waves can be sent to you via hand-held devices or piggy-backed in on cell phone and satellite towers.

Is it possible that someone(s) are very afraid of coming famines and riots due to the ongoing, man-induced failure of the ecological system, and they are saturating the earth with chemtrails for large- scale, gas plasma mind control? Is this the last grasp for the world's resources? Or, are they just control freaks and money mongers? Someone would like to get to that oil under the melting [due to chemtrail-trapped EM heat] Artic. And, I guess the Third World is not a part of this system. I don't think that the developed nations are going to let them in on this either.

Any country that joins this NATO system will become mind-controlled and diseased due to the associated, intense, oscillating, electromagnetic fields, electromagnetic soup, and the poisonous, toxic chemtrails. Our DNA will break. We risk the earth's spin and tilt becoming messed up due to mucking around with the magnetic fields through this military technology. Maybe, it is already messed up.

It constitutes U.S. global domination via NATO and the erosion of civil rights. According to Charlotte Iserbyt and Al Martin, there are ex-KGB and ex-STASI advising our new Office of Total Information Awareness. They are the ones creating our new internal passports [national ID]. And under "The Treaty on Open Skies," we have overflights by Russian and German military. Who exactly is flying those plasma-cloaked craft that are seen all over this country and mistaken for UFOs by people who do not know about this aerial deception technology? Obviously, we have another "Project Paperclip" in the making. We can add the new thugs to the 2,000 Iraqi brought into country by Daddy Bush who is now living in Nebraska.

The elitist corporate government is going to hold the rest of us hostage with directed energy weapons in space, if the Policy for a New American Century group - PNAC - Bush and cronies think tank has their way, along with directed energy attacks against any country or citizen that they decide they do not like. These weapons can create climate war, weather war, mind war, cyber war, disease war, disaster war, and undetectable war. Taken together they can create economic war.

If this system is not stopped, it will kill billions due to aluminum and barium poisoning. It will kill billions due to crop failures and world-wide famine. It will cause heart attacks, strokes, and

357

cancers. It will cause stillbirths, miscarriages, and infertility. The chemtrail sprays often have fungi, bacteria, viruses, desiccated red blood cells, crystalline substances, carbon, metal cations, lithium, other chemicals, heavy metals, and God knows what - probably smart dust, or nano crap. Years of bio warfare testing on the American public is no big secret anymore. Spraying germs in the sky where they mutate due to the ultra-violet light -- brilliant plan, my man. Are we acceptable losses or is this by design?

I know that many of the major players have big investments in pharmaceutical companies, GM seeds [seeds that can grow in an electromagnetic soup], weapons and directed energy development contracts, oil contracts, genetic research, and mind control research. Some of these people have had a familial history of financial and policy support for population control, eugenics, Hitler, Mao, Stalin, Lenin, Marx, Pinochet, Hussein, and various other dictators. Some of the major players were the masterminds of the death squads in Central and South America. They stand to make a big profit on our death and disease. Just take a look at Rumsfeld and Tamiflu.

I assume that they know the dangers of this system and that they take care to stay in their shielded, air-filtered offices, homes, bases, and cars. I assume they take chelating substances to remove the barium and aluminum from their bodies and minds.

If not, then they really do not understand the far-ranging implications of this destructive system. Congress may not understand just what a terrible weapons system and control grid they are funding.

As I understand it, Tesla towers attached to deep-earth, free-energy taps are to be created over the 10-12 magnetic poles and the GWEN system phased-out. Has this already been done? This should allow total control of the earth through giant, Tesla death ray-guns. This natural, electromagnetic earth was not meant to be an un-natural dynamo to power man's weapons or his utility companies.

Over-unity systems [Tesla devices]* are as of yet, another unexplored and probably not understood man-made energy. We should be very suspect of free energy. As we can see, the forms of man-made energy that have been created and used in the past have not been good for this planet. Maybe it is time to reconsider the options available to us through the development of crops for fuel, wind, solar, and water power. We need world-wide, different, more holistic, renewable, energy programs.

Is there any good news? Yes. There have been tons of particulate dumping through the spray operations for 8 years over the Americas, Europe, Scandinavia, Eastern Europe, and from what I can find out, over Russia. And, what goes around blows around, right? So, these substances are probably actually global. It sure makes a ton of sense to spray poisonous elements in 24 NATO countries and let the substances be carried around the earth on the jet streams to poison yourself, your enemies, and all neutral and non-combatant countries. Talk about making more enemies.

The water, air, and soil of all of these countries is so saturated with metal cations that these weapons freaks should be able to zap and mind f--k each other quite well now and as often as they wish. Once they have clobbered each other with light-saber beams for a few years and razed and scorched sections of the earth, they may start to realize that this foreign policy will lead to a defective human race and a rotten economy.

Do you think they will have knocked some sense into each other by then and will decide that non-proliferation and arms reduction is the more civilized and mature direction to take in world affairs? I doubt it, because only idiots would have developed horrific, planet-killer weapons like these. But, I'll bet the rest of the planet will finally rise up and tell these juvenile delinquents to quit playing with those ray guns right this second.

After further thought on Bearden + -- a big over-unity and free energy proponent of Tesla technology that makes energy off of boiling the ionosphere or stealing electricity from the mis-named "vacuum" called Life, I have decided that Bearden is telling us some, if not most, of the truth. Same for Eastlund.

Dear Diary,

"He, who represents himself in court, has a fool for a client."

This proverb is based on the opinion, probably first expressed by a lawyer, that self-representation in court is likely to end badly. I must concur although given little choice but to try and try.

It has been three months since I filed the Civil Complaint hoping that my Constitutional, Civil, and Human Rights would be upheld and honored. As I mentioned there was a six-month deadline determined by the final decision letter regarding denial of my Federal Tort Claim.

I used the Pro Se Clinic for the Central District of California which is located in downtown Los Angeles to file both. For those who cannot afford an attorney, many expect legal advice or help from this clinic. However, in accordance with strict guidelines, the volunteer attorneys, staffing the Pro Se Clinic, can only answer format questions or those about procedure. Anything outside of this realm, the Pro Se litigant is on their own.

I was told by the Pro Se Clinic that I had explained my situation well in the Pleading. The end result as stated by the judge after dismissal was:

"The case is legally and/or factually frivolous and Plaintiff has failed to competently allege the facts supporting any federal civil rights claim; largely unintelligible."

Dear Diary,

When I filed the initial Pleading for my life, I also submitted the first three books as Exhibits. I also filed a Motion to Appoint Counsel which, I had been given no response since filing on December 13, 2013 by March 24, 2014. Because of the intensity of the torture, I then filed a Motion for an Ex Parte Restraining and Order to Show Cause Re Preliminary Injunction as the Directed Energy Weapon attacks continue to escalate, without missing a beat, to deadly levels and began to focus on key areas which could result in instant, unexplained death such as a heart attack by lightly focused attacks which were just strong enough for me to notice as the beam scratched around in the wall to focus the optical lens..

There was also an attempt to transfer the case from judge to judge. In my opinion, it appeared that no one wanted to be involved. These super intelligent judges are most likely aware of what is factually happening today. The transferring to another judge was declined.

As the judge's opinions began to pour in, admittedly it was a battle to remain optimistic. However, from past experience, I was prepared and already knew what to expect. However, there is always hope.

The response to the Ex Parte Restraining order was DENIED with the following judge comment:

Pending before the Court is Ex Parte Application for a Temporary Restraining Order ("Application") filed on February 28, by pro se Plaintiff...Therein, Plaintiff contends that, in violation of her constitutional rights, the United States has been using "coercive physical torture and verbal abuse" (P1's Brief, 3:26-4) against her in an effort to deter her from publishing books about government surveillance and use of electronic weapons. In particular, Plaintiff alleges, that the United States has subjected her to electronic surveillance, direct surveillance systems information, "military technology," energy weapons, electronic torture, the Multifunctional Radio Frequency Energy Weapon System, and other invisible weapons technologies. Plaintiff seeks an order barring the United States from continuing these activities

The standard for issuing a TRO is similar to that required for a preliminary injunction. <u>Lockheed Missile & Space Co. v. Hughes Aircraft Co.</u>, 887 F. Supp. 1320, 1323, (N.D. Cal. 1995). Hence, a TRO may be granted when the moving party demonstrates either (1) a combination of probably success pm the merits and the possibility of irreparable injury, or (2) that serious questions are raised and the balance of hardship tips sharply in its favor. See Sun Microsystems, Inc. v. Microsoft Corp., 188_F.3d 1115, 1119 (9th Cir. 1999). In addition, because Plaintiff is seeking ex parte relief on an urgency basis, she must justify the urgency of his application. See Mission Power Engineering Co. v. Continental Casualty Co., 883 F. Supp. 488 (C.D. Cal. 1995) (discussing valid grounds for ex parte relief).

Plaintiff has not satisfied either test. Plaintiff's filing does little to substantiate her allegations and therefore neither demonstrates a probability of success on the merits, nor raises serious questions. Thus, the Plaintiff has not carried the burden.

Plaintiff's Ex Parte Application for a Temporary Restraining Order is therefore DENIED.

IT IS SO ORDERED.

Perhaps if I had a law degree I might have fared better attempting to inform a federal court what is happening today. But, unfortunately, for many targeted individuals, we are left with only a determination to take a stand fight and try to navigate through judicial experience and education.

Dear Diary,

I received a personal phone call from the Assistant District Attorney regarding the United States of America pending Motion to Dismiss the Case.

In the long run, I realized that in reality, positively, I was adding my name to numerous others, a part of history, who have acted and filed complaints in the Justice system and on the record. As documented, many continue, in light of Denials and Dismissals to do so, and most of all in the mist of painful discrediting.

If all things are working together for good, as they surely are, then our efforts may serve to help, or enlighten someone in the future.

In the grand scheme of these situations and efforts it would be foolish, under these circumstances, to not at least try

Dear Diary,

To the Targeted Individual community, do not dismay in the presence of this Goliath. Keep up a good fight for truth and credibility, for our children and our children's children in these God forsaken times. Remember it took just over 20 years before MK Ultra was eventually fully disclosed and believed to have stopped. We now know the truth. It did not! This program continues to thrive with MK Ultra as its foundation.

The battle rages!

BOOK
V

"I AM NOT LUNCH!"

RANDOM REFERENCE MATERIAL

United States Code, Title 50, Chapter 32, Section 1520a

DOD Regulation 5240.1.R

Executive Order 12333

PATRIOT Act

Foreign Intelligence Surveillance Act (FISA)

Electronic Communications Privacy Act (ECPA)

Electronic Surveillance by definition, Title 50, Chapter 36, Subchapter 1, § 1801 excerpt defining Electronic surveillance by law

****

In accordance with Department of Defense Directive Number 8521.01e, dated February 21, 2008, The United State Army is appointed the 'Executive Agent' (EA) for the DOD of Defense Biometric Program as stated in the excerpt below:

5.12. The Secretary of the Army is hereby designated the DOD EA for DOD Biometrics in accordance with DoDD 5101.1 (Reference (w)) and, in addition to the responsibilities in paragraph 5.11, shall:

5.12.1. Execute responsibilities of the DOD EA for DOD Biometrics in accordance with Reference (w) and this Directive.

5.12.2. Appoint an Executive Manager for DOD Biometrics, who shall be a G/FO or SES equivalent, with responsibilities as outlined in Enclosure 4. 9 DoDD 8521.01E, February 21, 2008 5.12.3. Provide for, manage, and maintain a biometrics center of excellence.

5.12.4. Appoint a single Program Management Office, under the authority of the Army Acquisition Executive, responsible for the development, acquisition, and fielding of common biometrics enterprise systems to support common, Service, and joint requirements.

5.12.5. In accordance with References (j), (k) and, when applicable, DoDD 5200.39 (Reference (x)), make recommendations to USD (AT&L) concerning acquisition category and milestone decisions for all biometric acquisition programs.

5.12.6. Program for and budget sufficient resources to support common enterprise requirements documentation, architecture development, materiel development, test and evaluation, lifecycle management, prototyping, exercises, records management, demonstrations, and evaluations to include efforts at maturing viable technologies and standards.

5.12.7. Program for and budget sufficient resources to support common biometric data management, training, operations, and lifecycle support.

5.12.8. Coordinate all component biometric requirements with DOD Component members of the DoD Biometrics EXCOM.

5.12.9. Develop, publish, and update as appropriate a DoD Biometrics Security Classification Guide.

More information centering on the DOD joint military role and Electromagnetic Spectrum operations, biometric / bio coded weapon operation and Department of Defense joint military role:

Electromagnetic Spectrum: Key to Success in Future Conflicts

Prepared Remarks of Emmett Paige Jr., assistant secretary of defense for command, control, communications and intelligence, Armed Forces Communications Electronics Association Spectrum Management Symposium, Washington, Wednesday, July 10, 1996

Defense Issues: Volume 11, Number 83-- Electromagnetic Spectrum: Key to Success in Future Conflicts The world is moving toward new warfighting paradigms and the electromagnetic spectrum holds the key to DoD's successful use of technological advantages of today and tomorrow.

Volume 11, Number 83

Electromagnetic Spectrum: Key to Success in Future Conflicts

Prepared remarks by Emmett Paige Jr., assistant secretary of defense for command, control, communications and intelligence, to the Armed Forces Communications Electronics Association Spectrum Management Symposium, Washington, and July 10, 1996.

The focus of my remarks today is on the radio frequency, or RF, portion of the electromagnetic spectrum. I will touch on some of the characteristics of the spectrum, review its importance to the DoD and outline how the DoD's experience and expertise in using the electromagnetic spectrum efficiently can point the way towards technical approaches that will ensure adequate spectrum access for both the private sector and the public sector of our society.

My objective today is to leave no doubt whatsoever about the importance of the spectrum to defense and national security.

I am not here to sell you some wolf tickets, but to give you the facts from the [perspective] of the person in DoD who has the charter responsibility.

Let's begin with some of the unique characteristics of the electromagnetic spectrum. We human beings cannot perceive it --- we cannot see it, taste it, hear it, smell it or feel it. Yet our everyday lives are tremendously affected by our use of the spectrum.

I'm talking about television, cellular telephones, weather satellites, cruise missiles, microwave ovens, the air traffic control system, police radars, and tornado tracking Doppler radars, MRIs [magnetic resonance images], baby monitors, command and control systems, car radios, pagers and reconnaissance/strike systems.

Through our tool making creativity, we have taken an intangible resource, the electromagnetic spectrum, and developed systems and devices that have immense tangible impact on our society and our national security. We may not be able see the RF spectrum, but we can see its utility. It is intangible, but it has immense value. Today, that value is measured not only in what we can do with the spectrum, but also in monetary value of that utility, both in terms of revenues for the U.S. Treasury and the market place value of spectrum use licenses.

This intangible but immensely useful resource, the electromagnetic spectrum, has another key characteristic -- it is finite. We have today all the spectrum we are ever going to have. But because of its immense utility, our use of the spectrum is growing every day, and by "our" I mean everybody: the private sector; local, state and federal government; domestic and international alike. This seeming paradox -- ever greater use of a finite resource -- is made possible by our technological advances. We are able to exploit the spectrum wisely and ever more efficiently. Through technological advances, such as the digital communications techniques initially developed by the military, we as a society are able to do more with the same amount of spectrum. It is this technology-enabled increase in efficient use of the spectrum that has enabled humankind to wring ever increasing usage out of the finite electromagnetic spectrum. So, let there be no doubt that the spectrum is an intangible and finite resource of ever-increasing utility and ever-increasing value to all of us. I am convinced that we still have a lot to learn and a long way to go in terms of getting more effective and more efficient use of the overall spectrum.

We in the Department of Defense and the intelligence community fully understand the ever-increasing utility and value of the electromagnetic spectrum. The DoD's needs are increasing too. Our tasks for the nation have become more challenging since the end of the Cold War, for we are being called upon to do more things in more places than ever before. Right now, the department has efforts under way across the breadth of the world, involving peacekeeping, humanitarian aid, disaster relief, counterterrorism, counter narcotics, counter proliferation, regional security and the protection of U.S. citizens. All of this is occurring while we are also maintaining our readiness to fight two nearly simultaneous major regional conflicts and continuing our deterrence of nuclear conflict.

These diverse and far-flung activities share at least two common features: First, they are being accomplished in defense of our nation and its citizens; second, they cannot be accomplished without use of the electromagnetic spectrum. That's a hard, cold fact that everyone must face up to. We are not "blowing smoke."

As our use of technology has advanced, enabling us to have greater impact with fewer forces, our dependence on the electromagnetic spectrum has increased.

Our military, just like much of our modern society, simply cannot function without adequate access to the electromagnetic spectrum. What does loss of spectrum access mean to our nation's military capability?

Essentially, the impact of diminished spectrum access will be a reduction in the effectiveness and overall capability of our military forces. It will impact our capacity to efficiently execute our mission. Losing spectrum is like losing any other resource, it costs.

Less spectrum access yields an increased expenditure of time, funds and other resources to develop, test and field alternative capabilities or work-arounds that in many cases will be less effective than the capabilities they replace.

Less spectrum access yields a degradation of military readiness while alternative capabilities are developed and due to more complicated training requirements. Each work-around is one more thing our young people must learn and remember, perhaps while under fire. Each time we are forced to "adjust" training in the United States away from operational norms to accommodate domestic spectrum constraints, our training realism and hence training effectiveness suffers.

Loss of spectrum access forces us to expend other resources to compensate or make expenditures that do not advance our capabilities.

The issue of spectrum stress is as great at home as it is with our deployed forces. With our permanent overseas presence significantly reduced, 85 percent of our forces train and exercise in the continental United States. If we cannot train as we fight, no matter how advanced our equipment may be, there can be little doctrinal development or organizational changes, and in the mind of the warrior, no confidence [in] the use of those advanced systems. As a result, our great technological advantage is squandered.

The reallocation of government spectrum executed over the past decade and the upcoming reallocation of spectrum associated with Title IV of the Omnibus Budget Reconciliation Act of 1993 are already forcing DoD to re-engineer or replace equipment that is still effective and long before the end of its planned life cycle.

From my perspective, the DoD and the nation are losing in two ways: the cost in lost military effectiveness and the financial cost of re-engineering, redesign or replacing existing systems. The ability of our target acquisition radars, remotely piloted vehicles, missile systems, shipboard air traffic control radars, long-range air surveillance radars and tactical radio relay to perform as intended in both peacetime and conflict is being directly affected. Further, we have not yet felt the impact of the 235 MHz [megahertz] reallocation of Title IV as those frequencies are not yet being used by the private sector. The department is concerned that even more reallocation and system relocation will be demanded before the impact of the 235 MHz reallocation of Title VI has been realized. We are concerned that decisions will be made without adequate consideration of impact on military capability and of the cost to relocate systems. I have the feeling that there are many folks on the [Capitol] Hill and in this country that do not care or at least do not believe us when we tell them that their military forces will be impacted.

The department fears the spectrum upon which our ability to execute national security missions depends will be reduced to the vanishing point; reduced to the point that we cross the threshold being unable to provide adequate support to our young men and women in the field and the units to which they are assigned. A hasty decision to reallocate government spectrum will be costly for the department -- costly financially, costly in readiness and costly in our ability to defend the nation.

There are some, not realizing these costs, who have suggested that we in the military just move our systems to "some other" frequency bands or replace existing systems with new ones using other bands of frequencies, but they are not the same folks who authorize and appropriate funds to DoD.

I submit that there are factors in addition to cost that must be considered. First, in some cases we use the bands we do because they are the frequencies that work for the purpose at hand. The physics of radio wave propagation is not something we can change. In other cases, our use of the spectrum is bound by international agreements since DoD operations are conducted worldwide. Relocation of systems is not trivial because each piece of equipment interacts with many others. Relocation and adjustment can have a domino effect. Changes in any single part of the system can force changes in other parts of the integrated military system. Then there is the cost factor. Changing the operating frequency of a piece of equipment is a re-engineering effort; replacing perfectly effective equipment just to affect a frequency change is costly. This is particularly difficult in an era of declining budgets. Lastly, the spectrum we move to often is less optimal for the functions concerned that the spectrum we leave. Hence, not only do we spend more, we get less.

There are some who accuse DoD of hoarding spectrum. This simply is not true. In the first place, DoD owns no spectrum. We are permitted access to specific bands of frequencies by joint agreement with NTIA [National Telecommunications Information Administration] and the FCC [Federal Communications Commission]. Overseas, we have similar agreements with each host nation within whose borders we operate. In the United States our frequency assignments are approved by NTIA. DoD has access to spectrum, we do not own it. Today, in the most desirable bands of frequency below three GHz [gigahertz], 30 percent of the frequencies are reserved for the exclusive use of the private sector. The private sector and the federal government share access to 56 percent of the frequencies. Thus, only 14 percent of the frequencies below three GHz are reserved for federal use. Over 86 percent of this valuable part of the RF spectrum is today available to the private sector, and that percentage will increase when the provisions of the Omnibus Budget Reconciliation Act of 1993 come into effect.

The need to review spectrum usage, to clearly articulate requirements and identify opportunities for sharing does not fall upon the DoD and other federal users alone, but also upon all users of the spectrum in the United States. Spectrum sharing is a way to satisfy the growing demands, both private and government, for this finite and increasingly important resource. We know this can be done because the Department of Defense does it daily. Our definition of sharing is using technology and coordination to enable disparate users to exploit the same spectrum; multiple users of the same frequencies whose individual uses are technically compatible; multiple reuse of the same frequencies through physical separation of users. We carefully examine the functions to be performed. We separate the high-powered or highly critical spectrum uses from other uses to prevent interference. We collocate compatible uses. We engineer our systems to operate compatibly -- tolerant of other uses in the same or nearby bands. We also employ dynamic management to maximize frequency reuse to meet our extensive requirements. To meet emerging military and intelligence data transfer requirements, which are expected to exceed multi gigabits of information, demands effective spectrum utilization on our part. We know that sharing of spectrum works because we do it every day throughout the world. Outside of the DoD in contrast, sharing often means highly inefficient band segmentation in which individual users are provided their own piece of the spectrum, often with additional, valuable spectrum squandered as unused "guard bands." Lastly, we know that spectrum sharing will work even better in the future with the advent of digital communications technology.

Drawing from DoD's national and worldwide experiences, two essential elements for successful spectrum sharing are performance criteria and standards for the technical design of receivers as well as transmitters. We have and use performance standards and receiver standards within the DoD. Many other nations in the world have both receiver standards and transmitter standards. Today, the U.S. employs only transmitter standards. The Omnibus Budget Reconciliation Act of 1995 did include language on the adoption of receiver standards. To date, the FCC has taken no action on this. ... The United States needs to implement and enforce such standards to ensure that commercial, federal and military systems can operate harmoniously when used within the United States or in other countries. The adoption of such standards by the United States would also aid the international competitiveness of our industry's spectrum-dependent products.

The Department of Defense is concerned that we are viewed as the only, or as the principal, source of relocatable spectrum for meeting the growing needs of the private sector. Instead of a national review of all spectrum use, there has been a persistent erosion of government spectrum and the apparent adoption of an implicit policy that concentrates on government spectrum as the default source to satisfy new private sector needs.

Our worldwide experience convinces us there is a better way to ensure adequate spectrum access for all users than the "zero sum game" of reallocation. But if that is the reallocation approach taken, it must be taken with great care. As Secretary [of Defense William J.] Perry stated in his Nov. 4, 1995, letter to Sens. [Trent] Lott [Miss.], [John] McCain [Ariz.] and [Kay B.] Hutchinson [Texas], before any further government spectrum is reallocated, target bands must be carefully reviewed. Consideration of the impacts on cost, military operations, intelligence operations and ultimately national security must be a priority.

The Department of Defense knows the value of the electromagnetic spectrum. In the gulf war, the coalition's first attacks were aimed at Iraq's use of the spectrum, Iraq's radars and communications. We sought to render our adversary blind, deaf and dumb by denying him access to the electromagnetic spectrum.

Without the spectrum, the Iraqis could not mount a coordinated offense and could not sustain any defense. Without immediate access to spectrum, neither could we.

The issue is more complex than summary statements regarding the relative ease or difficulty of reallocating DoD spectrum. [Army] Gen. [John M.] Shalikashvili [chairman, Joint Chiefs of Staff] strongly asserts that coalition warfare is our preferred strategy. Much of our current spectrum access is linked to international access afforded our alliance and coalition partners worldwide. Loss or reallocation of this access would have significant repercussions in our ability to operate effectively with other nations. As we shift to other less advantageous areas of the spectrum, our allies are left with awkward choices. Our commanders in the field and at sea must not be limited in either operational flexibility or ability to operate with allies.

Well over a decade ago, a Soviet general reportedly said something like "to prevail in the next conflict, one must control the electromagnetic spectrum." That statement proved true in the Bacca Valley and on deserts in Iraq.

The Department of Defense is committed to ensuring that "in the next conflict" it is we who will control the spectrum. We know its value.

Gen. Shalikashvili is fond of noting that the nature of war is unchanged, but its character is in constant change. He is exactly right. We are moving toward new warfighting paradigms. These opportunities are available only to those willing to boldly exploit the technological advantages of the type that we currently hold.

Remember that the electromagnetic spectrum hold[s] the key to our successful use of our technological advantages of today and tomorrow.

Thanks for letting me share a few minutes with you this afternoon.

Published for internal information use by the American Forces Information Service, a field activity of the Office of the Assistant Secretary of Defense (Public Affairs), Washington, D.C. Parenthetical entries are speaker/author notes; bracketed entries are editorial notes. This material is in the public domain and may be reprinted without permission. Defense Issues is available on the Internet via the World Wide Web at http://www.defenselink.mil/speeches/index.html.

****

Electromagnetic Spectrum and Biometric Operations

Department of Justice

Electronic Surveillance Unit (ESU) of the Criminal
Division's Office of Enforcement Operations - Criminal
Resource Manual:

US Attorneys > USAM > Title 9 > USAM Chapter 9-7.000

What exactly is Electronic Surveillance?

ELECTRONIC SURVEILLANCE

Over hearings

9-7.500 Prior Consultation with the Computer Crime and Intellectual Property Section of the Criminal Division (CCIPS) for Applications for Pen Register and Trap and Trace Orders Capable of Collecting Uniform Resource Locators (URLs) 9-7.010

Introduction:

This chapter contains Department of Justice policy on the use of electronic surveillance. The Federal electronic surveillance statutes (commonly referred to collectively as "Title III") are codified at 18 U.S.C. § 2510, et seq. Because of the well-recognized intrusive nature of many types of electronic surveillance, especially wiretaps and "bugs," and the Fourth Amendment implications of the government's use of these devices in the course of its investigations, the relevant statutes (and related Department of Justice guidelines) provide restrictions on the use of most electronic surveillance, including the requirement that a high-level Department official specifically approve the use of many of these types of electronic surveillance prior to an Assistant United States Attorney obtaining a court order authorizing interception.

Chapter 7 contains the specific mechanisms, including applicable approval requirements, for the use of wiretaps, "bugs" (oral interception devices), roving taps, video surveillance, and the consensual monitoring of wire or oral communications, as well as emergency interception procedures and restrictions on the disclosure and evidentiary use of information obtained through electronic surveillance. Additional information concerning use of the various types of electronic surveillance is also set forth in the Criminal Resource Manual at 27.

Attorneys in the Criminal Division's Electronic Surveillance Unit of the Office of Enforcement Operations are available to provide assistance concerning both the interpretation of Title III and the review process necessitated thereunder. The procedures are described in the Criminal Resource Manual at 27-37 and 89-92. The Electronic Surveillance Unit has developed a user-friendly DOJ Net site that contains training materials and sample Title III documents for review. Interceptions conducted pursuant to the Foreign Intelligence Surveillance Act of 1978, which is codified at 50 U.S.C. § 1801, et seq., are specifically excluded from the coverage of Title III. See 18 U.S.C. § 2511(2) (a) (ii), (2) (e), and (2) (f).

[Revised July 2012]

9-7.100

Authorization of Applications for Wire, Oral, and Electronic Interception Orders—Overview and History of Legislation

To understand the core concepts of the legislative scheme of Title III, one must appreciate the history of this legislation and the goals of Congress in enacting this comprehensive law. By enacting Title III in 1968, Congress prohibited private citizens from using certain electronic surveillance techniques. Congress exempted law enforcement from this prohibition, but required compliance with explicit directives that controlled the circumstances under which law enforcement's use of electronic surveillance would be permitted. Many of the restrictions upon the use of electronic surveillance by law enforcement agents were enacted in recognition of the strictures against unlawful searches and seizures contained in the Fourth Amendment to the United States Constitution. See, e.g., Katz v. United States, 389 U.S. 347 (1967). Still, several of Title III's provisions are more restrictive than what is required by the Fourth Amendment. At the same time, Congress preempted State law in this area, and mandated that States that sought to enact electronic surveillance laws would have to make their laws at least as restrictive as the Federal law.

One of Title III's most restrictive provisions is the requirement that Federal investigative agencies submit requests for the use of certain types of electronic surveillance (primarily the non-consensual interception of wire and oral communications) to the Department of Justice for review and approval before applications for such interception may be submitted to a court of competent jurisdiction for an order authorizing the interception. Specifically, in 18 U.S.C. § 2516(1), Title III explicitly assigns such review and approval powers to the Attorney General, but allows the Attorney General to delegate this review and approval authority to a limited number of high-level Justice Department officials, including Deputy Assistant Attorneys General for the Criminal Division ("DAAGs"). The DAAGs review and approve or deny proposed applications to conduct "wiretaps" (to intercept wire [telephone] communications, 18 U.S.C. § 2510(1)) and to install and monitor "bugs" (the use of microphones to intercept oral [face-to-face] communications, 18 U.S.C. § 2510(2)). It should be noted that only those crimes enumerated in 18 U.S.C. § 2516(1) may be investigated through the interception of wire or oral communications.

On those rare occasions when the government seeks to intercept oral or wire communications within premises or over a facility that cannot be identified with any particularity, and a "roving" interception of wire or oral communications is therefore being requested, the Assistant Attorney General or the Acting

Assistant Attorney General for the Criminal Division must be the one to review and approve or deny the application. (See the roving interception provision at 18 U.S.C. § 2518(11), discussed at USAM 9-7.111.)

In 1986, Congress amended Title III by enacting the Electronic Communications Privacy Act of 1986. Specifically, Congress added "electronic communications" as a new category of communications whose interception is covered by Title III. Electronic communications are non-voice communications made over a network in or affecting interstate commerce, and include text messages, electronic mail ("email"), facsimiles ("faxes"), other non-voice Internet traffic, and communications over digital-display pagers. See 18 U.S.C. § 2510(12).

Although the 1986 amendments permit any government attorney to authorize the making of an application to a Federal court to intercept electronic communications to investigate any Federal felony (18 U.S.C. § 2516(3)), the Department of Justice and Congress agreed informally at the time of ECPA's enactment that, for a three-year period, Department approval would nonetheless be required before applications could be submitted to a court to conduct interceptions of electronic communications. After that period, the Department rescinded the prior approval requirement for the interception of electronic communications over digital-display paging devices, but continued the need for Department approval prior to application to the court for the interception of any other type of electronic communications, including text messages, faxes, emails, and other non-voice communications over a computer. Applications to the court for authorization to intercept electronic communications over digital-display pagers may be made based solely upon the authorization of a United States Attorney. See 18 U.S.C. § 2516(3).

Because there are severe penalties for the improper and/or unlawful use and disclosure of electronic surveillance evidence, including criminal, civil, and administrative sanctions, as well as the suppression of evidence, it is essential that Federal prosecutors and law enforcement agents clearly understand when Departmental review and approval are required, and what such a process entails. See 18 U.S.C. §§ 2511, 2515, 2518(10), and 2520.

See the Criminal Resource Manual at 31 for citations to relevant legislation.

[Revised July 2012]

9-7.110

Format for the Authorization Request

When Justice Department review and approval of a proposed application for electronic surveillance is required, the Electronic Surveillance Unit (ESU) of the Criminal Division's Office of Enforcement Operations will conduct the initial review of the necessary pleadings, which include:

A. The affidavit of an "investigative or law enforcement officer" of the United States who is empowered by law to conduct investigations of, or to make arrests for, offenses enumerated in 18 U.S.C. § 2516(1) or (3) (which, for any application involving the interception of electronic communications, includes any Federal felony offense), with such affidavit setting forth the facts of the investigation that establish the basis for those probable cause (and other) statements required by Title III to be included in the application;

B. The application by any United States Attorney or his/her Assistant, or any other attorney authorized by law to prosecute or participate in the prosecution of offenses enumerated in 18 U.S.C. § 2516(1) or (3) that provides the basis for the court's jurisdiction to sign an order authorizing the requested interception of wire, oral, and/or electronic communications; and

C. The order to be signed by the court authorizing the government to intercept, or approving the interception of, the wire, oral, and/or electronic communications that are the subject of the application.

D. A completed Title III cover sheet that includes the signature of a supervising attorney who reviewed and approved the Title III papers. As of March 19, 2012, Department policy requires that all Title III submissions be approved by a supervising attorney other than the attorney submitting the application. That supervisory attorney must sign the Title III cover sheet, demonstrating that he or she has reviewed the affidavit, application, and draft order included in the submission packet, and that, in light of the overall investigative plan for the matter, and considering applicable Department policies and procedures, he or she supports the request and approves of it. The Title III cover sheet, with a space for the supervisor's signature, may be found on ESU's DOJ Net site.

[Revised July 2012] [Cited in Criminal Resource Manual 90]

9-7.111

Roving Interception

Pursuant to 18 U.S.C. § 2518(11)(a) and (b), the government may obtain authorization to intercept wire, oral, and electronic communications of specifically named subjects without specifying with particularity the premises within, or the facilities over which, the communications will be intercepted. (Such authorization is commonly referred to as "roving" authorization.)

As to the interception of oral communications, the government may seek authorization without specifying the location(s) of the interception when it can be shown that it is not practical to do so. See United States v. Bianco, 998 F.2d 1112 (2d Cir. 1993), cert. denied, 114 S. Ct. 1644 (1994); United States v. Orena, 883 F. Supp. 849 (E.D.N.Y. 1995). An application for the interception of wire and/or electronic communications of specifically named subjects may be made without specifying the facility or facilities over which the communications will be intercepted when it can be shown that there is probable cause to believe that the target subject's actions could have the effect of thwarting interception from a specified facility. 18 U.S.C. § 2518(11) (b) (ii).

When the government seeks authorization for roving interception, the Department's authorization must be made by the Attorney General, the Deputy Attorney General, the Associate Attorney General, an Assistant Attorney General, or an Acting Assistant Attorney General. See 18 U.S.C. § 2518(11) (a) (i) and (b) (i). Further guidance on roving interception may be found on ESU's DOJ Net site.

[Revised July 2012] [Cited in USAM 9-7.100; Criminal Resource Manual 28]

9-7.112

Emergency Interception

Title III contains a provision which allows for the warrantless, emergency interception of wire, oral, and/or electronic communications. Specifically, under 18 U.S.C. § 2518(7), the Attorney General (AG), the Deputy Attorney General (DAG), or the Associate Attorney General (AssocAG) may specially designate a law enforcement or investigative officer to determine whether an emergency situation exists that requires the interception of wire, oral, and/or electronic communications before a court order authorizing such interception can, with due diligence, be obtained. As defined by 18 U.S.C. § 2518(7), an emergency situation involves either: (1) immediate danger of death or serious bodily injury to any person; (2) conspiratorial activities threatening the national security interest; or (3) conspiratorial activities characteristic of organized crime. The only situations which will likely constitute an emergency are those involving an imminent threat to life, i.e., a kidnapping or hostage taking. See United States v. Crouch, 666 F. Supp. 1414 (N.D. Cal. 1987) (wiretap evidence suppressed because there was no imminent threat of death or serious injury); Nabozny v. Marshall, 781 F.2d 83 (6th Cir.)(Kidnapping and extortion scenario constituted an emergency situation), cert. denied, 476 U.S. 1161 (1986). The emergency provision also requires that grounds must exist under which an order could be entered (viz., probable cause, necessity, specificity of target location/facility) to authorize the interception.

Once the AG, the DAG, or the Assoc AG authorizes the law enforcement agency to proceed with the emergency Title III, the government then has forty-eight (48) hours, from the time the authorization was granted, to obtain a court order approving the emergency interception. 18 U.S.C. § 2518(7). The affidavit supporting the application for the order must contain only those facts known to the AG, the DAG, or the Assoc AG at the time his or her approval was given, and must be accompanied by a written verification from the requesting agency noting the date and time of the authorization. Failure to obtain the court order within the forty-eight-hour period will render any interceptions obtained during the emergency illegal.

Prior to the agency's contact with the AG, the DAG, or the Associate AG, oral approval to make the request must firt be obtained from the Assistant Attorney General (AAG) or a Deputy Assistant Attorney General (DAAG) of the Criminal Division. This approval is facilitated by the Office of Enforcement Operation's Electronic Surveillance Unit, which is the initial contact for the requesting United States Attorney's Office and the requesting agency. Once the Electronic Surveillance Unit attorney briefs and obtains oral approval from the AAG or the DAAG, the attorney notifies the agency representative and the Assistant United States Attorney that the Criminal Division recommends that the emergency authorization proceed. The agency then contacts the AG, the DAG, or the Assoc AG and seeks permission to proceed with the emergency Title III.

Please contact ESU prior to submitting a request for emergency authorization. In many situations, expedited review of a standard Title III application will better serve the needs of the investigation than would an emergency authorization.

[Revised July 2012] [Cited in Criminal Resource Manual 90]

9-7.200

Video Surveillance—Closed Circuit Television— Department of Justice Approval Required When There Is A Reasonable Expectation of Privacy

Pursuant to Department of Justice Order No. 985-82, dated August 6, 1982, certain officials of the Criminal Division have been delegated authority to review requests to use video surveillance for law enforcement purposes when there is a constitutionally protected expectation of privacy requiring judicial authorization. This authority was delegated to the Assistant Attorney General, any Deputy Assistant Attorney General, and the Director and Associate Directors of the Office of Enforcement Operations.

When court authorization for video surveillance is deemed necessary, it should be obtained by way of an application and order predicated on Fed. R. Crim. P. 41(b) and the All Writs Act (28 U.S.C. § 1651). The application and order should be based on an affidavit that establishes probable cause to believe that evidence of a Federal crime will be obtained by the surveillance. In addition, the affidavit should comply with certain provisions of the Federal electronic surveillance statutes. See the Criminal Resource Manual at 32 for additional discussion of video surveillance warrants.

Department policy requires that the video surveillance application and order be filed separately from, and not incorporated in, an application and order for electronic surveillance pursuant to 18 U.S.C. § 2518. When appropriate, the same affidavit may be submitted in support of both applications/orders.

[Cited in Criminal Resource Manual 32]

9-7.250

Use and Unsealing of Title III Affidavits

When the government terminates a Title III electronic surveillance investigation, it must maintain under seal all of the Title III applications and orders (including affidavits and accompanying material) that were filed in support of the electronic surveillance. See 18 U.S.C. § 2518(8) (b); In re Grand Jury Proceedings, 841 F.2d 1048, 1053 n.9 (11th Cir. 1988) (although 18 U.S.C. § 2518(8) (b) refers only to "applications" and "orders," "applications" is construed to include affidavits and any other related documentation).

The purpose of this sealing requirement is to ensure the integrity of the Title III materials and to protect the privacy rights of those individuals implicated in the Title III investigation. See S.

Rep. No. 1097, reprinted in 1968 U.S. Code Cong. & Admin. News 2112, 2193-2194. The applications may be unsealed only pursuant to a court order and only upon a showing of good cause under 18 U.S.C. § 2518(8) (b) or in the interest of justice under 18 U.S.C. § 2518(8) (d).

Thus, the government attorney should not attach Title III affidavits or other application material as exhibits to any search warrant affidavit, complaint, indictment, or trial brief. The government attorney may, nevertheless, use information from these materials or the Title III interceptions in documents such as search warrant affidavits, complaints, indictments, and trial briefs. See 18 U.S.C. § 2517(8) (a); 18 U.S.C. § 2517(1) and (2); and S. Rep. No. 1097 at 2188. In using this information, however, the government attorney must use care not to disclose publicly information from the Title III affidavits or interceptions that would either abridge the privacy interests of persons not charged with any crime or jeopardize ongoing investigations.

When Title III materials are sought by defense counsel or other persons and the privacy interests of uncharged persons are implicated by the contents of those materials, the government attorney should seek a protective order pursuant to Rule 16(d)(1), Fed. R. Crim. P. that will forbid public disclosure of the contents of the materials. Likewise, a Rule 16 protective order should be sought to deny or defer discovery of those portions of the affidavits and applications that reveal ongoing investigations when disclosure would jeopardize the success of any such investigation.

For discussion about disclosure of intercepted communications in civil litigation see the Criminal Resource

Manual at 33-34.

9-7.301

Consensual Monitoring—General Use

Section 2511(2)(c) of Title 18 provides that "It shall not be unlawful under this chapter for a person acting under color of law to intercept a wire, oral, or electronic communication, where such person is a party to the communication or one of the parties to the communication has given prior consent to such interception...." See United States v. White, 401 U.S. 745 (1971). As such, consensual interceptions need not be made under Title III procedures, interception orders under § 2518 are not available, and should not be sought in cases falling within § 2511(2) (c).

The Fourth Amendment to the U.S. Constitution, Title III of the Omnibus Crime Control and Safe Streets Act of 1968, as amended by the Electronic Communications Privacy Act of 1986 (18 U.S.C. § 2510, et seq.), and the Foreign Intelligence Surveillance Act of 1978 (50 U.S.C. 1801, et seq.) permit government agents, acting with the consent of a party to a communication, to engage in warrantless interceptions of telephone communications, as well as oral and electronic communications. White, supra; United States v. Caceres, 440 U.S. 741 (1979). Similarly, Title III, by its definition of oral communications, permits Federal agents to engage in warrantless interceptions of oral communications when the communicating parties have no justifiable expectation of privacy. 18 U.S.C. § 2510(2). (No similar exception is contained in the definition of wire communications and, therefore, the nonconsensual interception of wire communications violates 18 U.S.C. § 2511 regardless of the communicating parties' expectation of privacy, unless the interceptor complies with the court authorization procedures of Title III or with the provisions of the Foreign Intelligence Surveillance Act of 1978.) Since such interception techniques are particularly effective and reliable, the Department of Justice encourages their use by Federal agents for the purpose of gathering evidence of violations of Federal law, protecting the safety of informants and undercover law enforcement agents, or fulfilling other compelling needs. While these techniques are lawful and helpful, their use is frequently sensitive, so they must remain the subject of careful self-regulation by the agencies employing them.

The Department developed guidelines for the investigative use of consensual monitoring, which were promulgated most recently by the Attorney General on May 30, 2002. The guidelines do not apply to consensual monitoring of telephone conversations or radio transmissions. It was left to the enforcement agencies to develop adequate internal guidelines for the use of those aspects of this investigative tool. The following guidelines cover the investigative use of devices which intercept and record certain consensual verbal conversations where a body transmitter or recorder or a fixed location transmitter or recorder is used during a face-to-face conversation. In certain specified sensitive situations, under the regulations, the agencies must obtain advance written authorization from the Department of Justice. The guidelines on consensual monitoring set forth in the Attorney General's Memorandum of May 30, 2002, on that subject are contained in USAM 9-7.302.

[Updated September 2004]

9-7.302

Consensual Monitoring—"Procedures for Lawful, Warrantless Monitoring of Verbal Communications"

The following text was taken from a memorandum on "Procedures for Lawful, Warrantless Monitoring of Verbal Communications" issued by the Attorney General on May 30, 2002:

I. Definitions:

As used in this Memorandum, the term "agency" means all of the Executive Branch departments and agencies, and specifically includes United States Attorneys' Offices which utilize their own investigators, and the Offices of the Inspectors General.

As used in this Memorandum, the terms "interception" and "monitoring" mean the aural acquisition of oral communications by use of an electronic, mechanical, or other device. Cf. 18 U.S.C. §2510(4).

As used in this Memorandum, the term "public official" means an official of any public entity of government, including special districts, as well as all federal, state, county, and municipal governmental units.

IV.   Need for Written Authorization

    A. Investigations Where Written Department of Justice Approval is Required. A request for authorization to monitor an oral communication without the consent of all parties to the communication must be approved in writing by the Director or Associate Directors of the Office of Enforcement Operations, Criminal Division, U.S. Department of Justice, when it is known that:

(1) the monitoring relates to an investigation of a member of Congress, a federal judge, a member of the Executive Branch at Executive Level IV or above, or a person who has served in such capacity within the previous two years;

(2) the monitoring relates to an investigation of the Governor, Lieutenant Governor, or Attorney General of any State or Territory, or a judge or justice of the highest court of any State or Territory, and the offense investigated is one involving bribery, conflict of interest, or extortion relating to the performance of his or her official duties;

(3) any party to the communication is a member of the diplomatic corps of a foreign country;

(4) any party to the communication is or has been a member of the Witness Security Program and that fact is known to the agency involved or its officers;

(5) the consenting or non-consenting person is in the custody of the Bureau of Prisons or the United States Marshals Service; or

(6) the Attorney General, Deputy Attorney General, Associate Attorney General, any Assistant Attorney General, or the United States Attorney in the district where an investigation is being conducted has requested the investigating agency to obtain prior written consent before conducting consensual monitoring in a specific investigation.

In all other cases, approval of consensual monitoring will be in accordance with the procedures set forth in part V. below.

> A. Monitoring Not Within Scope of Memorandum. Even if the interception falls within one of the six categories above, the procedures and rules in this Memorandum do not apply to:

(1) extraterritorial interceptions;

(2) foreign intelligence interceptions, including interceptions pursuant to the Foreign Intelligence Surveillance Act of 1978 (50 U.S.C. §1801, et seq.);

(3) interceptions pursuant to the court-authorization procedures of Title III of the Omnibus Crime Control and Safe Streets Act of 1968, as amended (18 U.S.C. §2510, et seq.);

(4) routine Bureau of Prisons monitoring of oral communications that are not attended by a justifiable expectation of privacy;

(5) interceptions of radio communications; and

(6) interceptions of telephone communications.

III. Authorization Procedures and Rules

A. Required Information. The following information must be set forth in any request to monitor an oral communication pursuant to part II.

A.:

(1) Reasons for the Monitoring. The request must contain a reasonably detailed statement of the background and need for the monitoring.

(2) Offense. If the monitoring is for investigative purposes, the request must include a citation to the principal criminal statute involved.

(3) Danger. If the monitoring is intended to provide protection to the consenting party, the request must explain the nature of the danger to the consenting party.

(4) Location of Devices. The request must state where the monitoring device will be hidden: on the person, in personal effects, or in a fixed location.

(5) Location of Monitoring. The request must specify the location and primary judicial district where the monitoring will take place. A monitoring authorization is not restricted to the original district. However, if the location of monitoring changes, notice should be promptly given to the approving official. The record maintained on the request should reflect the location change.

(6) Time. The request must state the length of time needed for the monitoring. Initially, an authorization may be granted for up to 90 days from the day the monitoring is scheduled to begin. If there is the need for continued monitoring, extensions for additional periods of up to 90 days may be granted. In special cases (e.g., "fencing" operations run by law enforcement agents

or long-term investigations that are closely supervised by the Department's Criminal Division), authorization for up to 180 days may be granted with similar extensions.

(7) Names. The request must give the names of persons, if known, whose communications the department or agency expects to monitor and the relation of such persons to the matter under investigation or to the need for the monitoring.

(8) Attorney Advice. The request must state that the facts of the surveillance have been discussed with the United States Attorney, an Assistant United States Attorney, or the previously designated Department of Justice attorney responsible for a particular investigation, and that such attorney advises that the use of consensual monitoring is appropriate under this Memorandum (including the date of such advice).

The attorney must also advise that the use of consensual monitoring under the facts of the investigation does not raise the issue of entrapment. Such statements may be made orally. If the attorneys described above cannot provide the advice for reasons unrelated to the legality or propriety of the consensual monitoring, the advice must be sought and obtained from an attorney of the Criminal Division of the Department of Justice designated by the Assistant Attorney General in charge of that Division. Before providing such advice, a designated Criminal

Division attorney shall notify the appropriate United States Attorney or other attorney who would otherwise be authorized to provide the required advice under this paragraph.

(9) Renewals. A request for renewal authority to monitor oral communications must contain all the information required for an initial request. The renewal request must also refer to all previous authorizations and explain why an additional authorization is needed, as well as provide an updated statement that the attorney advice required under paragraph (8) has been obtained in connection with the proposed renewal.

B. Oral Requests. Unless a request is of an emergency nature, it must be in written form and contain all of the information set forth above. Emergency requests in cases in which written Department of Justice approval is required may be made by telephone to the Director or an Associate Director of the Criminal Division's Office of Enforcement Operations, or to the Assistant Attorney General, the Acting Assistant Attorney General, or a Deputy Assistant Attorney General for the Criminal Division, and should later be reduced to writing and submitted to the appropriate headquarters official as soon as practicable after authorization has been obtained. An appropriate headquarters filing system is to be maintained for consensual monitoring requests that have been received and approved in this manner. Oral requests must include all the information required for written requests as set forth above.

C. Authorization. Authority to engage in consensual monitoring in situations set forth in part II.A. of this Memorandum may be given by the Attorney General, the Deputy Attorney General, the Associate Attorney General, the Assistant Attorney General or Acting Assistant Attorney General in charge of the Criminal Division, a Deputy Assistant Attorney General in the Criminal Division, or the Director or an Associate Director of the Criminal Division's Office of Enforcement Operations. Requests for authorization will normally be submitted by the headquarters of the department or agency requesting the consensual monitoring to the Office of Enforcement Operations for review.

D. Emergency Monitoring. If an emergency situation requires consensual monitoring at a time when one of the individuals identified in part III.B. Above cannot be reached, the authorization may be given by the head of the responsible department or agency, or his or her designee. Such department or agency must then notify the Office of Enforcement Operations as soon as practicable after the emergency monitoring is authorized, but not later than three working days after the emergency authorization.

The notification shall explain the emergency and shall contain all other items required for a nonemergency request for authorization set forth in part III.A. above.

IV. Special Limitations

When a communicating party consents to the monitoring of his or her oral communications, the monitoring device may be concealed on his or her person, in personal effects, or in a fixed location. Each department and agency engaging in such consensual monitoring must ensure that the consenting party will be present at all times when the device is operating.

In addition, each department and agency must ensure: (1) that no agent or person cooperating with the department or agency trespasses while installing a device in a fixed location, unless that agent or person is acting pursuant to a court order that authorizes the entry and/or trespass, and (2) that as long as the device is installed in the fixed location, the premises remain under the control of the government or of the consenting party. See United States v. Yonn, 702 F.2d 1341, 1347 (11th Cir.), cert denied, 464 U.S. 917 (1983) (rejecting the First Circuit's holding in United States v. Padilla 520 F.2d 526 (1st Cir. 1975), and approving use of fixed monitoring devices that are activated only when the consenting party is present). But see United States v. Shabazz, 883 F. Supp. 422 (D. Minn. 1995).

Outside the scope of this Memorandum are interceptions of oral, nonwire communications when no party to the communication has consented. To be lawful, such interceptions generally may take place only when no party to the communication has a justifiable expectation of privacy—for example, burglars, while committing a burglary, have no justifiable expectation of privacy. Cf. United States v. Pui Kan Lam, 483 F.2d 1202 (2d. Cir. 1973), cert. denied, 415 U.S. 984 (1974) —or when authorization to intercept such communications has been obtained pursuant to Title III or the Omnibus Crime Control and Safe Streets Act of 1968 (18 U.S.C. § 2510, et seq.) or the Foreign Intelligence Surveillance Act of 1978 (50 U.S.C. § 1801, et seq. Each department or agency must ensure that no communication of any party who has a justifiable expectation of privacy is intercepted unless proper authorization has been obtained.

V. Procedures for Consensual Monitoring Where no Written Approval is Required

Prior to receiving approval for consensual monitoring from the head of the department or agency or his or her designee, a representative of the department or agency must obtain advice that the consensual monitoring is both legal and appropriate from the United States Attorney, an Assistant United States Attorney, or the Department of Justice attorney responsible for a particular investigation.

The advice may be obtained orally from the attorney. If the attorneys described above cannot provide the advice for reasons unrelated to the legality or propriety of the consensual monitoring, the advice must be sought and obtained from an attorney of the Criminal Division of the Department of Justice designated by the Assistant Attorney General in charge of that Division. Before providing such advice, a designated Criminal Division attorney shall notify the appropriate United States Attorney or other attorney who would otherwise be authorized to provide the required advice under this paragraph.

Even in cases in which no written authorization is required because they do not involve the sensitive circumstances discussed above, each agency must continue to maintain internal procedures for supervising, monitoring, and approving all consensual monitoring of oral communications. Approval for consensual monitoring must come from the head of the agency or his or her designee. Any designee should be a high-ranking supervisory official at headquarters level, but in the case of the FBI may be a Special Agent in Charge or Assistant Special Agent in Charge.

Similarly, each department or agency shall establish procedures for emergency authorizations in cases involving non-sensitive circumstances similar to those that apply with regard to cases that involve the sensitive circumstances described in part III.D, including obtaining follow-up advice of an appropriate attorney as set forth above concerning the legality and propriety of the consensual monitoring.

Records are to be maintained by the involved departments or agencies for each consensual monitoring that they have conducted. These records are to include the information set forth in part III.A. above.

VI. General Limitations

This Memorandum relates solely to the subject of consensual monitoring of oral communications except where otherwise indicated. This Memorandum does not alter or supersede any current policies or directives relating to the subject of obtaining necessary approval for engaging in nonconsensual electronic surveillance or any other form of nonconsensual interception.

[Cited in USAM 9-7.301]

[Updated September 2004]

9-7.400

Defendant Motion or Discovery Request for Disclosure of Defendant Overhearings and Attorney Over hearings

See the Criminal Resource Manual at 35 for a discussion of the law related to disclosure of defendant over hearings and attorney over hearings.

9-7.500

Prior Consultation with the Computer Crime and Intellectual Property Section of the Criminal Division (CCIPS) for Applications for Pen Register and Trap and Trace Orders Capable of Collecting Uniform Resource Locators (URLs)

In 2001, the USA PATRIOT Act (P.L. 107-56) amended the Pen Register and Trap and Trace Statute (pen/trap statute), 18 U.S.C. § 3121 et seq., to clarify that courts may issue pen/trap orders to collect the non-content information associated with Internet communications. One issue that has been raised in this regard is whether a pen register order may be used to collect (URLs), the terms that a person uses to request information on the World Wide Web (e.g., www.cybercrime.gov/PatriotAct.htm).

Because of privacy and other concerns relating to the use of pen register orders in this fashion, use of pen registers to collect all or part of a URL is prohibited without prior consultation with CCIPS. Among the factors that should be considered in deciding whether to apply for such a pen register are (1) the investigative need for the pen register order, (2) the litigation risk in the individual case, (3) how much of any given URL would be obtained, and (4) the impact of the order on the Department's policy goals.

Consultation with CCIPS can help resolve these issues, as well as ensuring that the contemplated use of a pen register would be consistent with the Deputy Attorney General's May 24, 2002 Memorandum on "Avoiding Collection and Investigative Use of 'Content' in the Operation of Pen Registers and Trap and Trace Devices."

This policy does not apply to applications for pen register orders that would merely authorize collection of Internet Protocol (IP) addresses, even if such IP addresses can be readily translated into URLs or portions of URLs. Similarly, this policy does not apply to the collection, at a web server, of tracing information indicating the source of requests to view a particular URL using a trap and trace order.

No employee of the Department will use the pen register authority to collect URLs without first consulting with the CCIPS of the Criminal Division. Absent emergency circumstances, such an employee will submit a memorandum to CCIPS that contains (a) the basic facts of the investigation, (b) the proposed application and order, (c) the investigative need for the collection of URLs, (d) an analysis of the litigation risk associated with obtaining the order in the context of the particular case, and (e) any other information relevant to evaluating the propriety of the application. In an emergency, such an employee may telephone CCIPS at (202) 514-1026 or, after hours at (202) 514-5000, and be prepared to describe the above information.

[New September 2003]

Below are moral, constitutional, civil and human rights, penal codes which appear to not apply to those, legally, maliciously accessing and deploying this highly advanced electromagnetic technology, in nationwide massive technology testing programs. Again, the technology is defined as "black bag" technology by our government, and the military industrial complex.

Electronic Stalking Penal Code 646.9 (g)

(g) For the purpose of this section, "Credible threat" means a verbal or written threat, including that performed through the use of an electronic communication device, or a threat implied by a pattern of conduct or a combination of verbal, written, or electronically communicated statements and conduct, made with the intent to place that person that is the target of the threat in reasonable fear for his or her safety or the safety of his or her family, and made with the apparent ability to carry out the threat so as to cause the person who is the target of the threat to reasonably fear for his or safety of his or her family. It is not necessary to prove that the defendant had the intent to actually carry out the threat.

(h) For the purpose of this section, the term "electronic communication device" includes, but is not limited to, telephones, cellar phones, computers, video recorders, fax machines, or pagers. "Electronic communications" has the same meaning as the term described in Subsection 12 of Section 2510 of Title 18 of the United States Code.

California Penal Code Section 653m, California Penal Code§653m (2001) - Obscene, Threatening or Annoying Communications

(a) Every person who, with intent to annoy, makes contact by means of an electronic communication device with another and addresses to or about the other person any obscene language or addresses to the other person any threat to inflict injury to the person or property of the person addressed or any member of his or her family, is guilty of a misdemeanor.

(b) Every person who makes repeated contact by means of an electronic communication device with intent to annoy another person at his or her residence, is, whether or not conversation ensues from electronic contact, IS guilty of a misdemeanor.

(c) Every person who makes contact by means of an electronic communication device with the intent to annoy another person at his or her place of work is guilty of a misdemeanor punishable by a fine of not more than one thousand dollars ($1,000), or by imprisonment in a county jail for not more than one year, or by both that fine and imprisonment.

(1) There is a temporary restraining order, an injunction, or any other court order, or any combination of these court orders, in effect prohibiting the behavior described in this section.

HISTORY:

Added Stats 1963 ch 801 §1. Amended Stats 1978 ch 1022 §1.Amended Stats 1990 ch 383 §1 (AB 3437); Stats 1992 ch 1136 §7 (SB 1541); Stats 1993 ch 589§ 116 (AB 2211); Stats 1998 ch 825 §5 (SB1796), ch 826§2 (AB 2351); Stats 1999 ch 83 § 147 (SB 966).

18 U.S.C. 2512 Manufacture Distribution, Possession, and advertising of wire, oral or electronic communication intercepting devices prohibited

(1) Except as otherwise specifically provided in this chapter, any person who intentionally—

    (a) sends through the mail, or sends or carries in interstate or foreign commerce, any electronic, mechanical, or other device, knowing or having reason to know that the design of such device renders it primarily useful for the purpose of the surreptitious interception of wire, oral, or electronic communications;

(b) manufactures, assembles, possesses, or sells any electronic, mechanical, or other device, knowing or having reason to know that the design of such device renders it primarily useful for the purpose of the surreptitious interception of wire, oral, or electronic communications, and that such device or any component thereof has been or will be sent through the mail or transported in interstate or foreign commerce; or

(c) places in any newspaper, magazine, handbill, or other publication or disseminates by electronic means any advertisement of,

(i)   any electronic, mechanical, or other device knowing or having reason to know that the design of such device renders it primarily useful for the purpose of the surreptitious interception of wire, oral, or electronic communications; or

(ii) any other electronic, mechanical, or other device, where such advertisement promotes the use of such device for the purpose of the surreptitious interception of wire, oral, or electronic communications, knowing the content of the advertisement and knowing or having reason to know that such advertisement will be sent through the mail or transported in interstate or foreign commerce, shall be fined under this title or imprisoned not more than five years, or both.

HISTORY:

(Added June 19, 1968, P.L. 90-351, Title III, §802, 82 Stat. 214; Oct. 21, 1986, P.L. 99-508, Title I, §101(c) (1), (7), (f) (2), 100 Stat. 1851.) (As amended Sept. 13, 1994, P.L. 103-322, Title XXXIII, §§330016 (1) (L), 330022, 108 Stat. 2147, 2150; Oct. 11, 1996, P.L. 104-294, Title VI, §604(b)(45), 110 Stat. 3509; Nov. 21, 1997, P.L.105-112, §2,111 Stat. 2273; Nov. 25, 2002, P.L. 107-296, Title II, Subtitle C, §25(f), 116 Stat. 2158.)

18 U.S.C. 2513 Confiscation of wire, oral or electronic communication intercepting devices

Any electronic, mechanical, or other device used, sent, carried, manufactured, assembled, possessed, sold, or advertised in violation of section 2511 or section2512 of this chapter may be seized and forfeited to the United States. All provisions of law relating to

(1) the seizure, summary and judicial forfeiture, and condemnation of vessels, vehicles, merchandise, and baggage for violations of the customs laws contained in title 19 of the United States Code,

(2) the disposition of such vessels, vehicles, merchandise, and baggage or the proceeds from the sale there of,

(3) the remission or mitigation of such forfeiture,

(4) the compromise of claims, and

(5) the award of compensation to informers in respect of such forfeitures, shall apply to seizures and forfeitures incurred, or alleged to have been incurred, under the provisions of this section, insofar as applicable and not inconsistent with the provisions of this section; except that such duties as are imposed upon the collector of customs or any other person with respect

to the seizure and forfeiture of vessels, vehicles, merchandise, and baggage under the provisions of the customs laws contained in title 19 of the United States Code shall be performed with respect to seizure and forfeiture of electronic, mechanical, or other intercepting devices under this section by such officers, agents, or other persons as may be authorized or designated for that purpose by the Attorney

GENERAL

HISTORY:

(Added June 19, 1968, P.L.90-351, Title III, §802, 82 Stat. 215; Oct. 21, 1986, PL. 99-508, Title I, § 101(c), 100 Stat. 1851.)

Dear Diary,

In December of 2019 posted online was a horrible review of this book. I immediately thought it was the discrediting tactic of this FBI Los Angeles Joint Resource Intelligence (JRIC) overseeing Sheriff and LAPD hoodlums and specifically a group of black men doing their dirty work. They were angered that I had gone through this book again, as they read long and made corrections to errors that was likely their doing. As I updated it, from the operation center, my left knee, was yet again under full attack to include my breasts. With an appointment, the next day at the VA hospital, I wondered would the gradual damage finally show?

When I moved to this location, purchasing this property, I jumped from the frying pan and into the fryer. I live now in a community where one neighbor factually is an LAPD employee, and personnel from the Air Force from the nearby military base were seen in 2015 seen entering several locations, and also renting the corner house behind me, and setting up their little shop of horrors. There was a large surveillance drone parked over my house 24/7 watching everything I do and when I move, both inside and outside my residence so did it.

ABOUT THE AUTHOR

Gratitude is sent, electromagnetically, to those targeting me from their state-of-the-art operation center that insures, through a combined effort around me, that I will have much to research, then write, and reveal to the general public. Thank you.

America needs to know.

Author Renee Pittman resides in Southern California and is the divorced mother of three daughters.

Ms. Pittman is also the author of a small metaphysically motivated, inspirational book, detailing her journey towards light, peace and greater understanding on her path, entitled "The Heart is Another Name for God." This book can be accessed on Amazon in printed form only.

Detailed information of the "Mind Control Technology" book series are available at the book's series website:

http://www.bigbrotherwatchingus.com.

Or, Amazon.com and as printed books and as Kindle eBook downloads.

Later written books, Book V and VI in this series are free eBooks at smashwords.com

CPSIA information can be obtained
at www.ICGtesting.com
Printed in the USA
BVHW040849090420
577263BV00013B/104